Still Kicking

Restorative Groups for Frail Older Adults

Still Kicking

Restorative Groups for Frail Older Adults

by Abby V. Brown-Watson, M.S.W.

Exercises developed by Cecile Freitas Morris, L.P.T.A.

Baltimore • London • Winnipeg • Sydney

Health Professions Press, Inc.
Post Office Box 10624
Baltimore, Maryland 21285-0624

Typeset by Barton Matheson Willse & Worthington, Baltimore, Maryland.
Printed in the United States of America by Versa Press, East Peoria, Illinois.

The photographs on pages 1, 7, 8, 15, 22, 31, 33, 64, 70, 85, and 107 are courtesy of John McNelly; those on pages 17, 44, and 51 are courtesy of Derek Wong.

Illustrations in Part 2 by Kathleen Gray Farthing, Farthing Graphic Design & Illustration, Alliance, Ohio.

Library of Congress Cataloging-in-Publication Data

Brown-Watson, Abby V.
Still Kicking : restorative groups for frail older adults / by Abby V. Brown-Watson.
p. cm.
Includes bibliographical references and index.
ISBN 1-878812-48-3

1. Aged—United States—Psychology. 2. Aged—Health and hygiene—United States. 3. Aged—United States—Life skills guides. 4. Social group work—United States. 5. Social work with the aged—United States. 6. Adjustment (Psychology) in old age—United States. I. Title.

HQ1064.U5B763 1998

613'.0438—dc21

98-36865
CIP

Contents

Part 3 The Support Sessions

Preface

For many years I was a member of the "sandwich generation," people who are caught between fulfilling the needs of their adolescent or young adult children and those of their parents. While raising my children, I spent almost as much time caring for older family members, sometimes from a distance of 9,000 miles. To add to my frustrations, no solutions seemed adequate or right. Finally, only my mother remained to be cared for, and she was becoming increasingly frail and dependent. After it became clear to her that she could not cope alone, she left behind longtime friendships and familiar places to move nearer to me. Perhaps that is why I feel with such passion the need for restorative groups and why I want to share their power with others. The restorative groups of the Honolulu Gerontology Program, begun in 1980, have helped thousands of older adults cope better with aging and continue to live independently in the community. In addition, I believe that the program has helped their adult children feel supported in their quest to make their parents' lives healthy, happy, and safe.

This book is the culmination of nearly 20 years of innovative and dynamic group work with frail people over age 65 who are coping with issues related to aging such as stroke effects, chronic illness, accidents, dysfunctional family relationships, or social isolation. As with many family caregivers I have worked with over the years, the dedicated staff of administrators, social workers, and group leaders at the Honolulu Gerontology Program tried various techniques to help older people acquire the knowledge, skills, and attitude needed to cope better with aging and to continue living independently. During twice-weekly sessions of exercise, discussion, and socializing, group members have improved both their motivation and their capacity to negotiate their "golden years."

Guiding older adults through their journey in the restorative group is the group leader. I came to group work through the back door, in a sense, and found that I love it. Some of us in the helping professions naturally gravitate toward working in a group setting rather than one-to-one. Maybe it is because there is more variety in a group. Maybe it is because the goals are more generalized and varied in order to reflect the needs of many rather than one. Maybe it is that I find working with groups is more rewarding than working with one client because the members help you and one another, relieving you of having to be the one with all of the answers. And, it is very rewarding for 20 people to appreciate your efforts.

Group work is rewarding, but it also has its challenges. Sometimes I feel that there is not enough of me to go around to meet the needs of all of the group members. In addition, with every new group, I must learn to judge another set of differences: who wants to talk and who does not; who likes to be touched and who does not; how to manage my time when some members are so demanding and others, who are just as needy, do not ask anything at all of me; how to deal with cultural differences when I do not know everything about all of the cultures that are represented; what to do when I cannot understand what someone is saying even after I have tried repeatedly to clarify it; how to decide whether to allow a client to air a very personal problem during the group discussion; what to do when a session falls flat. With experience, I found that the best ways to judge these differences appropriately are to accept my frailties, just as I accept the frailties of the members of my groups; practice, practice, practice; and draw on good materials, such as this book.

Still Kicking addresses a wide-ranging audience of professionals who work with older adults in various settings (e.g., community-based programs, rehabilitation hospitals, adult day programs, senior centers, churches, nursing facilities). Planners, administrators, and direct-service practitioners (e.g., nurses, social workers, senior center directors, physical and occupational therapists, recreation/activity therapists) can use both the experience-based practice guidelines and the exercise routines and actual session plans in setting up new programs or treatment groups. Instructors in associate's- or bachelor's-degree–level allied health, gerontology, and social work courses may adopt the book as a supplementary text, especially for courses in group work with older adults.

. . .

I would like to thank the many people who have contributed indirectly or directly to this book. Among them are the more than 1,500 older adults who shared their concerns and their insights during the Honolulu group sessions. All of us who work with these amazing individuals consider our work to be extremely gratifying. We feel that we have gained much more than we have given, and we have been rewarded hugely by these inspirational, wise, and determined people. Thanks also go to Dr. Oscar Kurren, a pioneer in identifying and obtaining grants for emerging community needs, who got the Honolulu Gerontology Program up and running; Mildred Ramsey, cofounder and current director of the Honolulu Gerontology Program, whose vision inspired the restorative group concept and who has kept us growing through her dedicated, tireless efforts; Hazel Beh, my mentor in social work, whose warmth and wisdom were the perfect model for restorative group discussions; all of the creative and nurturing group leaders who blazed the restorative group trail, particularly Beverly Csordas, Judy Armsby, Margaret Brown, Margie Durant, Karen Lanke, Janet Shigemura, and Gilda Zion; Cecile Freitas Morris, whose natural talent for leading exercises with frail older adults remains a model that we cherish; all of the exercise leaders, especially Miff Clowe, Linda Kidani, Debbie Merritt, and Rose Myers, each of whom added his or her own creative spark to enrich the exercise experience; the thinkers and teachers whose words and ideas have been my guides in group work—Irene Burnside, Gerald Corey, Ruth Middleman, Laurence Shulman, Marilee Tuifua, Celia Weissman, and Irvin Yalom; Jan Ferris Koltun, whose editorial suggestions on the original manual were an immense help in expanding the work; Earl White, whose wonderful children's book *Nourishing the Seeds of Self-Esteem* gave me the basic ideas for Sessions 2, 3, 5, and 19–21; and David L. Watson, whose creativity, patient editorial guidance, and persistence helped me through it all—it's safe to say that I would not have completed the book without his constant encouragement (thanks also for contributing ideas for Sessions 13, 14, and 22).

Foreword

It is a privilege for me to be invited to write a foreword for a colleague who, like me, has written a manual about the implementation of groups for older adults. It is so important to provide a manual or field guide for the complex intervention that group work with older people truly is. In the current environment health care providers are hard-pressed to find information or alternative methods quickly and easily. In addition, not many books have been written on group work with older adults since Kubie and Landau published their classic book in 1953. Yet, these individuals have such great and varied needs. As I read Abby Brown-Watson's approaches, I was reminded of something Dr. Francis Peabody once said: "One of the essential qualities of the clinician is interest in humanity, for the secret of the care of the patient is in caring for the patient." (Peabody, 1927, p. 882) Brown-Watson is a clinician who has spelled out the ways to care for frail older adults through the group modality. Not only does she offer 58 explicit plans for discussion sessions and illustrations for exercise routines, but she brings together in one place information that is available only by searching through a hopelessly wide variety of journals. This book will save invaluable time for busy practitioners.

I am impressed by the versatility of this manual. Because it contains exercise as part of the group intervention as well as discussions, the book should be a valuable resource for program planners, social workers, nurses, exercise group leaders, physical therapists, and students in health care.

Abby Brown-Watson has been a true pioneer in a wide-open field that will continue to grow as the size of our older adult population grows. Her efforts are worth emulating. Her own group work has been field tested since 1980; she knows what works and what does not. She began with one small group, which has grown into a network of 10 groups on the Hawaiian island of Oahu. This model can be translated easily into programs all over the country, if not the world.

I view this manual as a major contribution to the implementation and maintenance of groups for frail older adults. Brown-Watson and her team at the Honolulu Gerontology Program deserve thanks for their efforts to bring health care professionals to a fuller understanding of the meaning and value of group work with frail older people and, most important, for improving the quality of life for so many of them.

Irene Burnside, R.N., Ph.D., FAAN
El Cajon, California

REFERENCES

Kubie, S., & Landau, G. (1953). *Group work with the aged*. New York: International Universities Press.

Peabody, F.W. (1927). The care of the patient. *Journal of the American Medical Association, 88*, 882.

In memory of Jack, Peg, Hazel, and Evie

Part 1

Building a Restorative Group Program

1 Restorative Groups An Overview

Americans are living longer. This is a mixed blessing because living longer does not always mean living healthier. Longevity sometimes means a long, slow decline, with multiple chronic illnesses and social isolation that cause people to need an extended course of long-term care, either at home or in a nursing facility. The need for long-term care may be unavoidable, as in the late stages of Alzheimer's, Parkinson's, and other progressive diseases. However, some people are admitted to nursing facilities unnecessarily or prematurely.

The Honolulu Gerontology Program,[1] from which this book derives, was founded in 1980 to address the needs of vulnerable, frail older adults and to show them how to maintain well-being and independence. After nearly 20 years of service to older, frail adults, I believe that the program has developed some answers and service models that work. One of these models is the restorative group for frail older adults.

Restorative groups bring together frail older adults who are having difficulty because of physical, mental, or psychosocial problems that put them at risk for further decline (see p. 4). These older adults meet with age peers twice a week for a program of exercise (1 hour) and social support (30 minutes) that is designed to improve or maintain their physical and mental well-being. Approximately 20 members

[1]The Honolulu Gerontology Program is a program of Child and Family Service, 200 North Vineyard Boulevard, Honolulu, Hawaii 96817.

Restorative Groups at a Glance

Goals	Promote independent living for frail older adults Increase motivation and capacity for independence
Who	Older adults who are Trying to remain independent Chronically ill Isolated Neglected Depressed Frail or disabled Able to interact in a mutual help group Independent or accompanied Continent or incontinence is managed
What	Exercise: Range of motion, strength training, chair, standing Discussion: Reminiscing, and social and coping skills Education: Health and community resources Socialization: Mental stimulation and enjoyment
When	At least twice weekly, 90 minutes to 2 hours Year-round, continuous, and open-ended
Where	Social halls, public parks, churches, senior housing
Funding/ financing	Older Americans Act of 1965 State and local government United Way Client sliding-scale fees or donations
Features	In-home assessment Care plan Linkage to community services Physician consent Monitored over time
Staff	Director Case manager Group leader Exercise leader

are enrolled in each group. Participation in the groups is not time limited: Clients may stay as long as they are able physically and feel the need for the support of a group of peers. Many stay for years; some join for a month or two, either feeling better and moving on or becoming too frail to continue attending. (The restorative group model is described in detail in Chapter 2.)

The use of groups with frail older adults is not new. Burnside has used group work to build self-esteem among nursing facility residents since the 1970s (Burnside & Schmidt, 1994). In 1977 Kaplan, Cassel, and Gore wrote of the need for groups designed to help older adults improve their coping and affiliative skills (their ability to take steps to maintain good social support as they age). Lewis (1984) emphasized the need to rebuild frail older adults' motivation (i.e., desire) and capacity (i.e., physical and mental wellness). Restorative groups can help them do that.

One of the hallmarks of the restorative group program is the thorough client assessment and case management process, described in Chapter 3. This information is important for programs that are reaching out to new clients in the community; administrators of programs whose members are in place or known to the staff may not need to understand this process. The restorative group program identifies and assesses suitable clients through a psychosocial assessment and plan of care, which may include links to services that remove any barriers to client enrollment. Trained interviewers (see p. 41) visit the potential client's home to administer a psychosocial questionnaire and examine the home environment. The staff social worker develops the care plan. Once the care plan is carried out and the client is enrolled in the group program, program staff provide clients with ongoing case management. The identification and servicing of older adults for group participation is the subject of Chapter 3.

Each restorative group has two leaders: The group leader is the overall group coordinator and case manager for clients, and the exercise leader leads the group in an hour of exercise. Chapter 4 describes the two leader positions and covers a wealth of practical information on effective leadership, including working with older adult volunteers and high school and college practicum students.

Restorative groups, or variations thereof, may be started in numerous settings such as senior centers, adult day programs, churches, seniors housing, or nursing or rehabilitation facilities, or as a freestanding community program. The tasks involved in developing new restorative groups are explained in Chapter 5. Part 2 describes an illustrated series of exercises and games for improving range of motion, strength, and flexibility. Part 3 outlines 58 discussion, education, and socialization sessions that take place during the support portion. Each plan is complete, providing everything a group leader needs to conduct a 30- to 45-minute session.

Understanding the Benefits of Restorative Groups

The restorative groups are beneficial in two ways: favorable treatment outcomes and cost-effectiveness—a win–win situation for both the clients and the program. Favorable treatment outcomes were demonstrated via a formal, 6-month-long pretest–posttest study of one of the Honolulu restorative groups (Dungan, Brown, & Ramsey, 1996). The variables measured were individuals' hand strength; blood pressure; range of motion of the shoulders, knees, and ankles; self-esteem; and life satisfaction. Nearly all of the variables showed statistically significant improvement during the study, and those that did not improve initially were moving toward improvement. Dungan and associates related that merely maintaining one's level of fitness would be an accomplishment for frail older adults; improvement is a bonus.

Reducing or eliminating the period of institutionalization, acute hospitalization, and/or confinement to bed/home is a goal of the restorative group program. Some clients die each year, but only a few are admitted to long-term nursing facilities. This is a key indicator of the success of restorative groups. Ensuring that frail older people remain independent until they die is commendable. That so few need bear the high cost and indignities associated with institutionalization before death is impressive.

Group leaders report improvements in their group members' moods and physical fitness. On arrival at their first group session, some older adults may be groomed poorly and may keep their heads down. Their level of participation is minimal, if they participate at all. Attendance early on may be spotty. With continuing help and encouragement from the group leader, their attendance improves. As their strength increases and their spirits lift, they begin to look forward to the group sessions, and they attend more regularly, chatting with new-found friends before the day's program begins. They begin to care about regular attendance and their fellow members. Older adults whose motivation and capacity are improving will, for example, bring a treat for the group, help one another during the exercises, or telephone when someone in the group misses a session to check on him or her.

Group leaders use client-satisfaction questionnaires to determine whether group members believe that the program is effective. The questionnaire elicits specific comments about whether and how the group helps them physically, psychologically, and socially, and whether they have realized improvements in carrying out everyday activities. Reported improvements include strength, endurance, and flexibility; a sense of wellness; the ability to complete everyday chores more effectively; and a sense of belonging, a purpose in life. An arthritic former physician in her mid-80s wrote, "Meeting friendly, outgoing, intelligent people in my age range has improved my outlook, my appetite, and my zest for living." Other group members wrote, "better muscular strength"; "better balance"; "able to do chores and activities for longer, more complete periods"; "sharing aches and pains, laughing out our pain, talking, singing, sharing. . ."; "when I do not attend I feel left out—my shoulder begins to hurt again"; "emotionally, it has helped me to feel better about myself; socially, it has helped me to talk to people more in my age group"; and "speech is more clear; arms are stronger; no longer feel depressed."

The benefits of restorative groups extend to home life as well. Many family members report that their loved ones' mood and behavior at home have improved as a result of the group experience. As one adult daughter commented, "Now, my dad has something to contribute during dinner conversations. He, too, has a life."

In terms of cost-effectiveness, the restorative group is much less expensive than most long-term care services. One month's residence in a nursing facility in Hawaii costs from $3,000 to $6,000. One month's stay in a board and care home is $1,200–$2,500. One month's participation in adult day programs costs a family from $500 to $800—more if health or hospital services are provided. One month's attendance at a restorative group costs approximately $65. Preventing or even postponing the need for higher levels of care by attending a restorative group saves families and/or the state a great deal of money.

Identifying and Compensating for Losses

A restorative group is a powerful medium that is particularly suited to helping frail older people cope with the losses that they experience, such as loss of fitness, health, social support, purpose in life, and personal power (Mosher-Ashley & Barrett, 1997; Toseland, 1995).

Fitness

Although not a part of traditional group work with older adults, exercise is an important component of restorative groups, not only for its health benefits but also because offering exercise is one way to lure depressed and reclusive older people out of their homes. Research indicates that regular exercise improves the quality of life of older people and helps to prevent premature aging and physical and mental decline (Strawbridge, Shema, Balfour, Higby, & Kaplan, 1997; Zimmer, Hickey, & Searle, 1997). Shephard (1993) stated that exercise improves older adults' ability to carry out the everyday activities that are essential to living independently, which leads to a substantial reduction in demand for

Two Honolulu group members exercise, each in her own way.

both acute and chronic care services. Studies conducted since the early 1990s showed that even old old adults (age 85 and older) with impairments improve in strength and functional capacity by exercising, including resistance training with hand-held weights (Berdit, 1995; Fiatarone et al., 1990, 1994; Guralnik, Ferrucci, Simonsick, Salive, & Wallace, 1995; McAuley, 1993; Munnings, 1993). Studies by Dungan, Brown, and Ramsey (1996), Sharpe et al. (1997), and Stevenson and Topp (1990) regarding older adults who participated in exercise classes reported improvements in physical and psychosocial indicators in as little as 6 months to 1 year. Perkins-Carpenter (personal communication, 1998) has said that older adults can do much more than they think they can and much more than younger people think they can.

Health

Many older adults can expect to cope with numerous chronic conditions, such as stroke, arthritis, hypertension, osteoporosis, diabetes, heart disease, vision and hearing losses, and cancers. Zimmer, Hickey, and Searle (1997) reported that people with arthritis decreased their level of activity in accordance with the severity of their pain. Losses of vision, hearing, and speech also have negative effects on activity levels and the ability to engage others socially (Verbrugge, 1997). Numerous studies have found that health problems and disability are predictors of depression in older adults (Burnette & Mui, 1994; Mosher-Ashley & Barrett, 1997; Roberts, Kaplan, Shema, & Strawbridge, 1997; Robinson, Lipsey, & Price, 1984).

The restorative group helps older adult members cope with physical decline by providing a place where they can experience feelings of universality, can exercise to improve their health, and can become educated about health-related aging issues. They derive comfort in learning that they are not alone in struggling to maintain well-being despite their physical decline; many realize "it could be worse." One restorative group graduate wrote, "I've lost my mobility, but Joe can't speak, and Theresa can't remember anything. Each of us has limitations, but we still can adjust, cope, and grow." The social support that they receive in the group helps to protect them against the effects of stress and illness (Berkman, Leo-Summers, & Horwitz, 1992; Mor-Barak & Miller, 1991; Thompson &

Heller, 1990). Becoming educated about aging issues heightens their awareness of their health and self-care (Bonder & Wagner, 1994; Dychtwald, 1986; Haber, 1994; Lorig, 1993; Mazzuca, 1982). Learning and change come slowly to frail older people, so an ongoing group experience helps to encourage and reinforce learning and maintaining helpful knowledge, attitudes, and behaviors.

Social Support

Individuals who survive to an advanced age become less active socially and lose the support that had been provided by spouses, siblings, friends, children, and co-workers. Some older people find it difficult to accept their need to lean on family members and others. The loss of their social network and/or the struggle to cope with difficult family relationships leaves many older adults feeling isolated and lonely. The restorative group helps to alleviate their isolation and loneliness by creating a new social network of age peers. In Zimmer et al.'s study (1997), the older adults who maintained strong social networks through illness were likely to replace previous activities with those that were adapted to their remaining strengths. They also found that preserving a strong social network had a positive effect on older adults' health. Among older heart surgery patients who had strong social support systems, Oxman and Hull (1997) found less depression and less impairment in performing the activities of daily living. Individuals who did not maintain a social network (or never had one) and did not replace their former activities responded less flexibly to their illnesses, which affected their well-being.

Purpose in Life

The loss of purpose in life has been reported by nearly all of the older adults referred to the Honolulu Gerontology Program. They speak of feeling useless, feeling that being frail

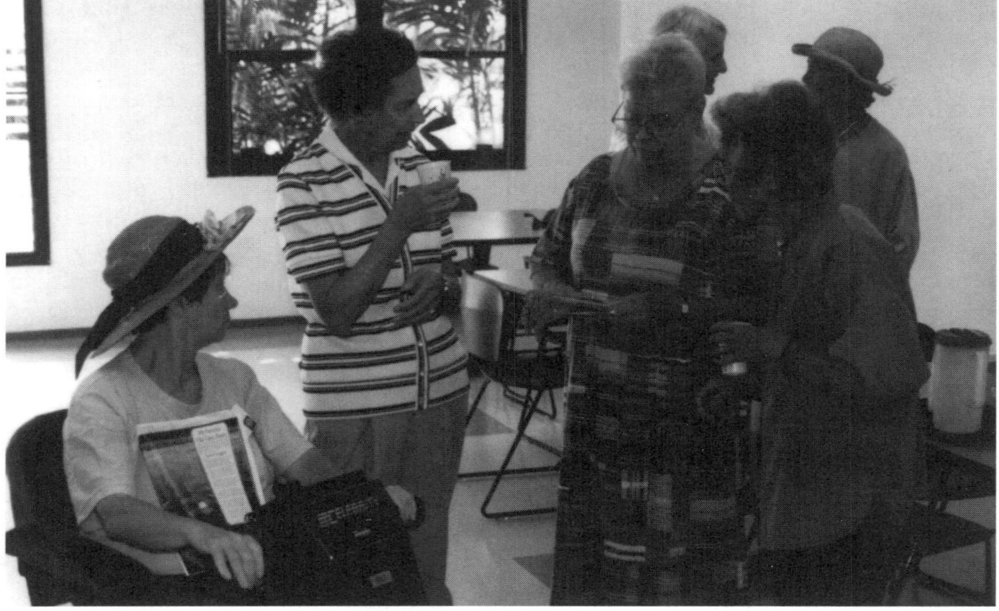

Upon arriving at the group meeting, members share news, which generates social support.

means saying goodbye to the things that they used to enjoy, and feeling that no one needs them anymore. The restorative group helps its members cope with this loss of purpose in life and, in many cases, to regain it. Group members say that they have a reason to get up in the morning and look forward to their future. As they begin to interact in the group setting and come to care about one another, they begin to feel needed once again.

Personal Power

As people become dependent on others because of impairments of vision, hearing, mobility, or cognition, they lose power, or control, over their own lives. No longer being able or allowed to drive a car means depending on others for transportation or staying home; being unable to handle the checkbook means letting someone else gain control over money; having to move closer to one's adult children means losing control over daily routines and social life. Participation in a restorative group of peers in similar circumstances helps older adults adjust to these losses of personal power. Together they seek ways to compensate, regain control, or maintain self-esteem. Along with good health, a sense of identity, self-reliance, and mastery are considered by older people to be important factors in helping them continue to live independently, which is one of the goals of the restorative group (Femia, Zarit, & Johansson, 1997; Mack, Salmoni, Viveras-Dressler, Porter, & Rashmi, 1997).

Successful performance of the developmental tasks of aging confers a sense of personal power on older adults. Peck (1968) believed that older adults must adjust to aging and the inevitability of death, that they should try not to become preoccupied with their limitations and discomforts but to focus on the positive aspects of their lives, and that they should find ways to gain a kind of immortality through social interactions and emotional giving. Research indicates that the generativity issues of caring, nurturing, and maintaining, described by Erikson as a task for adulthood, continue into old age (de St. Aubin & McAdams, 1995; Erikson, 1963; Erikson, Erikson, & Kivnick, 1986; McAdams, de St. Aubin, & Logan, 1993). Erikson recognized that older people need to reflect on their lives and reach a sense of integrity; that is, despite ups and downs, mistakes, and disappointments, they accept their life's journey (Erikson, 1963). If this conclusion is not reached, then older adults may feel despair about their lives. Butler called the process of reflecting on one's life "life review" and believed that reminiscing is necessary for older adults in order for them to adjust to the inevitability of the end of their lives (Butler, 1963, 1975, 1981; Butler & Lewis, 1982). Tobin (1988) believed that just surviving is a task of older adults and that this entitles them to be who they are, needing no excuses. Older adults need to feel good about themselves as they are, which may not be the message that they receive from their families and the community.

Understanding the Curative Powers of Restorative Groups

We know that restorative groups can help older adults to identify and cope with the losses that they experience, but we may not understand what causes this to happen. Yalom (1985) identified 12 curative factors that operate during the peer group psychotherapeutic process. At least 10 of these factors are particularly appropriate for restorative group work with frail older adults:

1. Cohesiveness—Yalom perceived cohesiveness, or a sense of belonging, as a preparatory stage that allows for more effective work in the actual group sessions. In the restorative groups achieving cohesiveness is also

an end in itself. Older people who are socially isolated once again feel as though they belong to a community of people who are like themselves.

2. Universality—To learn in the group setting that their pain is universal, that they are not the only ones going through hard times is comforting for most older adults. Because participants share a variety of diagnoses and psychosocial problems in a restorative group, they also learn that "it could be worse," and they gain relief from that knowledge.
3. Instillation of hope—Instillation of hope is a powerful factor for many group members. In the group setting, participants learn that their lives can, in fact, improve, that they do not need to "give up" on life, that they can enjoy life despite their limitations.
4. Catharsis—People who feel misunderstood at home and/or in the community are permitted emotional release in the safe environment of the restorative group. Some members arrive at the first meeting with a long list of complaints, which, once aired, dissipate; other members need to work for months in the group in order to achieve this result.
5. Interpersonal learning: Input—In contrast to the cliché, an old dog *can* learn new tricks. Members of restorative groups learn by listening to the problems of other participants and by sharing their own experiences.
6. Interpersonal learning: Output—In sharing their own experiences and the coping mechanisms that have worked for them, older adults find that they are helping other group members and that it feels good to do so.
7. Altruism—Participation in a restorative group allows members to find opportunities to fulfill their own needs for helping others by giving of themselves.
8. Identification—Group members may become sensitive to and adopt the positive attitudes and behaviors of other group members as well as the group leaders. These attitudes and behaviors include high self-esteem, positive regard for others, effective coping skills, and open sharing of concerns.
9. Reenactment of family—The group replaces a lost feeling of family for many participants. They nurture and support each other in the same way as they were supported and nurtured throughout their lives. In turn, sometimes a group member misbehaves as he or she may have in the family and finds that these behaviors also are not acceptable in the group, and group members reprimand him or her.
10. Insight—It is never too late to gain insight into some past event or behavior. In one of my groups a gentleman who had led a rather flamboyant life said, "If only I had known I was going to live so long, I would have taken better care of my body."

These curative factors find practical application in the restorative group setting, as the following vignettes demonstrate.

Aletha

While recuperating from a moderate stroke and feeling vulnerable emotionally, Aletha, 82, had been persuaded to sell her house in Oregon and move in with her daughter, Randa, and her family in Hawaii. Living with Randa was stressful for Aletha and for Randa and her husband, Josh, who worked more than full time in their family business. Aletha missed her home and her friends in Oregon and was desperately lonely, depressed, and angry. She wanted to go home to Oregon, but her home was gone. In despair, Randa called the Honolulu Gerontology Program looking for help. During the in-home assessment Aletha was able to express her feelings of frustration. The senior advisor told her that she might enjoy attending a restorative group two mornings a week with other people her own age. She would be able to exercise to improve her strength, learn about self-care, talk with group members about mutual concerns, socialize, and play games. Reluctantly, Aletha agreed to try the group.

At her first group meeting, she met another woman who had moved from her longtime home to be near her children, and she met several other people who were dealing with stroke effects. In the first few meetings Aletha could do only the first 15 minutes of exercise, but within 2 months, her strength had improved to the point that she could participate in the entire hour of exercise. During the half-hour support periods she learned useful information about preventing stroke and about housing options for older adults. She was able to express her feelings and learned to give herself permission to be sad about leaving her home and friends behind. At some of the support sessions she and the other members participated in life review, sharing stories of good times and bad. During the monthly group socials and during the informal visiting that group members did before group started each day, Aletha made new friends and enjoyed chatting with them. Within a few months her mood improved, and she began to feel a sense of control over her life. With her new-found sense of self, she made the decision to move into a nearby retirement residence, where she is now living quite contentedly. She did not return to the restorative group.

It is easy to see many of Yalom's principles at work in Aletha's case. Participation in the group addressed Aletha's need for friendships and community (*cohesiveness*). She noted that other group members' situations were worse than hers was, but that they were able to adjust to these new stages in their lives. She benefited from meeting another person who had left her roots behind and several others who were recuperating from stroke (*universality*), and thus was able to make adjustments herself. Through her group work, Aletha began to feel hopeful (*instillation of hope*) about her future. With fellow group members supporting her, she was able to carry out life review and come to accept life as it is, not as it used to be (*insight*). Although she had the support of her family, Aletha resented being dependent on them. She needed peer contact to feel a real sense of support, and thus she felt less dependent. In the group Aletha was able to vent her anger and frustration at her situation and felt that others understood (*catharsis*). Aletha listened to the stories of group members with problems who were learning to cope with them, and this helped her understand new ways of dealing with her difficulties (*interpersonal learning: input* and *identification*). As some additional benefits, Aletha improved her strength through exercise, she overcame her anger about leaving Oregon, and she learned practical information about preventing stroke through exercise and nutrition and finding different housing options.

Rita

A telephone call to the Honolulu Gerontology Program from Rita's daughter, Sally, sounded desperate: Sally said that her mother was driving her crazy. Rita, 84, had Alzheimer's disease. Mother and daughter had never gotten along, and now this situation was even more difficult. An in-home assessment showed that Rita had fairly advanced cognitive losses. Program staff decided to place Rita in a restorative group on a trial basis. In group she was pleasant and could contribute appropriately to discussions. Rita gained great satisfaction from reminiscing about her adventurous life on a Wyoming ranch. Because of her short-term memory loss she tended to repeat stories, but group members did not seem to mind, and the group leader was able to gently shift her away from too much repetition.

After 2 years in the group, Rita's condition deteriorated and she began to disrupt discussions. The group leader helped Sally to consider other resources for her mother. For a time, a volunteer companion brought Rita to group and then removed her when she became disruptive. Rita was also enrolled in an adult day program, attending once a week. Eventually, Rita was no longer appropriate for the group and was enrolled in the day program on a full-time basis. When her condition deteriorated further, she was placed in a board and care home.

Rita benefited in a more limited way than did Aletha from participating in the group. The exercise helped her to maintain physical fitness. Clearly, she enjoyed the peer support (*universality*). She enjoyed being a part of the group (*cohesion*) and was able to vent her problems with Sally (*catharsis*). She often shared her wisdom, using charming clichés, such as "laugh and the world laughs with you; cry and you cry alone" (*interpersonal learning—output*). Her dementia probably prevented her from working on developmental tasks or learning better self-care skills. The other beneficiary in this case was Rita's daughter, who was greatly relieved by having the program's support in providing care for her mother.

Roy

Healthy and independent until his only daughter died of cancer, Roy was without family support. Now in his 90s, he became depressed and began experiencing back pain, which kept him from pursuing what he loved best: helping homeless people. His physician recommended the restorative group.

The exercises helped to reduce his back pain and to increase his strength. The support period gave him a chance to be with others who were old and alone (*universality*). He found a sense of belonging (*cohesion*), and the group became his family and his community (*reenactment of family*). He found ways to help others by holding a chair for a female group member or reminding a forgetful member to bring a snack for the meeting (*altruism*). When he fell at home and fractured his hip, group members telephoned and sent cards, and the group leader arranged for in-home personal care. These supportive acts helped Roy to anticipate returning to the group (*instillation of hope*), and he did so in just 8 weeks.

. . .

Cases like these illustrate the benefits of restorative groups. Turn to Chapter 2 for a description of the components of a restorative group program.

2 What Are the Components?

This chapter describes in detail the exercise and support components of the restorative group program. Usually, the groups meet twice a week. Each group session includes 1 hour of exercise and a 30-minute support period. An additional 30 minutes is reserved for informal socializing, during which the group leader can catch up with clients on the significant events in their lives or help members reach out to one another. Most of the groups schedule the exercise portion before the support portion on the assumption that members are more inclined to arrive on time to exercise than they are to share personal, perhaps painful, information about themselves (see p. 47 for a discussion of older adults' resistance to support groups). Groups that schedule the support portion first usually do so because the leaders have found that the members are more alert—many are tired, even sleepy, after an hour of exercise. Use your judgment and knowledge of each member of your group of frail older adults to decide the appropriate and most beneficial order of the components.

Many, but not all, older adults prefer to meet in the morning because this is when they are the most alert and energetic. However, do not rule out afternoon groups; some potential members may not be motivated at 9 or 10 A.M., but they may be motivated at 12 noon or 1 P.M. Afternoon groups tend to grow more slowly than morning groups, but they do grow. A restorative group may be started with as few as three members, and it should meet even if only one person shows up. Start and end each session on time. Consistency is important to the development of the group specifically and to older adults in general because many of them have experienced numerous losses and need something on which they can depend. Members are more likely to attend group if they know that it is "there" for them, no matter what. It may take up to 2 years for a group leader to grow a group to full size (approximately 20 members).

Understanding the Components of a Complete Restorative Group

The Exercise Portion

Because of the age of restorative group participants (60–100), the variety of their impairments, and the size of the groups, the exercise leader should provide a 1-hour program of moderate nonaerobic exercise to promote good range of motion, flexibility, strength through resistance training using 1- to 5-pound hand weights, and endurance (for information on leading an exercise group, see p. 69; see Part 2 for illustrated exercise instructions). Games using playground balls, tennis balls, and beach balls promote good reaction responses and eye–hand coordination. The exercise program is not rehabilitative in that a particular impairment or disability is not addressed through a prescribed therapeutic regimen. Rather, people who have become weakened by illness or inactivity gain, regain, or maintain a level of fitness. Group members who are able to exercise at a higher level are encouraged to do so on their own (e.g., those who can walk at home on days on which the group does not meet are encouraged to do so). Frail clients maintain a good level of fitness as long as they participate regularly. Some fit members use the exercise portion as a starter class and then graduate to a higher-level class outside the restorative group program.

Group members' abilities and motivation to exercise range from low to high. The factors that may affect their ability to exercise include impairment of a limb or limbs, cognitive impairment from dementing illness or stroke, vision and/or hearing impairments, language barriers, and social isolation. The motivation to exercise varies among people, and illness, disability, and depression increase the variation. Some people want to give up, whereas others fight to improve. The exercise leader should try to learn as much as possible about each client in order to help maximize his or her participation in the exercise session.

In order for clients to participate in the exercise portion they must give the program written permission to obtain information from their physician about diagnoses, medications, and any special precautions that must be considered. Once they have granted permission (usually during the in-home assessment; see Chapter 3), their physician's consent must be obtained (see sample form on p. 16). Physician's consent is concrete reassurance to the client that he or she is capable of participating in exercise, and it protects the client and the program from legal liability. Consent is not free license, however. The physician may caution his or her patient against types of exercise or movements that may, because of the older adult's physical or mental limitations, cause injury or exacerbate the limitation. Clients should be (and usually are) aware of their own limitations and should work within them; occasionally, however, older adults try to do more than they should. The exercise leader should become familiar with these diagnoses and be prepared to caution members about exceeding any of their limitations and teach the proper way to exercise, including adaptations that can be made to compensate for limitations or disabilities. Special care should be taken with members who report balance disorders, rheumatoid arthritis, neck and back problems, hip replacements, knee

A 96-year-old and a 101-year-old woman maintain their range of motion using dowels.

replacements or pain, severe coronary artery disease, aneurysms, stroke effects, and Parkinson's disease.

The exercises are presented in four segments: chair exercises, standing exercises, weight-bearing exercises, and group games (see Part 2). The approximate length of the chair exercises is 20–30 minutes, the standing exercises take 10–15 minutes, the weight-bearing exercises take 10–15 minutes, the games last approximately 10 minutes, and the session ends with a 5-minute cool-down. "Deep-breathing breaks" are taken every 5–10 minutes. If group members are particularly frail, they may find it easier either to play a game or to use weights during a single session. The length of the chair and standing exercise segments can be shortened if the group is capable of participating in both the weight-bearing exercises and a game. More advanced exercises and additional repetitions can be added as members gain strength, and the length of the standing and weight-bearing exercises can be increased. (Floor exercises such as sit-ups greatly increase the strength-building aspect of an exercise program, but because many frail clients are not able to descend to and ascend from the floor, floor exercises are not used.)

The chair exercises provide a warm-up for muscles and joints, which promotes flexibility and an increased range of motion. The exercises begin at the head and move down through the shoulders, arms, elbows, wrists, fingers, spine, abdominal muscles, hips, knees, ankles, and feet. Motions are slow, smooth, and deliberate; fast, jerky motions do not build strength or endurance and may lead to injury. Shrugged shoulders should be lowered slowly, not dropped. Similarly, a leg lifted off the floor should be returned gently and slowly to the floor. Hand weights should be raised and lowered slowly and delib-

Client's and Physician's Authorization Form *(Sample)*

Part 1. Client Authorization to Release Information

I, ____, grant permission to

Dr. ____________________________________ to release medical information about me to the Honolulu Gerontology Program.

_______________________________ _______________________________

(Client's signature) (Witness's signature)

Address _______________________ Date __________________________

____

____

- -

Part 2. Physician's Authorization for Exercise

Client's Name: ____

Date of Birth: _____/_____/_____ may participate in a special exercise class for older adults sponsored by the Honolulu Gerontology Program.

Physician's Name (Please Print) ______________________________

Physician's Signature ____________________________________

Physician, please complete the following

Client's Diagnoses:

Client's Medications:

Specify any limitations or special precautions for exercise:

Please return completed form to the Honolulu Gerontology Program

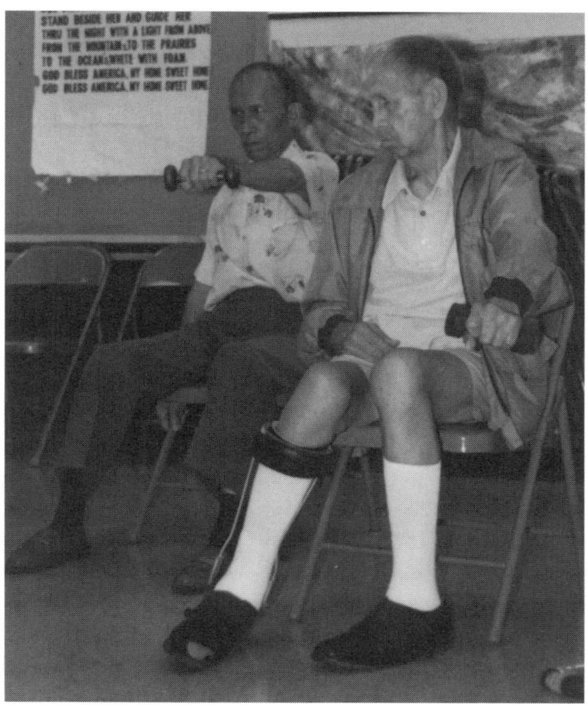

Two group members concentrate on weight routines.

erately. Each movement is repeated four to eight times, depending on the exercise and the group's level and comfort with the particular exercise.

When the chair exercises have been completed, clients who are able to do so are asked to stand behind their chairs, using chair backs for support, to complete a regimen of standing exercises. A chair should be placed in front of and behind group members with poor balance and stamina so that they can sit if necessary. Standing exercises build strength in the legs, hips, torso, and buttocks, which improves walking and balance; improved walking and balance prevents falls and fractures. These exercises also provide a more complete range of motion than do chair exercises.

Free weights are used from a seated position. One- to five-pound hand weights are used, depending on each client's strength. People with stroke-affected sides or severe arthritis should not use weights. Variety in the hour of exercise is provided via the use of games using dowels for stretching; tennis balls for squeezing, passing, and bouncing; and playground or beach balls for throwing and kicking. The final 5 minutes are reserved for the cool-down, which is done in the seated position.

Seating

The exercise portion is conducted in a large circle or semicircle. For safety purposes, ample space (two arm lengths apart) should be created between chairs. Sturdy chairs, preferably with armrests, are necessary in performing the chair exercises and for holding onto during the standing exercises. Some high-back chairs are needed for tall group members so that they are not required to lean over while performing the standing exercises.

Music

Music has therapeutic value and makes exercising rhythmic and smooth. Each exercise leader provides her own equipment and chooses her own music. Some exercise facilitators use the music simply as background so that it does not conflict with the routines and rhythm of the exercise; others use popular music (e.g., music from the big band era) to promote reminiscing among group members. Each exercise leader makes an audiotape copy of her favorite music, and the tape is placed in a library from which all of the leaders can choose.

Using music during the exercise portion is not without hazards. Music can conflict with verbal instruction and group interaction and can cause sensory overload in clients who, because of cognitive or auditory losses, need to concentrate even to follow the exercises. Individual musical preferences within a group also are of concern. Some participants love the music and want it to be played loudly; others are bothered by it. The exercise leader must remain aware of members' responses to the music. She must be innovative and diplomatic in order to satisfy everyone.

Safety

Ensuring client safety during exercise is of the utmost importance and is the responsibility of the exercise leader. Prior to each day's session, the exercise leader should check for hazards in the room (broken chair, damaged floor, objects in the way) and around each person (unlocked wheelchairs, canes on the floor) and remove them. Based on her knowledge of each participant, the leader decides who can stand, when they should stand, and whether they need someone to "spot" them (stand next to them) during the standing exercises. The exercise leader should spot new clients so that she can assess them for problems with balance or limb weakness. If there are problems, then she should counsel these clients and/or assign a family member or trained volunteer to assist them. Family members who are impatient or handle older adults roughly are counseled about or discouraged from spotting. Some clients may remain seated during standing exercises. Before asking group members to stand, the leader helps or arranges for help for participants to rise to a stable standing position. Some group leaders may be willing to assist during the standing exercises, although this is not part of their job and they may be occupied with other matters. The exercise and group leaders should discuss this possibility in advance so that they both have a clear understanding of needs.

At the beginning of each class, group members should be cautioned to do only what is comfortable for them; to stop if they experience pain; and to stop and inform the leader if they experience shortness of breath, chest pain, dizziness, or light-headedness. New members should be cautioned to start slowly and not try to keep up with those who have been with the group for a longer time. Group members should be observed closely during exercise to be sure they are executing the motions correctly and to encourage those who need it. Participants should be warned against executing the following movements:

- Backward head tilt—the vertebrae are close together at this location on the spine, and repetitive backward motion can irritate already frail, potentially arthritic, or osteoporotic vertebrae
- Dropping the head too low—blood rushing to the head can cause dizziness
- External rotation of the hip joint and adduction beyond the midpoint of the body, particularly for people with hip injuries or replacements
- Forward flexion (e.g., bending forward toward the floor), particularly for people with severe osteoporosis or arthritis of the spine

Participants should be reminded often to breathe naturally during exercise and never to hold their breath. In addition, approximately six to eight deep-breathing breaks should be taken during the 1-hour session. Group members should be instructed to breathe in through the nose slowly and deliberately and breathe out through the mouth gently. This style of breathing ensures the proper circulation of oxygen through the body tissues. Repeat once or twice during each deep-breathing break.

A Helping Handout

Handouts are helpful to group members for several reasons. First, reviewing them with participants during the meeting often leads to interesting exchanges of pertinent information, thereby increasing their power. Second, group members can continue learning about a topic after the session by reading the handout at their leisure. Third, handouts, including worksheets, that are sent home with clients (see, for example, Part 3, Session 16) help their caregivers to learn more about the subject as well. Fourth, a handout may list additional resources that interested members can pursue on their own.

Handouts that are not used during the session should be distributed at the end so that they do not detract from the activity or discussion. Suggestions for additional handouts, which can be ordered from organizations such as AARP and NCOA, are included at the end of some of the session descriptions in Part 3. For ordering information, see Appendix A.

The Support Portion

The best support period for a group of frail older adults is one that is balanced among the areas of discussion, education, and socialization. The 58 daily session plans in Part 3 form the core of the support portion. These sessions need not be undertaken in a particular order—the order that the group leader establishes depends on the needs of the group members. (The group leader should plan early in the group's history and often thereafter sessions that help members get to know one another [Sessions 1–11]. Some of these sessions can be repeated whenever a new member joins the group.) Many issues and activities of interest and importance to frail older adults are introduced in the support sessions. These sessions heighten awareness of the issues by introducing a topic and asking members to share their wisdom and experience. Each session plan provides everything a group leader needs to facilitate the session: objectives, materials/props, suggested seating, and instructions, which include a capsule summary and/or script that the leader can use to introduce and conclude the session. Some session plans include reproducible handouts (see p. 187) as well as recommendations for additional handouts that can be ordered at little or no cost from various organizations (see the display on p. 20). Selected session plans suggest sources for speakers and organizations that can be invited to teach subjects that interest group members. For the group leader who wants to learn more about the topic, some session plans contain a suggested reading list. Each month, a complete restorative group should offer two or three discussion sessions (see Sessions 1–22), two or three education sessions (see Sessions 23–45), and two or three socialization sessions (see Sessions 46–58). Some sessions, such as Sessions 46 and 48, can be repeated each month.

Sources for Speakers

The Honolulu Gerontology Program calls on many organizations and professionals who are happy to donate their speaker services to its restorative groups. The Honolulu program presents speakers about once a month or as the sessions in Part 3 demand. Here is a list of professional and organizational speakers that the program has used.

Professionals

Physicians Psychiatrists Psychologists
Social workers Dentists/dental hygienists
Physical therapists Speech therapists
Pharmacists Health educators
Nutritionists/dietitians Attorneys

Other Resources

American Cancer Society American Diabetes Association
Alzheimer's Association Arthritis Foundation
American Lung Association AARP
State/local departments of health Home care agency
Area Agency on Aging U.S. Census Bureau
Local fire department Local police department
Consumer protection agency Rehabilitation hospitals
Alcoholics Anonymous Mental health association
Medicare representative Medicaid
Medical supply company Legal Aid Society
Financial planners Long-term care insurance company
Local recreation department
Volunteer organizations (e.g., Meals on Wheels)

Appendix A provides a list of names, addresses, and telephone numbers of the national chapters of many organizations on which you can call.

Discussion sessions focus on reminiscing and life review so that older adults can put the past in perspective and on developing social skills in order to maintain a good quality of life. Education sessions include information about aging, health, chronic illness, safety, long-term care, and community resources for continued independent living. Socialization sessions promote self-esteem and feelings of belonging, which are so important for older adults who have withdrawn from the mainstream of life and other people. The social activities that are offered are designed to provide mental and social stimulation, which help to build motivation and capacity for social interaction and bonding among members.

Talking and sharing are encouraged not only in the discussion sessions but during educational and socialization sessions as well (e.g., an education session can feature a discussion of members' experiences with their medications or homes; a socialization session can feature verbal, participatory games such as charades or Wheel of Fortune). Sharing stories, ideas, and insights is a major goal of the restorative group, so the group leader should ensure that every group member has many opportunities to talk and share.

The methods that are used to implement the sessions depend on the type of group and on group members' interests and level of personal development or self-awareness. Creating a monthly calendar helps to maintain balance in the support period programming. The sample calendar on page 21 can be distributed to group members to help them remember and anticipate special days. They should be encouraged to post the calendar on their refrigerators or in a location that is special to them.

Variety in programming is important for a number of reasons. First, until the group leader gets to know the members of her group as individuals, she may not know which program or activity will touch a person. A good rule of thumb is that even if only one per-

Sample Calendar

Kailua Restorative Group

March 1998

4	***Education***	Scam Alert Review a handout and share your experiences
6	***Discussion***	Are You Making Progress Toward Your 1998 Goals? *(psychologist leads)*
11	***Education***	Taking Care of Our Hearts *(speaker from Castle Medical Center)*
13	***Socialization***	Bingo Bring a small prize if you can
18	***Socialization***	Brain Games Word Scramble *[Exercise 57]*
20	***Discussion***	Reminiscing Share a scary weather story
25	***Social***	Bring $3.50 for a soup/salad from the vegetarian deli
27	***Open Discussion***	What's On Your Mind?

son seemed to have gained something from a session or was able to shine, the session was worth scheduling. One day, one of my groups was playing a word game (see Part 3, Session 49) in which members were to think of a flower whose name began with the letter E. Everyone was stumped and about to give up when Ed, an aphasic client, said, "Edelweiss." Everyone marveled that Ed had thought of this tiny flower and was able to say the word. His contribution and the group's response to it gave Ed a huge dose of pride and helped group members realize that he was alert—only his ability to speak was impaired.

Second, variety in programming prevents monotony, both for group members and the group leader. Serious and lighter sessions should be interspersed because no one wants to dwell on the problems of aging and illness and no one wants to reminisce all of the time. Older adults *want* to live in the present and for the future, and this is the program's goal for them as well. Monotony can also be avoided by holding open discussions (see p. 24 for details on open discussions).

Discussion Sessions

The discussion sessions help older adults to build social support, review their life journeys, polish their daily living skills, and maintain their self-esteem. During these sessions group members are encouraged to talk about issues of importance to them and to share their concerns and wisdom. For these reasons the discussion sessions are the most directly therapeutic part of the program.

Building Social Support

Social support, knowing that one cares for/is cared for by others and that one belongs, is a key ingredient in well-being at any age, but particularly beyond age 60. Heightening older adults' awareness of the importance of social support and rebuilding their sense of support and belonging are goals of the discussion sessions. Becoming a member of a supportive group of peers helps isolated older adults to reconstruct a social network, even though the nature or quality of the new relationships may not be the same as the earlier relationships.

The social support–centered sessions in Part 3 focus on helping group members to become acquainted, develop a sense of belonging within the group setting, and become more comfortable expressing themselves. Session 1, "The Mingler," is a gentle icebreaker during which participants learn nonthreatening facts about one another. Session 2, "What Do We Have in Common?," Session 3, "What's in a Name?," and Session 4, "Learning Names," continue the process of members' becoming acquainted and building group cohesiveness. Session 5, "The Importance of Belonging," examines the value of

Group members socialize before the group meeting.

having social support. Session 6, "What I Like About Our Group," is a heartwarming exercise that can be conducted regularly once the group begins to sense cohesiveness. During the session, members express their heartfelt gratitude for the support of the group, and the group leader receives all of the positive "strokes" she needs to believe that her work is valued.

The group leader can plan other social support–centered discussions. Meaningful discussions could explore such questions as: What is the difference between aloneness and loneliness? What do you think about family relationships today? Can you talk about your past and present leisure interests? What is a friend, and how have your friendship needs changed over the years? What do we want from our families? The Ungame (see Appendix A) provides discussion starters ranging from simple icebreakers to thought-provoking questions about ideas and feelings. *The Book of Questions* (Stock, 1987, 1989, 1991) series is another tool that can be used to jump-start discussions.

Reviewing Life Journeys

Reminiscing in a group setting helps older adults to carry out the life-review process (see Chapter 3) and to bond with age peers who have already done so. In working through life review and sharing what they discover with others in the group, members eventually reach acceptance of their life journeys—that despite the "bumps in the road" of life they have survived and they are not alone. They reach acceptance by sharing their reminiscences with peers, who help each other to accept their successes and failures as, at least in part, a reflection of the times in which they lived.

The life-review–centered sessions in Part 3 help older adults to pinpoint areas on which they need to work. Session 7, "Where It All Began—Childhood Memories," takes group members back to the place of their birth or early childhood. Session 8, "In a Word—Reminisce," asks members to reminisce about their youth using the keyword "trouble." Session 9, "The Working Life," promotes sharing memories of the experience of work. Session 10, "The Best Years of Our Lives," is fun because people vary in their choice of which time period was best for them. Session 11, "Show and/or Tell," encourages members to share and reminisce about a special object brought from home. Other ideas for reminiscing sessions can be found in the article, "It's Your Story: Pass It On," in *Reminisce: The Magazine that Brings Back the Good Old Times*, a game called *Life Stories* (see References), and the American Association of Retired Persons' (AARP) publications *Reminiscence: Finding Meaning in Memories*, and *The Power of Memories: Creative Use of Reminiscence*. The following are some techniques that can be used to stimulate reminiscences:

1. Word association. Reminisce using a keyword such as "pet," "friend," "funeral," or "trouble," as in Session 8. Word association can trigger interesting memories.
2. Brainstorming. In small groups or one large group, brainstorm a topic (e.g., old cars, favorite movie stars, inventions, trips taken) and list them on the flip chart/easel or blackboard.
3. Visual prompts. "Coffee-table" books of pictures of past fashions, cars, grocery advertisements, or newspaper headlines help to stimulate memories. Group members can bring pictures and books from home or they can check the local library for historical picture books.

Reminiscing is an important function in restorative groups because it helps people to validate their past (which improves their quality of life in the present and future), but it must be kept in perspective. Not all older adults enjoy reminiscing: Some find the memories too distant, too boring, or too painful, and for some, the memory is no longer painful but the recounting is.

Polishing Daily Living Skills

The ability to cope with change and loss is a major determinant in making a positive adjustment to aging. Becoming aware of and practicing coping techniques and good social skills are the tools that older adults need to deal effectively with these events. Session 12, "Being Assertive," helps older adults learn to deal with people such as adult children and physicians in a way that protects their own rights while respecting the rights of others. Session 13, "Solving Problems," outlines a simple method that helps clients to analyze and find solutions to problems. The time-tested techniques in Session 14, "Making Good Decisions," help older people make some tough decisions: giving up driving, selling their home and moving nearer to their children or to a retirement residence/assisted living facility, accepting in-home assistance (e.g., chore assistance), changing physicians, or having elective surgery or undergoing chemotherapy. Session 15, "Grieving Losses," offers some ideas for coping with loss (e.g., death, loss of a job or home). Session 16, "Coping with the Holiday Blues," lists ways to handle sadness or depression at the holidays. In Session 17, "What Keeps Me Going?," members are asked to share their wisdom about remaining motivated in the face of adversity. For some participants, the activity touches on spiritual matters.

Maintaining Self-Esteem

Self-esteem evolves from parental love, peer relationships, personal accomplishments, and body image, among other factors. It is reinforced through being loved and valued by others, valuing oneself, and continuing to participate in satisfying activities. Maintaining self-esteem becomes more difficult as people age because these reinforcements are less available, and America's youth-worshipping society does not value its older members. The activities in Sessions 18–22 help group members to examine and analyze self-esteem issues: How do they view themselves as older adults (Sessions 18 and 22)? Who helped them to develop their self-images, and who have they influenced during their lives (Session 19)? Do they receive opportunities to maintain the self-esteem–promoting balance of being cared for, caring for others, and caring for themselves (Session 20)? Are they giving and receiving appreciation (Session 21)?

Open Discussions

Open discussions have no preset agenda and give group members a chance to discuss personal concerns or problems or even current events. Sharing concerns leads to closer bonding among group members, allowing them to admit to problems, to find others who share the same problems, and to give and receive help. Try to hold open discussions at least once each month so that you and the group members can become comfortable with this format. Start the open discussion by reminding members that the purpose of the restorative group is to help them cope with daily living and the problems of aging and chronic illness. Then ask what their concerns are today. You may need to endure a long period of silence before someone offers to discuss a concern. Do not be afraid of the silence; eventually, a group member will speak up. Often, after one person begins speaking another picks up the thread of conversation or is reminded of an issue he or she wants to discuss. Many times, open discussions produce a meaningful exchange of ideas among people in the group. For example, a Honolulu group member mentioned using a Catholic

An Open Discussion *(sample)*

GROUP LEADER: Every month, we have an open discussion so that you can share what's on your mind. Remember that the purpose of the restorative group is to help you cope with daily living and the problems of aging and chronic illness. Does anyone have something he or she would like to share?

[Long silence]

JOHN: I know I'm too sensitive and maybe you can help me with that. I remember that one time you suggested I go around the circle to each person at the start of each session so I could "see" through touch who's there. I wouldn't do it. My wife wants me to use a blindman's cane, but I don't want anyone to know I have a problem, so I won't use it. I don't want anyone to feel sorry for me. Sometimes my wife gets mad because her friends see me and I don't say hello.

ROSE: I know what you mean. My daughter thinks I ignore people, but I just don't see them well enough to remember if I know them. I hardly ever get out of the house.

MASAO: I understand how you feel about using the cane, John. People see me in my wheelchair and think I'm stupid or something.

MARY: John, I think people would admire you, not pity you, if they see that you have a cane but you're getting around so well. I think you should use it, especially now with the holidays. It's downright dangerous walking around town whether you're blind or not. People push and shove and don't give a darn.

JOE: I agree. Just for safety reasons, I think it's good to let people know you're disabled, otherwise they just run you down.

SUE: You know, John, you are really sensitive and that's good. You like to help people and everything. Ministers *[Sue's husband had been a minister]* tend to be that way, too. They are empathic about others but get hurt easily. You seem to be that kind of person.

HELEN: Yes. We're taught to give, but we get little training in how to receive. My mother used to say, "It is more important to give than to receive." Now we're in the position where we have to receive and we don't like it.

(continued on next page)

Charities van that transported older adults to the grocery store and pharmacy. Others in the group had never heard of this service and expressed interest in using it.

The open discussion sample on pages 25–26 concerns John, who is nearly blind. The open discussion format gave John a chance to express himself and to give himself permission to feel dependent on others. In addition, the exchange may have helped John to feel valued by other people and to learn another way of looking at his needs. The tone of the discussion freed John to delve deeper into his concerns—about how to cope with his

An Open Discussion *(sample) (continued)*

GROUP LEADER: That's a good point, Helen. John, how do you feel when you are able to help someone out?

JOHN: Good.

GROUP LEADER: That's good. Why don't you try thinking that someone helping you will give that person pleasure?

JOHN: I guess I could, but it's still hard. I've been a proud, hardworking man all my life and I can't stand the idea of being so helpless.

GROUP LEADER: Maybe many of you share John's feelings. You've always been the ones giving and now find it hard to be on the receiving end.

MARY: I know that's true for me. I hate being dependent. I don't drive anymore, and I just hate having to ask my daughter for a ride to the store. She's so busy.

GROUP LEADER: Yes, I can understand that it's hard to give up any independence. Independence is important to older people. One of the goals of this program is to help you find ways to compensate for various losses in your lives.

JOHN: How should I plan for the future? Should it be from physical to physical (3 to 6 months) or should I plan for 5 years?

GLADYS: Just live for each day.

HELEN: Right.

VIOLA: I agree. *[Stands up]* Each day I wake up and say, "I'm alive. I'm here. I can get up and walk and eat. Thank God."

JOE: I'd like to live to be 100!

GROUP LEADER: Thank you all for sharing your thoughts and ideas on the subjects of dependence and independence. I hope you got some new insights about them. Joe said that he wants to live to be 100, so one of these days we'll do a longevity quiz and watch a film about living to be 140. John, thank you especially for sharing your concerns with us, which led us into a subject that seemed to interest us all. How do you feel now?

JOHN: Fine. No one at home will talk to me about things like this.

[A few others thanked and praised John, and a few approached him after group to talk more about the subject.]

aging and mortality. Learning to take one day at a time and to be grateful for each day may be helpful to John at this point in his life. John was not the only group member to gain from the open discussion, however. Other members were able to help John and show him that they cared. Also, they realized that other people struggle with dependency and mortality. Finally, John raised the issue of not being understood at home. This comment was a red flag to the group leader, who realized she needed to understand John's support system better and look for ways to counsel John and his wife about caregiving and care receiving. Following an open discussion such as this one, a group facilitator could plan a session on longevity and/or conduct Session 20, "A Balance in Caring."

Open discussions also help facilitators to brainstorm ideas for support sessions. During one open discussion in the Honolulu program, a group member brought up the problem of dressing after recovering from a stroke. A stroke had left this individual with left-sided weakness, and he had trouble pulling up his pants and zipping them. His contribution became a discussion of what clothes are practical, easy to care for, and affordable, and of the difficulty of going shopping. The discussion continued for two support periods. The facilitator had not thought of discussing this topic and was surprised by the group's interest. You can also draw a sample calendar for the following month on a flip chart and ask participants to fill in the open dates. Because it may be hard for some of the group members to think of activities, hand out a list of possible topics (see p. 28) or the table of contents for Part 3 and discuss it. Another way to approach brainstorming is to toss around ideas to motivate the group's thinking: What shall we reminisce about next month? Let's talk about your favorite teachers or your closest friend. What service would you like to learn about—home-delivered meals or the bath service? Members may choose one of these topics or think of another one. Although somewhat laborious, this activity helps the group to develop a sense of control over the activities of the group and, therefore, their lives.

Education Sessions

The educational component of the support portion entails understanding the aging process, developing a healthful lifestyle, managing chronic illness, understanding emotional problems, staying safe, using community resources, and planning for long-term care. This component also requires group members to discuss and share their knowledge and wisdom. The group leader guides the education discussions, although she is not expected to be an expert in any of the topics. She arranges for outside speakers and videos/films that supplement the discussions and enhance learning. The videos/films can either precede or follow the discussion. The Honolulu groups invite speakers to address them at least once a month. They have found that they need to familiarize speakers with the techniques of communicating effectively with frail older adults. One method that the group leaders have used is the sample letter that appears on page 30 (this information can be provided verbally as well). Numerous resource organizations and professionals can provide films and videos, but these media should be used sparingly. Often, the film dialog is too fast and the material covered is not targeted to frail older adults. Also, because most films and videos are approximately 25 minutes long—5 minutes shorter than the length of the support portion—they do not permit sufficient time for group response and discussion. The organizations that provide films and videos are listed in Appendix A.

Understanding the Aging Process

The sessions from Part 3 that concern understanding the aging process help restorative group members to think about the physical and social changes that occur in normal aging and to distinguish those changes from changes caused by disease or psychosocial problems. Understanding the difference is difficult for some older adults because some aspects of normal aging may give rise to disease and psychosocial problems. For example, many participants worry about their memory; they wonder when is forgetting normal and when is it a problem. Myths and attitudes about aging affect objective thinking as

Possible Topics for Future Sessions

To help plan sessions, please circle the topics in which you are interested/on which you would like more information. Add other topics, as desired.

Health

Vitamins	Fiber	Budget cooking	Cooking for one
Grocery shopping	Healthful snacks	Sleep problems	Stress
Special diets:	Diabetes	Low fat	Low sodium

Other ______________________________

Exercise	Massage	Foot care	Dental care
Glaucoma	Cataracts	Macular degeneration	Hearing loss
Arthritis	Stroke	Heart disease	High blood pressure
Diabetes	Depression	Alcoholism	Medications
Smoking	Memory loss	Parkinson's disease	Alzheimer's disease
Skin care	Hair care		

Other ______________________________

Community Services

Legal services	In-home companions	Chore services	Home-delivered meals
Group dining	Medicare	Medicaid	Food stamps
Social Security	SSI	Employment	Volunteering
College courses	Nursing facilities	Long-term care	Other ______

____

Recreation

Senior clubs	Music	Art	Arts and crafts
Games	Leisure ideas	Programs for older adults	

Other ______________________________

Discussion Topics

Living alone	Living on a budget	Loss and grief	Tasks of aging
Sexuality	Problems of aging	Relationships (friends, family)	Fears
Crime	Living wills	Reminiscing	Health care costs

Other ______________________________

do ageist attitudes, which are held even by physicians and older adults themselves. Dispelling myths and learning more about the aging process help an older person to put aging in perspective. Session 23, "What's Your Aging IQ?," is an examination of some of the myths of aging. The problems of older adults are compared with those of teenagers in Session 24, "'Seniors' and 'Teeners'." In Session 25 group members share their views of the losses and gains of aging. Session 26 helps participants to look realistically at aging-related memory problems and learn tips for coping with memory loss.

That Sinking Feeling

Once in a while, a session falls flat. All group leaders have been frustrated or panicked by a session that just wasn't reaching any of the group members—they act disinterested and perhaps disrupt the session; some may even sleep through the support portion. The thought, What do I do *now*?, has occurred to even experienced leaders.

First, take a deep breath and tell yourself that it's okay that the topic doesn't interest the group today. Then, acknowledge that thought to the members. You may be surprised by their reactions: They do not understand the topic, or they are not ready to share. In such cases try to explain the topic in another way or give group members more time to think. If their reactions are that the topic is boring to them or they just don't want to talk about "that" today, then "go with the flow": Acknowledge their feelings by saying, "Let's talk about something else. What's on your minds today?" An alternative is to use some of the ideas found in the section on conducting open discussions (pp. 24–27).

Developing a Healthful Lifestyle

In the sessions that are related to developing a healthful lifestyle, group members become aware of the many elements of this lifestyle and discuss ways to improve their own lifestyles. They learn that incorporating these elements has an impact on the quality and, perhaps, the length of their lives. They find that it is not too late to pursue a healthful lifestyle through exercise, nutrition, and attitude adjustment, even if they have abused their bodies in the past. Session 27, "What Is a Healthful Lifestyle?," looks at the many aspects of healthful living. Session 28 uses the popular game show "Wheel of Fortune" to reinforce good nutritional habits. Speakers can be invited to address the aspects of a healthful lifestyle, such as disease prevention, adapted exercise, smoking cessation, alcohol use and abuse, self-care skills, medical quackery, stress management, nutrition, and avoidance of constipation.

Managing Chronic Illness

As noted in the Introduction, the trade-off for living longer is the probability of enduring chronic illness or illnesses. Most adults older than age 65 have one or more chronic diseases and many have multiple conditions (American Association for Retired Persons,

Letter to Invited Speakers *(Sample)*

Group: ______________________________

Date: ______________________________

Start time: ______________________________

Length: ______________________________

Subject: ______________________________

Dear ______________________________:

Thank you for agreeing to speak to our restorative group for frail older adults. Below are a few tips that we recommend to speakers addressing our groups:

- Try to arrive 5–10 minutes early. We will help you set up. Also, allow us a few minutes to arrange the group in the best configuration for your presentation.
- Please use our mini-Vox sound system. Ask whether members can see and hear you so that you can adjust the level of your speaking voice and reposition yourself or your audiovisual aids.
- Ask group members what they know about the subject or if they have any questions. Make eye contact with group members while you wait for a response.
- Because time is short, limit the amount of information you present. Stick to your key points.
- Ask for feedback occasionally.
- Use visual aids and pass them among the group members.
- Leave enough time for questions and discussion.
- If possible, create handouts for group members. Unless you plan to review them with participants, distribute them at the end of the session.

We hope that these tips will help you to feel "at home" with our group members, and we look forward to having you with us.

Sincerely yours,

Your Name and Affiliation

Using the hand-held mini-Vox, a group member shares a story as the exercise leader and other group members listen.

1996). Some group members worry that talking about illness in the group will be depressing, but the Honolulu groups have not found that perception to be true. On the contrary, participants are hungry for information. By learning about the prevention, care, and management of chronic illnesses, members learn how to develop a "take-charge" attitude toward maintaining their health. The relevant sessions in Part 3 are merely a "starter kit" for dealing with this wide-ranging topic. Session 29, "What Do I Know About High Blood Pressure?," Session 30, "What Do I Know About Diabetes?," and Session 31, "What Do I Know About Osteoporosis?," model ways to introduce discussions about chronic illness in order to assess members' knowledge and interest. Depending on the group's interest, the leader can plan other activities and speakers on additional conditions, such as incontinence, shingles, arthritis, hearing and vision impairments, heart disease, stroke, Parkinson's disease, and Alzheimer's disease and other dementias. Session 32, "Coping with Pain," asks members to share their experiences with and their cures for chronic pain. Session 33, "Managing My Medications," introduces the important concept of a partnership between clients and their doctors in managing their regimen of medicines. Group members discuss problems related to the use of medicines in Session 34, and Session 35, "Do I Have the Right Doctor?," examines the doctor–patient relationship and suggests ways to improve it.

Understanding Emotional Problems

Maintaining good mental health is a challenge at any age, but especially in old age, because physical and/or emotional problems can affect mental capabilities. Becoming more aware of mental health problems helps older people to distinguish between good and poor or failing mental health and to realize the importance of early intervention. Most psychological problems are treatable with therapy that is appropriately matched to the complaint. Session 36, "Symptoms We Shouldn't Ignore," provides an introduction to mental health, and Session 37, "When I'm Depressed," addresses the most common mental health concern among older adults. Depending on the group's needs and interest level, speakers can be invited to address such related topics as anxiety; paranoia; medication or substance abuse; alcoholism; elder abuse, exploitation, and neglect (including self-neglect); sleep problems; stress management; and emotional disturbances.

Staying Safe

As older adults experience losses in mobility, vision, hearing, and reaction time, they become vulnerable. Thus, their safety becomes an important issue. Two major safety concerns of older adults are addressed in Sessions 38 and 39. Session 38, "A Safe Home Is No Accident," provides a checklist that group members can follow in conducting a safety survey of their residences. Session 39, "Preventing Falls," focuses on the many causes of and ways to prevent falls, which are a significant danger for older adults. Invited speakers can undertake other relevant topics such as the following:

Natural disasters—Invite a representative from the local civil defense agency or local chapter of the American Red Cross to talk about what frail older people can do in case of a natural disaster (e.g., tornado, earthquake, flood).

Crime prevention—The public relations office of the local police may be able to provide speakers on ensuring pedestrian safety, burglarproofing the home, and avoiding scam artists who prey on older people.

Fire prevention—A captain or the chief of the local fire department can be contacted to speak on preventing and reacting to fires in the home.

Using Community Resources

Learning about community services and how to use them helps older adults to feel more confident about reaching out for help, even in emergency situations. Most communities make available myriad services, however, contacting them can be frustrating. Some older adults cannot articulate their needs, and some telephone representatives are unhelpful. Thus, older people become discouraged and fail to follow up. By familiarizing themselves with the kinds of services that are available, older people understand that there are better ways through the system. Session 40 reviews some of the systems available for emergency help. Session 41 helps group members to think about what help they need or anticipate needing. Session 42 helps to familiarize members with the types of community services available. The local Area Agency on Aging can help the group leader to find speakers on various services such as the use of 911, 311, and other telephone emergency/information lines; personal alarm systems; emergency room procedures; ambulance use; and the signs and symptoms of emergency medical conditions.

Planning for Life Care

Some older adults have not considered planning for their life care needs in the areas of housing, estate, finances, health, and social welfare. Careful planning helps to prevent problems for them and for their families should these older adults become dependent and vulnerable. This area is complex, and participants' ability to plan depends on their level of independence and cognition. Speakers can be invited to group sessions to address estate planning, financial planning, wills and probate, trusts, advance directives, power of attorney and living wills, guardianship, transfers of assets to children, funeral planning, entitlement programs (e.g., Social Security, Medicare, Medicaid), spousal impoverishment, long-term care legislation, long-term care insurance, protective services for older adults, housing (landlord/tenant issues) and consumer protection, age discrimination, and pa-

A small group reviews a handout.

tients' or residents' rights. Session 43, "Developing an Independent Spirit," encourages group members to adopt a take-charge attitude, which is so important in continuing to live independently. This attitude encourages the idea that accepting a little help to remain independent does not mean that they are giving up. Session 44, "Where Shall I Live?," raises a question that often worries older adults. Session 45 helps members to become familiar with the documents and programs that are involved in life care planning.

Socialization Sessions

Participating in social and leisure activities is therapeutic and provides mental and social stimulation and fun. Although the socialization component is listed last, it is an important part of the program because it helps group members to become comfortable with one another, which facilitates the other parts of the restorative program. The socialization sessions have two components, socials and games, and the planned activities for each are found in Part 3.

Socials

Socials give group members a chance to interact informally. Session 46 offers ideas for planning a simple and effective monthly social event that centers on food. This type of event helps to continue the tradition of celebrating with food—from a casual dinner with friends to formal occasions such as weddings—which eases the social anxiety that is a part of interacting with others. How do you throw a party in 30 minutes? It *can* be done. Another social that can be planned is a sing-along (Session 47). Music is a powerful unifying force.

Games

Besides providing a mental challenge and competition, games are fun and help people to interact in a nonthreatening way. Even a simple game such as bingo helps older people to maintain vital cognitive abilities (Freiberg, 1995). The latter section of Part 3 provides suggestions for games that are mildly competitive, including an adapted version of bingo (Session 48), a word game (Session 49), a memory game (Session 50), a famous couples quiz (Session 51), an adaptation of charades (Session 52), silly skits (Session 53), an old-fashioned spelling bee (Session 54), a sedentary scavenger hunt (Session 55), a three-letter-word game (Session 56), a word scramble (Session 57), and a trivia game based on the popular board game, Trivial Pursuit (Session 58).

Seating

A large circle is often the most effective seating arrangement for restorative group discussions. Groups that have achieved cohesion like to be seated in a large circle because members enjoy hearing what others have to say; they do not want to feel left out of the action. Although a large circle is effective in most cases, in other cases a different seating arrangement is necessary.

Semicircle

Forming a semicircle is appropriate when discussing certain topics, for example, brainstorming or listing all of the games that group members played as children (which facilitates the life-review process). One or two small semicircles may facilitate viewing a video or film. A semicircle is preferable when the group leader will be using a blackboard or flip chart during one of the sessions in Part 3.

Small Groups

On certain occasions and in certain situations the group leader will place older adults in small groups rather than one large circle (e.g., team games, shy people seem to cope better and participate more in small groups). The leader can begin by giving instructions in the larger group and then breaking it into a number of small groups. Groups can be divided by several methods:

1. Allow group members to form their own small groups.
2. Ask group members to count off by 3s (i.e., "1, 2, 3, 1, 2, 3") and then form small groups of all of the 1s, the 2s, and the 3s.
3. Gather together certain group members for one purpose (e.g., all of the women together for a discussion of favorite hair or clothing styles of their youth; all of the men together for a discussion of favorite cars).
4. Form groups by stated commonalities (e.g., individuals who never worked outside the home, individuals who worked on a farm).

One drawback to seating participants in small groups is that the overall noise level in the room can become distracting. Small groups should be positioned as far apart as possible.

Dyads and Triads

In a dyad, two group members share with one another. The triad configuration may be preferred over the dyad in groups of frail older adults because if one participant has trouble communicating because of hearing, vision, or memory impairments, the other two can carry on and/or help the frailer member. Dyads or triads are effective for reminiscence sessions when personal information is shared. In addition, more people get a chance to share their stories when there are two or three people in a group.

Tables

Some sessions work best when group members are seated at tables. For example, the group leader may ask members to bring in family pictures or may bring in photography books from the library for a reminiscing session. The group may be seated at one large, round table, which makes it easier to pass around the pictures or books. This configuration encourages looking and informal conversation and discourages whole-group discussion. An alternative is to set out the pictures or books before the beginning of the group meeting so that participants can look at them. Then the leader can ask members to sit in the circle without the pictures and prompt them for their memories.

The Honolulu groups have found that it is easier to conduct writing assignments at tables. For example, in Session 18, "Being an Older Adult Is. . . ," members write completions to this open-ended statement. After writing, members share what they wrote. Also, it is more efficient to conduct craft activities at tables. (Craft activities are not often used in restorative groups because the time period is too short, many members are not interested, and people with arthritic and stroke-affected hands have trouble with fine motor activities. Talking about and/or showing crafts is beneficial, however, as members enjoy sharing their past craft work.)

Safety

Ensuring client safety during the support sessions is of the utmost importance and is the responsibility of the group leader. The restorative group program encourages clients to remain as independent as possible within the scope of their limitations. Because many group members have impaired ambulation as the result of stroke, Parkinson's disease, arthritis, hip fracture, or other medical problems, clients who require assistance should be accompanied by a caregiver or another escort (see p. 67). In addition, program staff and volunteers may help with ambulation and transfers, but only if they are trained and strong and healthy enough to do so. Sometimes deciding whether and when to help is difficult. For example, Gladys is capable of ambulating without help, but she enjoys walking arm in arm with a volunteer because she lives alone and is without any nurturing touch in her life. In other words, the restorative group program does not encourage dependence on help for walking, but touch for the joy of touching is. Some clients do not judge well what they can do safely and try to do too much; some caregivers help because it is faster and easier than letting clients do it themselves. If a client can ambulate or transfer safely alone, then he or she should do so. The group leader should test this theory; for example, the group leader can ask a male client to lock his wheelchair, give him a chance to do so, and give him a little help if he needs it. With time and practice, the client's ability to lock his wheelchair may improve.

With clients in fragile states of health, medical emergencies will occur. Both the group leader and exercise leader should be certified in CPR and first aid and should call for emergency services when necessary. The Honolulu program's experience with emergency services has been positive: Group leaders have never been criticized for calling for help even if the emergency turns out to be gastritis or the flu. Because older adults do not always present with classic symptoms in medical emergencies, it is better to err on the side of caution and call for help.

Caution must be exercised when a member enters or leaves the support group circle. Participants should remain seated during games that require a lot of movement because it is easy to lose balance during the excitement of play.

3 Whom Are We Serving?

One of the keys to the success of a restorative group is the thorough, caring attention that is given to identifying, screening, and preparing older adults who can benefit from participation in the group, and then continuing to help them with concerns as they arise. This chapter considers the kinds of people who are appropriate for group participation and reviews the steps involved in assessing, admitting, and working with them.

Identifying Potential Group Members

Most of the individuals who participate in the restorative group have health problems, and most of them have not one but several diagnoses. The most common diagnoses are, in approximate order of occurrence, stroke effects, hypertension, heart disease, arthritis, diabetes, a dementing illness, depression, Parkinson's disease, and anxiety. (The display on pp. 38–39 identifies and briefly describes these conditions.) Some participants also have various levels of hearing and vision impairment. For many of these older adults, the health problems are severe enough to have caused an alteration in their lifestyle, a reduction in physical and social activities, and/or an increased dependence on others to carry out everyday activities. Many have become isolated or reclusive; others have moved closer to or in with their adult children and find the adjustment difficult to make. Sometimes it is the adult child/caregiver who has difficulty adjusting to his or her parent's (or parents') dependence and is looking for ways to restore their independence.

Common Medical Problems of Restorative Group Members

Anxiety Anxiety is a vague, uneasy feeling, the source of which is often unknown to the individual. It may be a signal that a person is having difficulty coping in his or her usual way. Physical illness, personal loss, and psychological or environmental distress can bring on anxiety. Anxiety disorder is characterized by persistent worry with symptoms of chronic tension, timidity, fatigue, apprehension, indecisiveness, restlessness, and irritability.

Arthritis Arthritis of various types causes stiffness and pain in joints and muscles. At least half of all older adults have some form of arthritis. Osteoarthritis, the most common form, is a degeneration of cartilage and bone that comes from wear and tear of the joints of the hands, hips, and knees.

Dementia Dementia is a progressive mental disorder that is characterized by chronic disintegration of personality, confusion, disorientation, deterioration of cognitive capacity and function, and memory impairment. Dementia may be caused by a variety of disorders, including Alzheimer's and Parkinson's diseases, drug intoxication, vascular conditions such as small mini-strokes, depression, alcoholism, vitamin B_{12} deficiency, and fluid in the brain (normal pressure hydrocephalus). Some dementias are reversible, although dementia caused by Alzheimer's, Pick's, and Huntington's diseases and traumatic brain injury are irreversible.

Depression Depression is a treatable mood disorder or low mood that is characterized by exaggerated feelings of sadness, despair, melancholy, worthlessness, hopelessness, and sometimes thoughts of suicide. There are many causes, including genetic predisposition, environmental triggers, and responses to treatment of an illness. It is the most common psychological disorder among older people and may be mistaken for a dementing illness (Mosher-Ashley & Barrett, 1997).

Diabetes Mellitus Diabetes is a disorder of carbohydrate metabolism that is characterized by the inadequate use of insulin by the body; high levels of glucose in the blood; and excessive urination, thirst, and hunger. Its prevalence increases with age, from 8% of people over 65 to 25% of people over 85. Advanced diabetes places people at risk for complications such as cardiovascular disease and problems with the eyes, the nervous system, the kidneys, and the circulatory system.

continued

The group program seems to appeal to all types of people, regardless of advanced age, gender, ethnic group, or condition. Men like the idea of rebuilding their strength through the exercises, whereas others simply want to get out of the house for a few hours each week. Some like to have a "destination," which, for them, imitates their preretirement work schedule. Some of the group's youngest clients are those who have had disabling strokes. Some of the oldest are nonagenarians who are healthy but have become isolated. Various ethnic groups get along well in the group. Perhaps the commonalities that people share in coping with aging are more binding than the cultural differences are

Heart Disease Two of the most commonly seen heart diseases are congestive heart failure (CHF) and coronary artery disease (CAD). CHF occurs when the heart is unable to maintain an adequate circulation of blood in the body's tissues. CAD is any one of the abnormal conditions that can affect the arteries of the heart and produce effects such as reduced oxygen and nutrient flow. Coronary atherosclerosis, the leading cause of death in the Western world, is the progressive narrowing of arteries supplying blood to the heart. A third heart disease is peripheral vascular disease, or poor circulation, which is a reduced flow of blood to the lower extremities (e.g., legs, feet).

High Blood Pressure (Hypertension) Often called a "silent disease" because of the lack of symptoms, hypertension is an elevated blood pressure consistently in excess of 140/90. Hypertension is caused by aging or clogged arterial walls (atherosclerosis). Nearly half of all older adults in industrialized societies have at least mildly elevated blood pressure, and African Americans and men are more likely than Caucasians and other ethnic groups and women to be hypertensive. High blood pressure increases the risk of heart attack and stroke.

Osteoporosis Osteoporosis is decreased bone strength with decreased bone density and enlarged bone spaces that produce porosity and fragility. These abnormalities increase the risk of bone fracture, particularly of the hip. Back pain, decreased height, and stooped posture are symptomatic of osteoporosis-related compression fractures of the back. Hip fractures can have serious complications; for example, up to 25% of all people with hip fracture are dead within 1 year of their injury (Tideiksaar, 1998).

Parkinson's Disease Parkinson's disease is a slowly progressive degenerative disease of the nervous system featuring a slowing of the ability to initiate and control movement (bradykinesia); a resting tremor; shuffling when walking; and muscle stiffness, including the inability to smile. In later stages of the disease, the risk of falls increases. Parkinson's disease can result in symptoms of dementia, although it is important not to confuse the symptoms of Parkinson's disease with the symptoms of dementia.

Stroke The most common medical problem among group members is stroke (cerebrovascular accident, or CVA). Stroke is an injury to the brain tissue that occurs when the blood supply to the brain is inadequate or blocked. Many participants experience weakness or paralysis, sensory changes, aphasia (difficulty in speaking), a change in personality, or memory loss.

separating. Differences among some cultures have been diluted after years of living together in one environment. The maturity that comes from living a long life permits people to relax their misunderstandings and fears. The only barrier that seems to affect participation in a group of mixed ethnicity has been language. The Honolulu restorative groups are conducted in English, and most groups have several members who speak little or no English. Although most of the non–English-speaking participants are able to manage the exercise portion of the program because of the reliance on following musical beats and the movements of the leader, they have a hard time participating in the support portion. Language barriers must be weighed by the leader. Not understanding or not being able to speak the prevailing language detracts from full participation and may cause a person to feel excluded. In addition, translating discussions into a second (or third) language is a challenge that most group leaders cannot meet. They report that it is difficult enough to moderate group discussions among people with a variety of physical impairments without also doing it in two (or more) languages. Nevertheless, some non–English-speaking clients have managed to benefit from participating in the group despite gaining little from the verbal portion. Perhaps they understand a little more English than they let on, or perhaps being part of a group of peers meets their needs. A Korean man who understood no English became a much-loved member of one of the Honolulu groups. He was able to do the exercises from visual cues and received minimal help with translation from a volunteer who spoke Japanese, which he understood slightly. In another group a 93-year-old Japanese-speaking woman decided to forgo the support period (except on bingo or social days) after an experiment in simultaneous translation of discussions proved to be disruptive to the group process.

Other people who benefit in only a limited way from group participation are those with speech, hearing, or visual impairments. People with speech or hearing impairments have some difficulty during discussion and education sessions, and people with visual impairments have difficulty following the exercises. Many learn to cope with their disability and enjoy the group. It is best to give people with disabilities a chance to participate if they are motivated to do so. You must maintain a balance in enrollment in the group, however, and not admit more people with speech, hearing, or visual impairments than you are capable of handling.

Although many loners may not be willing to join a group, those who have participated have found that they became comfortable in a nonthreatening, nurturing group setting. Some have even blossomed. In one of my groups, a professional writer who had been a loner for most of his life surprised himself by revealing a long-dormant social side.

People in the early stages of Alzheimer's disease or other dementias can participate in restorative groups as long as their behavior continues to be appropriate and nondisruptive. Older people with dementia benefit from the stability and companionship provided by the group experience. Their number in each group must be limited to approximately 20% in order to avoid frightening away people who are cognitively intact. People in more advanced stages of dementia are not appropriate for the restorative group because their cognitive losses make it difficult or impossible for them to participate in discussions.

Some group members are frail caregivers who use the group as their respite from a difficult or demanding spouse at home. One Japanese American client, feisty but frail from multiple strokes, reported that she valued the support of the group as she cared for her frailer husband, whose lack of hearing and sensitivity drove her crazy at home. Sometimes, a couple joins the group. On the one hand, both may be looking for peer support and the benefits of exercise. On the other hand, a healthy spouse may need to accompany a spouse who is not independent enough to come to group unaccompanied. The healthier spouse can be helpful in the group and can socialize with other caregivers. Refer the caregivers of people who are very dependent or have advanced dementia to the local Alzheimer's Association for information on respite resources. Contact the national Alzheimer's Association for the location of the local chapter.

Assessing, Admitting, and Working with Clients

Prior to admitting a person to the restorative group, the program staff need to know about his or her strengths, problems, and ability to participate in a group program. This information is derived from a comprehensive assessment. Knowledge gained through the assessment is important for several reasons: to determine whether the client is, in fact, appropriate for the group; to develop a care plan to help overcome barriers that could preclude attendance; and to enable the group leader to work effectively with the client as a member of the group and as an individual who may need case management help in the future.

Assessing, admitting, and working with older adults in the restorative group occurs in six stages: referral, in-home assessment, developing and implementing a care plan, orientation to the group/client's first day in the group, follow-up, and ongoing case management.

Referral

Referrals of frail older adults to the restorative group come from aging network agencies, hospital social workers and discharge planners, home health agencies, physicians (especially geriatricians and geriatric specialists), family members, and potential clients themselves. Often, the referrals come by telephone, but occasionally someone will appear at the group meeting site to investigate the group. After listening to an informal presentation of the client's situation, the staff member can conduct an initial screening (see p. 42) to determine appropriateness for the group. To be eligible for membership in a restorative group, an older adult should

- Be of an appropriate age (60–100 years old)
- Have a physical, social, or mental need for exercise and peer support
- Be alert enough to interact with his or her peers in group discussions
- Be independent enough to attend group on his or her own or be accompanied by an escort
- Be continent or have managed incontinence
- Not behave disruptively
- Not exhibit wandering behaviors

If the individual meets these criteria, a written intake form can be completed (see p. 43 for a sample form). A written intake should include the client's name, date of birth, address, and telephone number; the name and telephone number of a responsible family member; the name, agency, address, and telephone number of the referring party; the client's physician's name, address, and telephone number; a list of the client's diagnoses; and a brief description of the presenting problem and any perceived barriers to attending a group. These barriers may include incontinence, lack of mobility, lack of cognitive skills, severe hearing impairment or vision loss, and client or caregiver resistance to being interviewed or joining a group. The assessment and casework steps of the process determine whether the barriers can be overcome.

In-Home Assessment

An in-home visit and psychosocial assessment determine further the older adult's suitability for membership in the group. Meeting with the individual in his or her home helps to provide a wide-ranging picture of the person's living situation, relationships, remaining strengths, and any problems. The in-home visit also establishes a relationship with the client and his or her family/caregiver and educates them about the restorative group. Some families may resist the in-home visit initially; often, with encouragement and an explanation of the group's purpose, a visit is approved and, later, greatly appreciated. (Some older adults report to group leaders that they were happy to spend more than an hour talking to someone about their concerns because they believed that most people had little time for them.) During the in-home assessment the interviewer can begin to dispel the older adult's fears about the restorative group program and begin to deal with

Referral Checklist

Name of referral (older adult) ______________________________

Name of person referring/affiliation ______________________________

____

Is the older adult of an appropriate age (age 60–100)? _____ Yes _____ No

Does the older adult have a need physically, socially, or mentally for exercise and peer support? _____ Yes _____ No

Describe the need:

Is the older adult alert enough to interact with his or her peers in group discussions? _____ Yes _____ No

Is the older adult independent enough to attend group on his or her own? _____ Yes _____ No

Would the older adult be accompanied by an escort? _____ Yes _____ No

Name of escort? ______________________________

Relationship to the older adult ______________________________

Is the older adult continent? _____ Yes _____ No

Is the older adult's incontinence managed? _____ Yes _____ No

Does the older adult display disruptive behaviors? _____ Yes _____ No

Does the older adult display wandering behavior? _____ Yes _____ No

Is the older adult so severely hearing impaired as to preclude group participation? _____ Yes _____ No

Is the older adult so visually impaired as to preclude group participation? _____ Yes _____ No

Notes

Client Intake Form

Name ____

Date of birth ______________________________

Address ____

____

Telephone ______________________________

Family member name/telephone ___________________________

____

Referring party name/agency/address/telephone __________________

____

Physician's name/address/telephone___________________________

____

Physician's diagnoses ___________________________________

____

Briefly describe the presenting problem and perceived barriers to group attendance (e.g., incontinence, lack of mobility, lack of cognitive skills, lack of social support, severe hearing or visual impairment, client or caregiver resistance to being interviewed or joining a group):

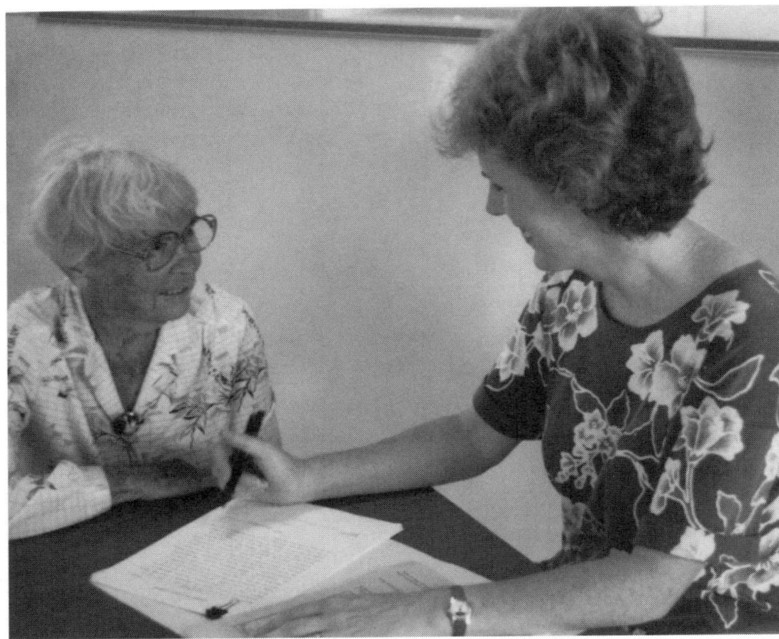

A group leader conducts an in-home assessment to determine the potential client's strengths and needs.

any resistance to it (see p. 47). This is also a good time to secure the older adult's written permission to obtain pertinent information from his or her physician with regard to participation in the exercise program; see page 16 for a sample form.

The in-home assessment is conducted by an age peer of the potential client, referred to by the Honolulu program as a "senior advisor." Senior advisors are retired social services professionals who are trained in the use of the assessment questionnaire. They are individuals who are sensitive to older adults' fears and tread carefully when discussing areas of potential resistance. For example, if the older adult is ashamed about the condition of his or her house, then the interviewer can conduct the questionnaire in the kitchen or even on the porch. If the older adult is reluctant to disclose information about his or her finances, then the interviewer can explain that there is an important reason for gathering financial information: to determine whether the individual needs financial assistance (in general, older people with low incomes divulge financial information more readily than do people with higher incomes). The older adult also can be asked to suggest a range of income, should the information be required for the program's statistical purposes or to help in setting a sliding-scale fee or donation level. If the individual is adamant in his or her resistance, then the senior advisor should move on to the next section of the questionnaire.

For use in interviewing potential clients and their caregivers, the Honolulu program adapted the Multidimensional Functional Assessment Questionnaire (MFAQ), which was developed in the 1970s as part of the Older Americans Resources and Services (OARS) program at the Duke University Center for the Study of Aging and Human Development (Fillenbaum, 1988).[1] Using the questionnaire, the senior advisor asks the client about his or her physical and mental health, social resources, financial status, and the physical and

[1]For further information, write OARS, Center for the Study of Aging and Human Development, Box 3003, Duke University Medical Center, Durham, North Carolina 27710. Telephone: (919) 660-7500. FAX: (919) 684-8569. Training in the use of the OARS questionnaire is offered at Duke on a monthly, as-needed basis.

Senior Advisors Program

The Honolulu Gerontology Program has trained a number of older adult volunteers, called senior advisors, to administer home-assessment questionnaires to potential group members. The program has recruited retired nurses, social workers, and others with human relations skills through word of mouth or through professional organizations' newsletters. The qualifications for senior advisor include the ability to understand and empathize with frail older adults, objectivity and a nonjudgmental attitude, and the creativity to work through barriers such as client or caregiver resistance. Senior advisors must possess the time and the stamina to work 4-hour days. At least one interviewer is recruited from each community so that these individuals are not required to travel outside their area. The ideal number of interviewers is one for each ethnic group so that culture and language are understood. Six hours of training in the use of the assessment questionnaire is provided to each senior advisor.

Using senior advisors saves the program money and the staff time. Senior advisors are paid a small stipend (in 1998, $15.00) and transportation expenses for each home visit. Having senior advisors explain and recommend the restorative group program helps the potential group members to understand the program and increases the likelihood that they will join.

Being a senior advisor is meaningful volunteer work for retired older adults. Helping to encourage depressed, possibly isolated, frail older adults to join a program that improves their physical and mental health is satisfying. They are able to maintain their skills and satisfy their desire to work with people. That the volunteering takes place only on a part-time basis means that it does not interfere with other activities, which is important to many older people. Senior advisors tend to stay with the program for many years, often until their stamina or health problems prevent their participation.

instrumental activities of daily living (ADLs). The questionnaire begins with a brief mental status examination, which determines whether the older adult is sufficiently cognitively alert to complete the assessment. It also contains a short psychiatric evaluation schedule, which allows the interviewer to ascertain whether the individual is depressed or paranoid or exhibits an anxiety syndrome.

The questionnaire continues with the interviewer recording his or her observations of the ways in which family members interact. A caregiver who hovers over the older adult may need respite care, and thus would be encouraged not to attend group with the potential client. Alternatively, a caregiving spouse may be in poor health and also in need of the restorative group. Some couples flourish in the group, whereas others need and enjoy time away from one another. Other observations include ADLs such as ambulation (walking). If the potential client's ambulation is unstable, then the interviewer should encourage him or her to use a walker or wheelchair (the program can arrange for the rental of an assistive device) or the program can try to arrange for an escort to bring the older adult to the group. The older adult's physician should be consulted if the individual's ability to attend the restorative group unescorted is questioned.

Ideally, the older adult and his or her caregiver are interviewed separately in order to determine whether either has concerns that he or she does not want to share in the presence of the other. The senior advisor can detect additional information from the older adult's or caregiver's reactions and interactions to the proposal of separate interviews. Some older adults do not want to be interviewed alone because they have become dependent on their caregiver and are fearful of not being able to cope with it. The senior advisor can gently remind the older adult and the caregiver that the potential client's own answers are needed to assess accurately his or her strengths and limitations. The caregiver who insists on being present during the older adult's interview may be trying to protect him or her because of the person's frailty and/or cognitive losses, or he or she may fear that the care receiver will divulge family secrets. The senior advisor must be alert to the latter possibility, especially to hints of physical, psychological, or financial abuse and should note any suspicious behaviors or responses. The program staff and group leader should continue to try to identify the causes of any such behaviors or responses. Participation in the restorative group helps to prevent elder abuse and neglect. The education, counseling, linkage to outside services, and the feeling of being part of a supportive community of peers helps to defuse tensions and improve the client's coping skills.

Unless the potential client or his or her caregiver objects, the interviewer should ascertain the condition of the home. For example, the pantry and refrigerator can be examined for signs of nutritional problems or alcohol abuse; inspection of the bathroom may reveal a lack of safety devices (e.g., toilet safety frame, bathtub grab bars) or careless control over medications; driveways or stairwells may be determined to be potential barriers to attending the group (i.e., a steep driveway or too many steps may be a deterrent to exiting the home).

Developing and Implementing a Care Plan

On completion of the in-home visit and assessment the staff social worker or the group leader writes a summary of findings from the questionnaire, as well as information received from the potential client's physician, caregiver, or other sources (see p. 41 for a discussion of the process for obtaining physician consent). The summary lists findings for each area—physical health, mental health, social resources, financial status, and ability to perform ADLs (see p. 47). The written care plan outlines the steps involved in resolving concerns about and eliminating barriers to group attendance. The group leader uses a checklist of potential barriers (see p. 48), which can be helpful in drawing up a care plan. All of the items checked should be resolved before the client's first day in the group. Weeks, even months, may pass before the older adult is capable of being admitted to a group. In addition, points in the summary may lead to other areas of concern. For example, the physician's response may raise questions about whether exercise is appropri-

Summary of MFAQ Findings/Care Plan *(Sample)*

Name: Richard Smith

Presenting problem: 70-year-old Caucasian male, retired teacher, Parkinson's disease, self-referred to restorative group

Assessment

Physical health: Parkinson's disease since 1984; heart bypass, 1986; degenerative arthritis in hip, with severe pain at times; cataract surgery with lens implant, 1990; intestinal cancer with colostomy, 1992; hypertension; shingles, 1995

Mental health: Perfect score on Mini-Mental Status Exam; Short Psychiatric Scale score of 11 indicates severe depression and anxiety; self-reports fair life satisfaction, poor emotional health, frequent depression, fear and anxiety, occasional loneliness; in therapy with psychiatrist

Social resources: Lives with wife; four adult children live in other states; likes to watch television; takes walks daily; no out-of-home activities

Financial status: Reports adequate income and assets (still paying mortgage); has Medicare and supplemental medical insurance

Activities of daily living: Independent in self-care (bathing, grooming, eating, toileting); ambulation is independent but unstable; independent in use of telephone but needs help with other instrumental ADLs, including use of medications, housekeeping, meal preparation, and shopping

Transportation: Still drives, but only distances close to home (wife drives distances farther from home); does not hold public van permit

Escort: Not needed at present

Care Plan

1. Refer to restorative group for exercise and peer support
2. Refer to Parkinson's disease support group
3. Refer for public van transportation permit so that Mrs. Smith has respite when he comes to group
4. Refer Mrs. Smith for caregiver support group
5. Counsel Mrs. Smith regarding other respite options
6. Provide information on personal emergency response systems (PERS)
7. Contact physician for any limitations in exercise
8. Contact physician about possible use of cane or walker
9. Contact psychiatrist for any suggestions regarding participation in restorative group

ate for the older adult, or the individual's score on a mental status examination may raise questions about his or her cognitive ability to participate.

Initially, many clients seem resistant to the idea of a group program. It is the responsibility of the program staff to work through their resistance while respecting clients'

Potential Barriers to Group Attendance

- ❒ Client's social support is inadequate to prepare him or her for group
- ❒ No escort is available to assist client
- ❒ Client is too weak physically to attend group unescorted
- ❒ Client's cognitive losses prevent him or her from attending group unescorted
- ❒ Client's visual losses prevent him or her from attending group unescorted
- ❒ Client's hearing ability is inadequate for group participation
- ❒ Client cannot walk alone safely
- ❒ Client cannot operate wheelchair independently
- ❒ Physical barriers in the home prevent client from attending group
- ❒ Physical barriers in the home prevent client from returning home after group meeting
- ❒ Client does not have or cannot afford a mode of transportation
- ❒ Client has bladder or bowel incontinence
- ❒ Client cannot use the toilet independently
- ❒ Client's cognitive abilities are inadequate for participation in a 2-hour-long program
- ❒ Client does not behave appropriately for group participation
- ❒ Client's social abilities are inadequate for group participation
- ❒ Client's resistance to group cannot be overcome
- ❒ Caregiver's resistance to group cannot be overcome
- ❒ Client's ability to speak English (or dominant language) is inadequate for interaction with peers

rights to self-determination. Working through the understandable resistance of a depressed and unmotivated person is one of the greatest challenges of working with frail older adults. Nurturing the most reluctant older adults so that they want to return to living and functioning provides great rewards for you and for them. Change is possible, but it comes slowly to older adults. One of the most powerful weapons in your arsenal is persistence, a gentle refusal to take no for an answer, as in the following example.

Severio

A widower in his late 70s, Severio was referred to a restorative group because he had become depressed and a recluse following a leg amputation. Initially, he expressed willingness to come to group, but every time the group leader called, he would claim that he had the flu or that his arthritis was bothering him too much to attend. After numerous calls the group leader reasonably could have concluded that Severio would never come to the meetings. However, she persisted in telephone contact with him. After 6 months of periodic calls he relented and attended a group session. Much to his surprise, he enjoyed the camaraderie and, especially, the exercise. The group became a powerful support system for this lonely man. He ceased complaining about his "aches and pains" and proved to be a warm personality. After 5 years in the restorative group, Severio graduated to an exercise club for older adults in the community.

Some candidates may simply be fearful or timid. For instance, in describing the group you may use the word "exercise." Some older adults may picture a roomful of sweaty, gasping people doing vigorous aerobics; they may think that they need special clothes or shoes; they may fear that they are too shy to be with other people and that the "regulars" will not be friendly; they may believe that they cannot cope with making friends; or they may think that they cannot afford the expense of joining a group. Your job as group leader is to correct these mistaken impressions and to do so early on. By dealing with these issues head-on the older adult is likely to consider the program with an open mind.

Potential clients are not the only individuals who exhibit resistance. Caregivers, for a variety of reasons, may respond negatively to the restorative group. Often, the caregiver has been the only one caring for the potential client, and he or she may feel indispensable to the person's safety and well-being. The caregiver's concerns are legitimate and should be addressed by reassuring the caregiver of the program's ability to protect the older adult. The caregiver may accompany the client to the group meeting and stay with him or her until the caregiver feels that safety is assured. Another reason for resistance is that the caregiver may be trying to stretch limited finances to meet present and anticipated future needs and may not understand the value in spending money for the program or the transportation to the program. The caregiver may feel that it is too much trouble to bathe, dress, and groom the frail older adult for group; the caregiver may doubt the ability of the public van transportation staff to handle the client; or the caregiver may be ashamed of the client's appearance or even of his or her own appearance after a period of being a recluse. You can work through the caregiver's concerns in one telephone call or in weeks or months of gentle education and nurturing through periodic telephone calls or home visits. The caregiver also needs to know that having some separation and respite from the care receiver will be beneficial for both of them.

If both caregiver and older adult demonstrate resistance, then approach another respected family member to intervene, or ask the older adult's primary physician to recommend the exercise program. Because of the revered, authoritarian role that doctors play in many older adults' lives, their suggestions seem to be followed when no one else is able to penetrate the wall of resistance.

An outside care management agency may be able to help prepare a reluctant older adult for group, as in the following example.

Lucy

Lucy was referred to the group program by a case management agency. She was on welfare and was living with her daughter and her daughter's drug-using boyfriend. Communicating with Lucy was problematic because the family had no telephone and they harbored an uncooperative attitude toward authority. Lucy, an insulin-dependent diabetic with one leg amputation, was hospitalized frequently because she failed to comply with her medical regimen. After some effort, Lucy's assessment was finally completed, and she was persuaded to attend the group. Her attendance was erratic, however. Undeterred, the group leader and the case management agency continued to work with Lucy and her family. Months later, the situation was stabilized sufficiently and Lucy began to attend the group regularly. She received continuous monitoring and reinforcement for better self-care.

In Lucy's case a seemingly marginal client worked out well. At other times clients who seem on paper to be appropriate group members sometimes do not work out. They may be too frail, they do not mesh with peers, or they find that they cannot work within the confines of a group setting. Again, use judgment, even intuition, to admit whoever seems suitable for the group. Set up membership on a trial basis if you have doubts.

Orientation to the Group

When the barriers to attending the group have been overcome, the older adult is ready for orientation to the group. Throughout the initial casework process, staff members educate the older adult about the value of participation in the restorative group: the benefits of exercise for physical wellness, the value of peer support for coping, and the possibility of making new friends. The educational process continues with orientation. To begin, reiterate the benefits of the restorative group. In many cases it is best to emphasize the exercise aspect of the program over the other components. Most people can understand the value of exercise, whereas the value of peer support and socialization may be less well understood and, as mentioned earlier, resisted: Even though the client is willing to attend a group session, he or she may not be committed completely to the program. Reinforcing the basic principles of the program helps the client to deepen his or her commitment.

A description of a typical restorative group meeting follows this reiteration of the basic group principles. Because clients' attention may be focused more on the exercise portion of the program than on the support group discussion, it is important for the group leader to clarify that exercise is only part of the program and that group members are expected to participate in both parts. Initially, some clients may try to avoid attending the support period because it seems unimportant or threatening to them. Reassure them that the support period is nonthreatening and is enjoyed by the group members. Mention various program activities that might appeal to them, such as parties, bingo, or speakers. In addition, the group leader must explain whether any fees or donations are required and when and how they are to be paid, as well as what the appropriate dress is for the exercise portion (casual).

Transportation to and from the group meeting facility must be arranged, and the arrangements must be clear to the client, the caregiver, and the group leader. A secondary but no less important transportation issue is how frail clients travel from the facility's front door to the meeting room. If a group member's ability to do so is in question because of his or her ambulation or cognitive deficits, then the caregiver should be asked to escort the individual to the first few meetings until a secure arrival system can be established. Another arrangement to make in advance is the incontinent client's bladder or bowel management method (e.g., using timed toileting, using adult incontinence pads, asking his or her escort to assist with toileting).

Unless the client is eager to attend the very next group meeting, select a starting date that is at least 1 week ahead of the next meeting. The client and/or caregiver may find it less threatening to set a later date. Not enough lead time may cause feelings of anxiety, whereas too much lead time may cause the client's readiness to slip. To reinforce the caregiver's resolve, he or she should be invited to come to the first meeting to understand more completely what the program is about.

Client's First Day in the Group

The group leader must plan carefully for the new member's arrival in the group. A negative impression made on the new member may negate the possibility of his or her joining the group. The client and his or her caregiver should be asked to arrive around 45 minutes before the group's starting time so that there is sufficient opportunity to greet and talk one-to-one with the member to review the group format, transportation, bathroom arrangements, fees, and any other concerns or questions. In addition, this time can be used to set both the client's physical and psychosocial goals (see pp. 52 and 53), which will increase the effectiveness of the group experience. Ask the client how he or she hopes to benefit physically and mentally from participating in the group. The group leader may need to probe, but, often, extra questions and patience help the client to focus his or her work in group. For example, a stroke-affected person may concentrate on strengthening a disabled side or improving speech; a woman with arthritis may want to improve her ability to perform ADLs. To help the client focus on psychosocial goals, you can draw from

A group leader gently facilitates this client's first day in the restorative group.

Physical Goals for Group Participation

____ Increase my overall strength and endurance

____ Increase my strength in one area (e.g., stroke-affected leg)

____ Increase my range of motion to specific area

____ Reduce pain

____ Improve my ability to walk safely

____ Improve my ability to carry out household chores

____ Improve my ability to do yard work

____ Improve my ability to ride the bus or drive a car

____ Improve my ability to transfer from the bed or chair

____ Get rid of my wheelchair/walker/cane

____ Other ____

____

____

the results of the individual's in-home assessment and prompt him or her with questions: "You told me that you feel very lonely at home. Would you like to feel less lonely?" If the client answers yes, then meeting new people can be one of his or her goals.

Seat the new client in the room and introduce him or her to the person seated on either side. Starting in this way helps new members to feel welcome by the group members without overwhelming them. Before the exercise class begins, the exercise leader should welcome the client and ask whether he or she has any special concerns about exercising this first day. (The exercise leader should have already reviewed the client's physician consent form—see sample on p. 16—and should be aware of the person's diagnoses, medications, and limitations or special precautions for exercise.) The exercise leader explains that he or she will remind new members throughout the hour not to exert themselves as strenuously as the longtime group members, who are in better physical condition and have learned in the group how to avoid injury. Leaders in the Honolulu program have noted that some new members may feel ashamed or embarrassed (some even feel competitive) about their inability to work as hard as longtime members. The exercise leader must dispel these negative feelings and reassure new members that their conditioning will improve.

Psychosocial Goals for Group Participation

____ Reduce my feelings of depression

____ Reduce my sense of isolation

____ Talk to people my own age

____ Talk to people with problems identical to mine

____ Learn more about aging

____ Learn more about how to stay healthy

____ Learn more about my chronic condition(s)

____ Learn about services for older adults

____ Feel a sense of belonging

____ Improve self-esteem

____ Improve self-confidence

____ Make new friends

____ Accept my limitations

____ Appreciate my strengths

____ Develop new interests

____ Learn to get along with others

____ Return to enjoying life

____ Return to traveling

____ Return to being happy

____ Other ____

____

____

Once the exercise portion of the group begins, the group leader should sit and talk with the client's caregiver to learn of his or her concerns and expectations for the group experience. If the caregiver has been resistant to the group, then he or she may express some unfair criticisms of and unrealistic expectations for the client. Such negativity gives the group leader an opportunity to counsel the caregiver about what is reasonable to expect given the limitations imposed on the client by the condition of his or her health. It may take time, but the group leader can help the caregiver to understand the client's situation and to be more accepting of his or her limitations.

During the half-hour support period, give the new client the opportunity to introduce him- or herself and say a few words if desired. Many clients are too depressed or overwhelmed to say anything the first day, but some come with a need to express pent-up emotions. Let the client ease into the rhythms and dynamic of the group rather than challenge the person by asking him or her to contribute. Sometimes it is helpful to conduct nonthreatening social interaction when a new member is admitted to the group.

Follow-Up

Making a follow-up telephone call a day or so after a client's first group meeting is extremely important. The group leader's call may reveal problems that the client experienced with the group or the group process. Sensitive probing on the part of the group leader may persuade the client to disclose that he or she had forgotten that the program charged a fee, that the exercises were too hard, that entry to the meeting room was difficult, that a roomful of people was intimidating, and so forth. The group leader should rectify any misconceptions or reassure the client so that he or she feels more positive about the group experience. Maybe some of the barriers that were thought to have been overcome in the casework phase still require work. Whatever the case, the client should be urged to try the group several times before declining membership. Some frail older people need more time than others do to develop feelings of belonging and appreciation for the benefits of the group. In addition, there may be other reasons that frail older adults do not "click" with the program from the first day in the group, as in the following example.

Ruth

After living for several years in a board and care home because of poor physical function and double hip fractures, Ruth, 84, returned to independent living in a seniors housing project, where a restorative group met twice each week. Her daughter referred her to the group because she seemed isolated in her new apartment. The in-home assessment showed that Ruth was mentally alert but had poor short-term memory. She attended one or two restorative group meetings with a companion, but did not return. During her follow-up telephone call, Robin, the group leader, found that Ruth simply could not remember from week to week to come to the meeting. She and Robin decided that Robin would call Ruth 30 minutes before group started to remind her to attend. After a few weeks of reminders, Ruth began to remember on her own and came to group regularly.

Ongoing Case Management

The restorative group leader is the case manager for group members. Either the group leader or the exercise leader may notice a change in an individual's behavior during the group sessions and can intervene early to identify the cause and look for solutions, as in the following example.

Dorothy

Dorothy began falling asleep during group sessions. The group leader was concerned, so she spoke with Dorothy and her caregiver and suggested that Dorothy consult with her physician. Dorothy made an appointment to see her doctor to explain her symptoms. The doctor reduced the dosage of one of Dorothy's medications, and Dorothy stopped sleeping during group. Early intervention prevented the crisis that could have resulted from Dorothy's being overmedicated (many falls and hip fractures result from older adults' being overmedicated).

Absences commonly hint at some kind of problem. A group leader may hesitate to call the client, thinking that he or she has tired of the group program, and sometimes this is the case. More often, however, there is a physical barrier to attendance: Perhaps the caregiver is ill and is not able to ready the client for group; perhaps the client has had a minor stroke.

Myrtle

Myrtle, 75, joined a restorative group after a moderate stroke. She was improving rapidly and continued to attend group faithfully until she broke her foot during her first poststroke adventure, a trip to Las Vegas. The incident set Myrtle back physically and psychologically. Recovery from the fracture was slow, and she kept delaying her return to the group. After being absent for 6 months, the group leader considered her terminated but telephoned her one last time, a few days before the next group meeting. Sounding very depressed, Myrtle said, "I'll never be able to come back. I just have too much pain." The leader was surprised but pleased when Myrtle attended the next group session. "You won't believe it," she said to the leader. "The pain went away the next day!" Perhaps knowing that someone cared "cured" Myrtle.

Jack

Jack, 81, attended a restorative group for several months after he experienced a stroke. A second stroke made him feel so weak that he believed that he would not be able to return to the group. In addition, Jack had no family support. Repeated case management calls from his group leader revealed that Jack was increasingly depressed and reclusive. The leader referred him for support services such as chore service, home-delivered meals, in-home visitors, and counseling for his depression. Jack eventually returned to his group in good spirits.

The group leader should telephone clients who live alone. If, after several attempts, the client cannot be reached, someone on staff should be assigned to go to the client's home to check on him or her. In my restorative group program, staff have found clients who had fallen and fractured their hips.

Terminating Group Members

Except in rare cases, clients are not terminated from the restorative group program. Frail older adults need the continuing support of the group to maintain wellness. Members eventually stop attending group for a variety of reasons, including "graduation," physical or mental deterioration, and death.

"Graduation"

Clients may improve their physical and mental health and seek activities outside the restorative group (e.g., a more challenging exercise class), or they may resume their pre-illness lifestyles gradually, making the group unnecessary. For example, Ignacio was admitted to the program with a diagnosis of Alzheimer's disease. After 6 months in the program, it became clear that depression actually caused his symptoms of dementia. (In his career he had been a highly placed professional with many responsibilities, so when he retired, he became depressed.) During Ignacio's tenure in the group, his physical and mental health improved dramatically and his symptoms of dementia disappeared. He "graduated" himself from group and led an active life.

Physical or Mental Deterioration

Because of the aging process and progressive diseases, some clients become too frail or their behavior becomes too erratic for them to continue in the group. As group leader, you should speak with these clients and their families about terminating the person's membership and help them to identify other, more appropriate long-term care services, such as full-time day services and chore services. Try to remain in periodic telephone contact with the client and family for support. It is a sign of the restorative groups' success that, often, current members stay in touch with former members, enabling the latter to continue to feel supported.

Death

Although the death of a group member is sad for the group and for family members, it is remarkable that seriously ill or frail people can remain active and feel supported by the group program until their death. An example is Joe, a retired musician whose multiple strokes gradually robbed him of his physical stamina and cognitive status. Despite the disabilities, Joe persevered in attending group sessions, at first on his own and later with a companion, until he died of a massive stroke. Another example is Lillian. When her first stroke made living alone impossible, she moved cross-country to live with her adult daughter and son-in-law. The group became her only social outlet, and she was well loved by fellow members. Lillian died one morning as she prepared for group. Later, Lillian's daughter and son-in-law, who greatly appreciated the group's support, shared memories and pictures of Lillian's life with group members. Sharing these memories helped Lillian's family and the group members to achieve closure, an important step in coping with death and one that is so often missing in older adults' lives.

4
How Do I Lead a Restorative Group?

Restorative groups for frail older adults need leaders: a group leader and an exercise leader. The most compelling personal qualification for both kinds of leader, beyond professional qualifications, is empathy with frail older adults. Leaders must enjoy, respect, and relate to frail older people as adults. Ageism, whether demonstrated by older or younger people, has no place in facilitating restorative groups for older adults.

Leading the Restorative Group

The group leader (see p. 58 for group leader job description) is the overall coordinator for the restorative group and is responsible for helping members to develop into a supportive group of peers who work together to improve their motivation and capacity for remaining in charge of their lives. She oversees the program, meets with site managers, opens and closes the meeting room each day, greets arriving group members, stands by during the exercise program, handles clients' and caregivers' concerns, plans and leads the half-hour support session, maintains client's and attendance records, and remains on-site until the last participant has departed. She also provides ongoing case management to clients as needed. Restorative group leaders should work under the supervision of a master's degree–level administra-

Job Description
Restorative Group Leader

Job Summary
Under the supervision of the Program Director, the Restorative Group Leader is primarily responsible for coordinating the operations of one or more Restorative Groups.

Duties and Responsibilities
Coordinates all operations of the assigned Restorative Group(s). Coordinates class schedules, logistical arrangements, first aid, and safety with site personnel. Plans and carries out discussion, education, and socialization portions of group program; recruits speakers; leads therapeutic discussions. Provides ongoing counseling and case management for group clients and/or caregivers as necessary. Provides periodic reports of progress to clients' physicians. Attends group staff and planning meetings. Provides monthly attendance statistics and narratives to Program Director. Supervises volunteers and students assigned to groups. Conducts public relations and education with site personnel, community groups, and medical/health practitioners in the area. Attends agency staff meetings and selected staff development meetings as needed. Maintains client confidentiality at all times. Performs other related duties as assigned.

Minimum Qualifications
Bachelor's degree in social work or a related human services field from an accredited school. A minimum of two years' experience working with frail older adults and leading support groups. Knowledge of physical and psychosocial aspects of aging. Good verbal communication and writing skills. Valid driver's license and access to an insured vehicle. Up-to-date CPR and first aid certification.

1/95

Reasonable accommodation will be provided to enable the qualified applicant or qualified employee to perform the essential functions of this position.

tor (social worker) with experience in gerontology. Group leaders should hold a bachelor's degree in social work or a related field; be certified in CPR and first aid; and be knowledgeable about aging, chronic illness, and aging network services. He or she must understand the group process and group dynamics and be able to moderate group discussions. These qualifications are of little use, however, unless the leader can express creativity in planning interesting sessions. The session plans outlined in Part 3 are helpful, but they are just an outline, a guide to get the leader started. Honolulu group leaders are paid for 5 hours of work for each session that they lead: They work with the group for approximately $2\frac{1}{2}$ hours and plan future sessions and do casework for the other $2\frac{1}{2}$ hours. The exercise leaders are paid for each hour of exercise that they lead.

Group leaders grow on the job, so even beginners should not be daunted, as long as they possess empathy and respect for frail older adults, knowledge about aging issues, and leadership tendencies. As they grow on the job, group leaders form close attachments to their clients, which is a good quality, but they must remember to encourage empowerment, not dependency. In forming these attachments, group leaders model attitudes and behaviors that help group members gain the most benefit from the restorative group program. One of these attitudes is "modeling 'we-ness'."

"Modeling 'We-ness'"

The group leader is a listener, a comforter, a supporter, an encourager, a teacher, an administrator, a matchmaker, an interaction broker (i.e., interactions between group members), a respectful adult friend, and the creator of a nurturing environment—the restorative group. The group leader helps to create the nurturing environment of the restorative group and fosters its cohesion by setting the tone, or, as Middleman (1987) termed it, "models 'we-ness'." Modeling we-ness in a group for frail older adults means believing in and encouraging the following feelings:

We are people who are worthy of respect.
We care about one another.
We have stories to tell.
We have needs.
We have wisdom.
We have disabilities, but they do not demean us.
We can improve our lives.
We can cope.
We can have fun.

Group Discussions

The importance of modeling we-ness does not diminish the importance of learning the techniques of facilitating good restorative group discussions. Fourteen techniques are listed below.

Seat members closely together in the discussion circle. If the exercise period precedes the support period, then you should take a few minutes after exercise to move the chairs closer together. Doing so brings members closer psychologically and helps them to hear a speaker and one another during discussions.

Use a co-leader. A co-leader should be seated across the circle from the group leader in order to involve clients on that side and also to observe and involve clients seated next to the group leader. A volunteer, a student, or even an appropriate group member can be encouraged and trained to fill the role of co-leader.

Consider the ability of the group members. A group leader may need to lower her expectations for what can be accomplished in a half-hour discussion (Weisman & Schwartz, 1989). Every "step" of a discussion requires time: repositioning the chairs, explaining the topic, considering responses, repeating or clarifying quiet comments, and so forth. Trying to cram too much into a half hour is the biggest mistake made by beginners. To quote Thoreau, simplify, simplify.

Keep presentations brief. Speak slowly and clearly and stick to the essence of the presentation. Always present a brief overview of the topic and ask whether everyone understands. A summary before the group leaves for the day also helps to reinforce what has been discussed during the session.

Permit silence. Allowing silence is important in groups of frail older adults—many times, thoughts come slowly because they have a lifetime of memories to sift through. The Honolulu groups use a technique called "close your eyes for a few moments" (see p. 62) to give group members sufficient time to consider the topic. This technique also prevents overly eager, vocal members from jumping in before others have time to think.

Help each member to feel included. All group members should be recognized during a group meeting even if they do not have an opportunity to speak. The group leader should call each person by name, make eye contact with each person, and give the person at least a moment or two of attention. The group leader must help bring out the best in each participant by providing frequent praise, comfort, support, and encouragement. Some sessions are set up to allow the group leader to go around the circle and give each older adult a chance to contribute to the discussion. The advantage of this technique is that it encourages quiet or shy members to speak while it prevents a monopolizer from gaining control over the discussion. The group leader should interrupt a long offering with a statement similar to the following: "Thanks for sharing, Louise. We need to move on to hear from everyone today."

Encourage members to speak to one another, not only to the group leader. One way to encourage members to speak to one another is for the group leader to look around the circle while someone is talking, which helps her notice whether group members are paying attention to the speaker. It also prevents the speaker from directing comments only to the leader because she is not looking at him or her all of the time. The speaker may then look to someone else for attention.

Encourage members to speak, but respect their wish not to. Margaret, a retired teacher, had undergone brain surgery. The procedure caused her to have difficulty articulating her speech, and she was very embarrassed by it. Because of the shame she felt, she would leave group immediately after the exercise portion. The group leader recognized that Margaret had a lot to offer the group and encouraged her to stay. After several efforts Margaret agreed, but asked not to be called on in group. Margaret not only stayed but gradually began to contribute without being asked. Her speech and her self-confidence improved with practice and the generous praise of the group leader and other members. Eventually, she graduated from the group and rejoined her organization of retired teachers.

Watch for attention lapses. Some clues to lapses of attention are nodding off; talking to a neighbor; and looking around, hoping to sneak out. Giving the offender a little direct but gentle attention redirects his or her wandering mind: "How are you doing, Mabel?" "Juan, let's hear your ideas about your best job."

Manage side conversations. Side conversations are disruptive. They occur for various reasons: People with impaired hearing may turn to their neighbor to ask what was said. Some participants enjoy making sarcastic comments, or they become excited and want to talk about the topic. One solution to such situations is to conduct an "official" side conversation: "Today we are talking about stress in our lives. Turn to your neighbor and talk about what stress you have in your life." Or, "I can see this topic really interests you. Take a few minutes to talk to your neighbor about it and then we'll go on." After a few minutes of conversation the group leader needs to be firm in order to get everyone back on track, which includes waiting for or prompting all eyes to focus on her before resuming.

Help clients who have visual limitations or losses. Special care must be taken with group members with visual impairments. There are several ways to make them more comfortable. The close-seating configuration mentioned at the beginning of this section is helpful, as is seating the person with low vision at the proper angle so that he or she can hear the speaker or leader (the client should decide what that angle is). The group leader should let the participants with visual impairments know that she is supportive of their need to see and should encourage them to choose the right seat. Handouts should be made available in large-print format, and any writing that is done on the blackboard or flip chart should be large.

Help clients who have hearing loss. Special care must be taken with group members with hearing impairments. There are several ways to make them more comfortable. The group leader must control outside or background noise and side conversations. Sometimes volunteers and caregivers sitting outside the circle but near the group converse loudly. The group leader must be direct in reminding them to keep their voices low, or she can invite them to join the discussion or move to another room. The group leader should not raise her voice to compensate for hearing losses; rather, she should speak clearly and slowly in a normal tone. A microphone is highly recommended for use in all groups. Many members resist the idea of using a microphone themselves, but they readily acknowledge that they hear others better when they use it. Encourage them to do so; they will become comfortable using it and appreciate hearing what is going on. Many guest speakers resist using a microphone, but they should be encouraged to use it as well. A mini-Vox, a small battery-operated sound system that can be fitted with a 20-foot-long cord, is an inexpensive sound system. Visual aids are also helpful. The leader must continually remind group members to speak up and restate or clarify for the group the mumbled or quiet offerings of soft-spoken members.

Help clients with memory loss. Some group members are ashamed of their memory loss and will try to hide it. Working with them proceeds more smoothly when the memory loss is acknowledged. One way for the group leader to help is to repeat the assignment often: "Remember, today we're thinking back to our first job." Question the person with memory loss first, but be careful of the phrasing. Do not ask, "What is your memory of. . . ," or, "What do you think?" Rather, spell out the question: "Ruth, do you remember your first job as a young woman?" Encourage the person to keep a pad on his or her lap and jot down thoughts as they come (unfortunately, some participants' memory loss is so pronounced that they will not be able to do this). Handouts also help to reinforce what has been said. Another suggestion is for the group leader to write down the discussion topic on a slip of paper and hand it out at the beginning of the meeting. The group leader can call and remind the caregiver or send home a written note about any homework assignments (e.g., "Remember to bring in a picture of your pet next time").

Help clients who are aphasic (problems with speaking and/or understanding speech). Communicating with a person who has aphasia is difficult, yet they must be included in the discussion to the greatest extent possible. One way to include them is to ask questions to which they can respond "yes" or "no" or make statements to which they can nod agreement. The group leader should learn as much as she can about the person so that she can speak for him or her when necessary. During a discussion on leisure activities, for example, she could say, "Bill, I know you and your wife love to travel to some of the national parks for vacation." The group leader can call the caregiver or send home a note asking for input on a forthcoming session. She could ask Bill's wife, for example, to write down a memory for a reminiscing discussion about school days. Games should be adapted for the person with aphasia; for example, a bag of letters from which the aphasic person can pull a letter could be created for the word game in Part 3, Session 49. Some older adults with aphasia can speak, but they need practice to improve and gain confidence. The group leader must make the group a safe place for the aphasic person to practice his or her speech. Often, group members model the leader's approach and are extremely supportive of the member's efforts to talk.

Discussion Techniques

Members should be taught to follow basic rules for communicating in a group. Some of these can be taught by leader modeling, but it is wise to review the rules with members from time to time or even involve the group in a discussion on effective communication skills. Some of the discussion rules are

1. Give the speaker your full attention.
2. Avoid side conversations.
3. Share your ideas and feelings, although you are not required to do so.
4. Do not criticize others' ideas and feelings.

5. Guard your impulse to give advice. Tell what works for you.
6. It is okay to be sad and to cry.
7. Do not monopolize the discussion.
8. Raise your hand if you cannot hear.

Structuring Discussions

A half hour may seem like a short period of time for a discussion, but with careful planning, much can be accomplished. Discussions are usually structured in six basic steps, which can be adapted according to the subject.

Step 1: Organize the seating. At the end of the exercise period group members may be sitting too far apart. The group leader should take a few minutes to reorganize the circle, moving clients into a tight circle to promote a closer feeling and to facilitate hearing and seeing.

Step 2: Introduce the topic. Choose a single, clear, simple subject to which members can relate. When discussing nutrition, for example, the group leader can ask each participant to share what he or she usually eats for breakfast. Note, however, that trying to pin down what the person ate that morning may be too threatening for participants with memory loss or Alzheimer's disease. If the discussion never progresses beyond hearing what others eat, then people will learn by modeling from the healthful eaters. Group members can be given further guidance for discussion from a handout that lists alternative topics or subtopics. For example, the handout in Part 3, Session 9 lists subtopics. These subtopics may help to stimulate memories and add variety to the discussion.

Step 3: Focus. The group leader should give members a few minutes to think about the subject. A good method is the "close your eyes for a few moments" technique. Group members should be asked to close their eyes for a few minutes to think about the topic and then talk about what memories surfaced (Step 4). Some groups enjoy writing as a way of collecting their thoughts.

Step 4: Share. Ask members to open their eyes and talk about what memories surfaced. Go around the circle and call on each person, allow members to volunteer a memory, call on people at random, or begin the discussion with the member with short-term memory loss before he or she forgets.

Step 5: Summarize. At the end of the discussion, the group leader should thank the participants for sharing and recap what they learned during the session. For example, "I see that nearly everyone in this group worked outside the home, many of you on farms, and that your work life was sometimes very hard. Yet your memories seem to reflect pride in your work."

Step 6: Evaluate (optional). At the end of the session, the group leader should ask members whether the session was meaningful, helpful, or fun for them (depending on what goals were set for the session). Gathering this input on a regular basis helps in planning sessions. For example, "Yes, it was fun to talk about work, but what about the years during the Depression, when there was no work. Let's talk about that."

Progress Report to Client's Physician

The group leader, with input from the exercise leader, prepares a progress report to each client's physician (the primary physician or the physician who signed the release for the older adult to participate in exercise; see p. 16) after the client has been a group member for 6 months. This brief report (see display on p. 63) helps the physician to determine whether the older adult is improving, maintaining, or declining in fitness as well as in psychosocial issues of personal adjustment, social skills, cognitive level, and self-help

Progress Report to Dr. ______________________

Client's name ______________________________

Date of birth ________________ Today's date ______________

Dear Dr. ______________________:

The following is a report on your patient's progress in the

____

restorative group. As you know, the program provides nonaerobic exercise for strength, endurance, and improved range of motion, as well as education for self-care and mental and social stimulation in a supportive group of peers.

Date of entry ________________

Attendance record (circle one): Regular Irregular Days per week ____

Has not attended since ________________

Comments of Exercise Leader on Participation in Exercise Program

- ❑ Participates actively and is showing progress
- ❑ Participates actively and is maintaining abilities
- ❑ Lacks motivation
- ❑ Has declined in abilities
- ❑ Is unable to participate effectively
- ❑ Other: ______________________________

____

Comments of Group Leader on Client's Psychosocial Adjustment

M = Maintained I = Improved
D = Declined

Personal adjustment (acceptance of limitations, adequate coping skills) ____

Social skills (participation in group; interaction with peers and staff) ____

Cognitive level (ability to comprehend proceedings) ____

Self-help skills (independence in attitude and effort) ____

Other: ______________________________

____

Group volunteers always are ready to listen.

skills. The report also serves as a way to build a partnership with the physician for the client's ongoing care.

Working with Volunteers

Including volunteers in the restorative group program enriches everyone's experience. In large groups, volunteers are essential to maintaining order and serving as extra eyes and ears for the group and exercise leaders. The task of finding, training, and keeping good volunteers can be initiated and supported by the administrative staff, but, often, the crucial work is completed by the group leader.

The three types of people who are most suitable to be recruited as volunteers are older adults, students, and people who are recovering from physical or emotional problems. The most dedicated volunteers are older adults who were referred to the restorative program by their physicians in order to improve their health and well-being. These individuals had situational depression that resulted from experiencing a loss or losses, or they were caregivers for a spouse who attends the restorative group program. They feel the need for social support and exercise, which they receive by helping and participating in the group. Some examples from the Honolulu program: Peggy was having a hard time coping with the death of her husband; Ruth brought her husband, who needed exercise to reduce his high blood pressure. Peggy and Ruth soon "graduated" (see p. 56) from the group and became volunteers. Paul, another longtime volunteer, started as a group member with Parkinsonian symptoms, which later turned out to be a treatable illness. After surgery, he graduated from the group to become a volunteer and later a Senior Companion (a federally funded program of companions who help frail older adults). Dr. Wolfe, a retired physician, was a volunteer speaker for several of the Honolulu groups in the 1980s. In 1992 he became a group member and participated enthusiastically until just before his death from heart disease.

Recruiting healthy older people as volunteers is sometimes difficult because many resist working with older people who are unwell. Some report that it reminds them too much of their own mortality, whereas others believe that the program is nothing more than a nursing facility outpost. The Honolulu program has found that if they can be convinced to observe the group throughout the session, then they will learn that these frail-looking people are just like them: motivated, loving, wise, and fun.

Student volunteers are either assigned by their schools to work with the program as a practicum experience for credit or persuaded by their curiosity about working with older adults. The restorative group provides students with an excellent direct-practice "laboratory" and, at the same time, provides the group with a pool of substitute group leaders and exercise leaders for summer and part-time work.

People in recovery are referred to the group by counselors to build self-esteem and confidence before returning to school or the workforce. Some referrals have found success in the group program and later became respite aides. They credit their experience in the group as crucial to the rebuilding of their self-confidence.

Volunteers assist the group and exercise leaders before, during, and after the group session in many ways, but one of the most important is greeting and chatting with frail clients who need someone to talk to. (The display on page 66 lists some of the many ways volunteers help the leaders, and the display on page 67 lists preferred qualifications for group volunteers.) Because most of the volunteers join the program one at a time, initial training often occurs on the job. The group and exercise leaders teach hands-on safety in assisting mobility-impaired clients (see the display on pp. 67–68). Volunteers are asked to participate in the group session as though they were clients so that they receive the same benefits as do real clients and understand the experience. Physician consents are required for older volunteers. (The physician consent form on p. 16 can be adapted to suit the needs of volunteers.)

Like paid staff, volunteers need guidance to perform their jobs correctly. Some volunteers want to do too much, others not enough, and some want to come only when they feel like it. Volunteers should make a commitment to come regularly—either one or two days each week. Of course, group and exercise leaders need to recognize that volunteers are just that, and there will be occasions when other priorities take precedence over working with the group. Some volunteers become territorial and need to be counseled to share their "turf" with a new volunteer. The display on page 69 helps volunteers to understand that the purpose of the restorative group program is to build clients' self-reliance—volunteers should help only when help is needed. This lesson is sometimes difficult to teach because many volunteers are nurturers who feel that helping is what they should do, whether it is locking someone's wheelchair or playing someone's bingo numbers.

Most volunteers report that their work in the restorative group offers great personal satisfaction. Group leaders and group members are appreciative of the help given by volunteers, who become part of the group "family." Many of the volunteers take on leadership roles in their groups, which helps to fulfill their own needs for leading a useful life. Sometimes the group volunteers develop supportive relationships with clients that go beyond the group experience. For example, a volunteer in one of the Honolulu groups told the group leader about the death of a former client to whom she had become extremely

How to Assist in a Restorative Group

Thank you for volunteering to help in our group. Remember that the goal of the restorative group program is to help frail older adults maintain as much dignity and independence as possible. Some clients are rebuilding their independent living skills after a stroke, fracture, or other illness or injury. Others are fighting to hang on to their independence as a progressive illness takes its toll. Therefore, sometimes it's best to help by not helping. For the times that you'll want or need to be helpful, here are some suggestions:

Emergencies. Group and exercise leaders are prepared to handle any emergency situation. You should be prepared to assist them. You may be asked to place a telephone call or to calm members who may be upset. Your calm manner can help others to remain calm.

Assisting clients with disabilities. Do not provide physical assistance to clients unless you are in good health (no recurrent back problems) and you have been trained by the group leader or exercise leader. If the client is able to transfer safely from a wheelchair, allow him or her to do so. Stand by to remind the client to lock the chair or move to the appropriate position to make the transfer. Never pull on a client's arm in an attempt to lift him or her as this may cause injury.

Games. In games designed to provide mental stimulation for clients, you should not answer questions yourself but rather encourage clients to do so, being sure to give them enough time to think, as thought processes may be slowed by age and illness.

> *Bingo.* Most clients are able to manage their own bingo cards, although they may be much slower to spot the numbers than are you. Let them try. If they miss a number, just remind them of it. If the caller is going too fast, then ask him or her to slow down. A few clients may be unable to spot the numbers without your assistance. If in doubt, ask the group leader to help. When a client gets BINGO, let him or her read the numbers even if this slows down the game. For some clients, this may be the only time they speak up. A little inefficiency is okay in the interest of promoting clients' independence.

During group discussions. Sit across from the group leader so that you can bring the clients sitting on your side into the discussion. Invite them to contribute and, if necessary, repeat their comments so that the whole group can hear. You are welcome to offer your stories and opinions, but be sure to give precedence to clients. Beware of side conversations—it's easy to be drawn into side conversations with a group member, but they are distracting and make it difficult for everyone to hear. If the side conversation is relevant, you could announce that the client has a story to tell. If the conversation is not relevant, signal the client to wait until after group.

Lead a small group. The group leader may ask you to facilitate a small group. Your task is to be sure that each client has a chance to talk and share. You must be careful not to spend too much time talking.

Volunteer Qualifications

Interest in working with frail older adults.

Knowledge, ability, and judgment to assist frail older adults with walking; riding elevators; using wheelchairs, walkers, or canes; and so forth (you will receive training from program leaders).

Willingness to talk and listen one-to-one.

Ability to speak English; knowledge of other languages is welcome.

Training in CPR and first aid is helpful but not required.

Willingness to volunteer on a regular basis (1–2 times each week).

Willingness to take part in some of the training opportunities that are offered by the restorative group program.

Assisting Clients with Mobility Impairments

Wheelchair

At rest. Train the client to lock the wheelchair on both sides when it is idle. Check that the client has done so and help the client who is not able to do so. If the chair is sitting on a downward slope, point the chair at an angle to the wall to prevent rolling.

Pushing the wheelchair. Before pushing a client in a wheelchair, check that the footrests are in position and that the client's legs and feet are placed on the footrests. Be sure that the seat belt is fastened and that umbrellas, canes, or purses will not accidentally catch the spokes of the wheels. Tell the client that you are about to push the chair and ask him or her to release the locks. Push the chair slowly, looking ahead to anticipate turns, obstacles, and other people.

Ascending a curb/step. Place the chair facing the curb/step and push the chair against it. Step down on one of the rear foot braces while holding onto the guides with the hands. Gently lift and push the rear end of the chair until it is entirely on the higher level.

Descending a curb/step. Place the chair close to the curb/step and turn the chair so that the rear is to the curb. Gently pull the chair over the curb/step edge until the front end gently descends to the lower level.

Transfers. Position the wheelchair either directly facing or angled toward the bed or seat. Be sure that the chair is locked on both sides. Ask the client to push up from the wheelchair, not to reach across to the chair and pull up his or her body. (Stroke-affected people should turn their unaffected side toward the wheelchair.) Once balanced, ask the client to pivot slowly toward the chair, reaching across to hold onto the armrest. Ask the client to feel the back of his or her legs on the front of the chair and hold onto both armrests before sitting.

continued

WALKER

A client who uses a walker usually does not need assistance. Monitor the client's gait and the pathway ahead of him or her. The rhythm of the gait should be walker→unaffected side→affected side. If a client is not using the walker properly, ask the exercise leader to instruct the client on its proper use. If the client is shaky or uncoordinated, provide extra security by holding firmly to the back of his or her waistband. Do not hold onto the walker because this could throw off the client's balance.

CANE

A client who uses a cane usually does not need assistance. Holding the cane in the hand of the unaffected side (unless the hand or arm is missing) enables the client to form an arch between the affected side and the cane, which supports his or her weight. If the client seems to have poor balance or be weak, then provide extra security by holding firmly to the back of his or her waistband. Some clients may want to hold a volunteer's arm for added assurance.

INDEPENDENT AMBULATION

Some clients need assistance in order to ambulate safely. Some should use assistive devices but refuse to do so; others, for cognitive or physical reasons, cannot manage the use of these devices. There are several ways to assist a person to ambulate independently:

Allow the client to hold onto you. This makes the client feel secure, but if he or she falls, it would be difficult for you to break the fall. *(Least secure)*

Stand to the left of the client and hold his or her right hand with your right hand. Stand to the right of the client and hold his or her left hand with your left hand. *(Less secure)*

Stand to the left of the client. Place your right hand under his or her left upper arm, hold the back of the waistband, or hold onto his or her left lower arm with your left hand. *(More secure)*

Stand to the left of the client. Wrap your arm around the client's back and grasp the far side of his or her waist, lodging the client's body against your right hip. Hold his or her left arm with your left hand. *(Most secure)*

close, providing invaluable social support through several years of weekly telephone calls and visits.

Periodically, group leaders give volunteers special recognition. Each year the staff of the Honolulu Gerontology Program honors all of the volunteers by preparing and serving a volunteer recognition luncheon. The volunteers receive certificates and other awards for longtime or special service. The volunteers also participate in statewide volunteer recognition ceremonies.

Monthly Meeting

Group leaders should meet monthly to share program ideas and new material. Meeting this way helps to take the burden of developing 8–10 sessions every month off each leader. The curriculum guide in Part 3 helps to ensure that all relevant areas are covered during the course of a year.

Jobs for Volunteers

Greet group members as they arrive and help them to travel to the meeting room.

Help the leader to set up the room (e.g., chairs, tables, lights, windows) and equipment (e.g., projectors, screens) and close up when the session is over.

Help set up for, serve at, and clean up after socials.

Help clients to be seated and to transfer from wheelchairs to chairs and vice versa (if volunteer's health allows and after proper training).

Help clients to ambulate to and from bathroom as needed.

Help clients with exercises as directed by exercise leader.

Talk to clients who want/need more time to talk or who have requests.

Help group or exercise leader to carry out any incident or emergency procedures.

Tell the group or exercise leader, as appropriate, when you notice any changes in client behavior or hear of concerns expressed by clients.

During the support portion, encourage group members to participate in games or discussions and join in the discussions yourself. Be careful not to dominate the discussion.

Lead small discussion groups if requested by the group leader.

Help clients to meet their rides after the group meeting.

Leading the Exercise Group

Finding an exercise leader for the restorative group (see p. 71 for exercise leader job description) is often more difficult than finding a group leader, especially in community programs. In-house programs may be able to use staff physical or occupational therapists or their assistants, who can be called away to lead the hour of exercise. The majority of the Honolulu program's exercise leaders are occupational therapy assistants or therapeutic recreation specialists.

Often, exercise leaders in community programs are paid only for leading the hour of exercise, and locating someone who is willing to work only 2 hours a week is not easy, although the Honolulu program has managed to do so for 24 sessions a week for more than 10 years. Another challenge in identifying an exercise leader is that the job calls on three traits or skills that are not always found in one person: a strong yet nurturing personality, the ability to lead *group* exercise, and the ability to give attention to individuals. These areas are discussed more fully in the following paragraphs.

Because the exercise leader spends more structured program time with the group than does the group leader, he or she must possess a personality that is strong enough to attract and hold the group's attention—the hour of exercise must be fun as well as productive. The leader must demonstrate the kind of social and leadership skills that make conversation lively and make members feel comfortable enough to want to come to the

The exercise leader (right) demonstrates ways to work weak arms.

next group meeting. A nurturing personality can help foster individual self-esteem as well as group cohesion and feelings of belonging (see p. 72).

A person may be trained in physical rehabilitation and exercise but have no experience in leading a group in exercises. The most important tasks of a leader are to know the exercises that are appropriate for frail older adults and to ensure that the exercises are done correctly and safely. The exercises must flow smoothly from warm-up through cool-down, and there must be variety from session to session to prevent boredom. As with the group's leader, the exercise leader must demonstrate creativity in planning sessions and in selecting and using appropriate accompanying music.

Exercise leaders are not required to be registered physical therapists (RPT), but they must have knowledge of the limitations and disabilities imposed on people by aging, chronic illness, and disease. They must possess the ability to be attentive and sensitive to those limitations and to the needs of and differences among frail individuals. They must direct special attention at these individuals to caution, reassure, encourage, praise, and guide them. The exercise leader also must be able to communicate effectively and discuss his or her concerns about particular clients' behaviors or diagnoses with the group leader.

Although it may seem impossible to find one person who possesses all of these traits and skills, it can be and has been accomplished. One way to locate this multifaceted person is to develop him or her. The Honolulu Gerontology Program did this by creating a relationship with a local community college's certified occupational therapy assistant (COTA) and physical therapy assistant (PTA) programs. The Honolulu program provided COTA students with a first-year practicum in return for the community college's help in recruiting appropriate graduates to be the program's exercise leaders. Another avenue for recruiting instructors is locating unemployed, underemployed, or retired fitness or aerobics instructors. The most qualified instructors are people who are empathic toward and knowledgeable about the limitations of frail older adults and are able to tone down the high level of energy they may have used in teaching in health clubs. In fact, some fitness or aerobics instructors are beginning to specialize in working with older adults. Some of these candidates are themselves older adults, who make good role models for and can

Job Description
Restorative Group Exercise Leader

Job Summary

Under the supervision of the Program Director, the Restorative Group Exercise Leader promotes physical fitness for frail older adults by leading an approved regimen of nonaerobic group exercises for strength, endurance, and range of motion.

Duties and Responsibilities

Maintains safe environment during exercise sessions. Reviews Physician Authorization forms prior to leading nonaerobic exercises for groups of frail older adults. Supervises aides and caregivers who assist clients during exercise. Prepares and periodically revises Information Sheet for (visiting) Exercise Leaders and Helpers. Performs CPR and first aid in emergencies. Monitors each client's diagnosis, abilities, and limitations. Ensures that each client exercises within his or her prescribed limitations. Encourages clients to perform to their optimal level by working to overcome barriers to participation caused by impairments of speech, hearing, vision, or other impairments. Varies exercises by utilizing sticks, balls, parachutes, and weights. Promotes group cohesion by encouraging light conversation, anecdotes, humor, and so forth. Consults periodically with the Restorative Group Leader concerning client abilities, interactions, attitudes, and behaviors. Completes exercise portion of Progress Report to Physician. Participates in in-service and other training activities. Attends agency staff meetings and selected staff development meetings as needed. Maintains client confidentiality at all times. Performs other duties as assigned.

Minimum Qualifications

High school diploma or equivalency. Education in physical therapy, exercise physiology, rehabilitation, or related field. Experience in working with older adults with chronic illnesses and experience teaching group exercise. Up-to-date CPR and first aid certification.

1/95

Reasonable accommodation will be provided to enable the qualified applicant or qualified employee to perform the essential functions of this position.

empathize with restorative group members. Other resources are mothers who do not want to work full-time, retirees who want to work part-time, students who can fit an exercise class into their academic programs, and exercise instructors who fill their days with many part-time jobs.

Combining Group Leader/Exercise Leader

It is possible for one person to act as both group leader and exercise leader, but much depends on the size of the group (small), the kind of support staff that are available (supportive), and whether the person possesses both the technical exercise qualifications and the knowledge and interpersonal skills of a social worker. In general, it is better for group

Therapeutic Techniques for Group Exercise Leaders

Fostering individual self-esteem

Learn clients' names and call each person by name at least once a session.

Walk around the circle, standing in front of and acknowledging and encouraging each person during some of the easier sessions.

Be sure to include in each session some activities that even the most frail member can perform successfully.

Touch members often. (Not all older adults like to be touched, so get to know your clients before you make unwelcome gestures.)

Remind stroke-affected members to work their affected side.

Praise participants for a good effort, a smile, or a new hairdo.

Greet new members by approaching them, shaking their hand, and asking about special concerns or limitations.

Make an effort to notice positive things about each person.

Pay extra attention to the most withdrawn or depressed members of the group.

Fostering group cohesion (feelings of belonging)

Use the pronoun "we" when talking about the group.

Talk about subjects of common interest: "Are we all ready to vote tomorrow?"

Point out commonalities among members: "Look! Three members are wearing purple today."

Praise the group in general for performing particularly well or for its happy mood.

Acknowledge feelings of sadness or worry in the group: "I know we're all worried about George since he went into the hospital."

Help members relate to one another: "Well, Joe and Mike, how'd the football team do last night?" "Ruth, did you know that Ida is also from Long Island?"

members to work with two separate leaders because, often, both leaders are needed at one time. For example, the exercise portion has been in progress for 10 minutes when a group member arrives late and upset because he fell on exiting the van. The exercise leader can continue to lead the exercises while the group leader calms the panicked gentleman and tends to his needs. Group leaders often spend much of the exercise session interviewing a prospective member, listening to a caregiver vent his or her frustrations, or helping caregivers to meet with other caregivers.

Establishing Program Policies

The Honolulu Gerontology Program has established policies to ensure smooth program function and, in some cases, prevent ambiguity or controversy. Group leaders also set rules for their own groups. The policies are examined briefly in the following paragraphs.

First Names

The Honolulu program has chosen to use first names with clients as a means of establishing intimacy and informality in the group. In turn, clients are encouraged to call program staff by their first names. Initially, some group leaders and clients are uncomfortable using first names, but many report feeling more comfortable over time. Occasionally, a member may express a strong preference for more formality. Such wishes should be honored by calling these individuals by their titles and last names: Mr. Smith, Mrs. Hernández, or Dr. Simon.

Disability-Neutral Language

Program staff should use language that is disability neutral. For example, a client is *stroke-affected,* not a *stroke victim*; a person is a *wheelchair user* or *uses a wheelchair,* not *wheelchair bound*; a person *has* Parkinson's disease, he or she does not *suffer from* Parkinson's disease. Use of such positive, "people-first" language helps to promote the program's goal of empowerment and confers dignity onto clients.

Reliability and Consistency

Reliability and consistency, which are important in helping group members to make a commitment to the group, are developed in the program in many small ways: The group always meets, even if sometimes only a few people show up. The components start and end on time. If the exercise portion starts at 10:30, then the support portion starts at 11:30 and ends at noon. If occasional schedule changes need to be made, then the group is notified in advance. If the group session must be canceled (e.g., due to inclement weather), then each member is called at home. As few changes as possible are made in the group's leadership positions.

Taboo Subjects

The restorative group program operates on the premise that, during group discussions, there is no such thing as a taboo subject (Shulman, 1984). Group members must feel free to speak about any subject, even if it seems controversial or delicate. Older adults in a number of the Honolulu groups have reported that they cannot talk about "taboo" subjects at home with loved ones, so they are grateful for the forum provided by the group. Some older adults find these sorts of topics distasteful. One group member became upset because a local funeral director was invited to discuss funeral planning. "That," he said, very emotionally, "is for families to take care of once we're gone." The presentation was scheduled anyway because the majority of the group members were interested in learning about this topic. On the day of the funeral director's presentation, the offended individual chose to leave after the exercise portion. On occasion, a group member will raise a personal issue that is out of kilter with the tone of the discussion; the group leader may explain that the topic would be handled better in another way, perhaps one-to-one after the group meeting.

Sometimes the group leader, not the group, is shocked by the raising of delicate subjects, such as sexuality or death. She must be careful not to judge the topic or those discussing it but to facilitate the discussion without prejudice. What subjects the program chooses to offer may depend on the program's sponsorship (see Chapter 5).

Religion

The Honolulu program's policy is not to sponsor talks by religious leaders or to schedule presentations on the subject of religion per se because group members are from many or no religious background. Whatever their beliefs, they should be honored. If religious or spiritual issues arise during any discussion (e.g., see Part 3, Session 17), the group leader's role is to prevent members from proselytizing or belittling others' beliefs.

Health Education

Throughout its history the Honolulu program has offered group members health education presentations that conform to conventional medical practices, although the program's emphasis on prevention exceeds that of most of the medical community. Nontraditional, or alternative, health practices are not offered through the group program. Some of these practices are valid, but others are questionable or even dangerous. The group members can investigate alternative therapies on their own.

Unacceptable Behavior

Incidents of unacceptable behavior should be handled on a case-by-case basis. If the behavior is harmful, uncomfortable, and/or detrimental to the group, then the disruptive member is counseled to improve his or her behavior. When counseling is not effective, the client should be referred to other community sources for the good of the group. In the Honolulu program one member was counseled out of group because of unacceptable language, which could not be corrected after much effort. One alcoholic client was terminated because he continually arrived at group in an inebriated condition. A few clients with diagnoses of Alzheimer's disease were transferred to adult day services or in-home help because they demonstrated disruptive or wandering behaviors. A schizophrenic client with obsessive-compulsive hand-washing behavior was terminated because she left the group meeting every 5 minutes to wash her hands and returned to group without turning off the hot water. Sexually disinhibited group members have offended leaders or other members with words or touch. Group leaders are taught to be assertive and direct but nonjudgmental and caring in discouraging sexual behaviors, although they do not discourage the occasional romance between members unless one or the other is offended by it or one is at risk for abuse because of cognitive or emotional losses.

Money

Occasions arise when a group member becomes ill or loses a loved one, and the group wants to send a get-well or sympathy card. In addition, holding the group's socials may call for expenses that are not covered by the program's budget (e.g., paper plates, plastic spoons). Some general guidelines are that members can be invited but not be required to contribute, and that an amount can be suggested but compliance should not be monitored. Each person should give according to his or her desire or ability. Some older adults do not cope well with this guideline and can be rather rigid in wanting everyone to give equally and/or give generously. The leader should monitor this behavior carefully so that no one is pressured unduly—an individual's wishes for giving (or not giving) must be respected. Each group should establish its own petty cash supply for miscellaneous expenses. In some groups the leader serves as keeper of the petty cash, whereas in others an alert, organized member or volunteer handles this task. A person who acts as the group's treasurer should keep records and report to the group or group leader periodically.

Commercial Activities

The group leader is certain to receive calls from representatives of businesses that are related to the work of the restorative group: A medical equipment company manufactures products that improve the functioning and comfort of an older adult with a disability; an attorney specializing in estate planning would like to share information with group members; a business representative or professional may present information to the group only if the topic is related to the program's goals. They may leave their business cards at the front of the room so that members who wish to contact the business at a later time may do so. They may not collect the names, addresses, or telephone numbers of group members and may not sell their wares during their time with the group.

Group Address and Telephone List

Because the building of a social support network is a primary goal of the program, most groups decide to compile a list of members' addresses and telephone numbers so that members can contact one another outside the group meetings. This list is prepared by the group leader. Each group member must give permission for the release of his or her name and information. Members are cautioned not to release the list to anyone outside the group or to use it for any purpose outside the group because of the potential for abuse of the system.

5 How Do I Start a Restorative Group?

Restorative groups for frail older adults can be initiated either by an established organization or a new organization. Established organizations include health maintenance organizations (HMOs), seniors housing projects, retirement communities, long-term care facilities, adult day centers, senior centers, churches or synagogues, group dining programs (provided under the Older Americans Act of 1965, PL 89-73), or church coalitions. The restorative group program that is set up in an established organization is referred to as an "inhouse program." (This is not to say that the group should or would be closed to outside members, simply that some of the structure of a group may or would be in place.) A staff social worker or activity director could coordinate the group and conduct the support portion, a staff physical therapist could conduct the exercise portion, and a room in the building that is little used could house the program.

Restorative groups also can be initiated in a new agency created expressly for this purpose. The restorative group program established in a new agency is referred to as a "community program." This program could be either independent or established under the umbrella of another organization (e.g., the Honolulu Gerontology Program was founded under the umbrella of the nonprofit research arm of a private medical clinic; later, the program moved to a nonprofit family services agency).

The challenges of establishing a restorative group program differ depending on whether the sponsorship is in-house–based or community-based. As an example, an in-house program already may have staff on board and a site in which to hold the group sessions, whereas a community program may be required to raise funds for all aspects of the program, including personnel and meeting site.

Deciding on Group Program Type

One of the first decisions to be made when starting a restorative group program is the type of group: a complete restorative group, with exercise, discussion, education, and socialization components, or a modified version of the group: exercise only, exercise and informal support only, or support only. Undoubtedly, funding limitations will be a factor in making this decision. The "support only" group can be structured informally, by holding a weekly luncheon or potluck supper at which members discuss or reminisce, or it can be structured more formally, by scheduling a time-limited program of discussion or reminiscence. The "support only" group is appropriate for recently widowed men and women. For example, a church with a large group of fairly healthy older adults could sponsor a 10-week-long exercise-and-socialize group to raise their awareness of healthful lifestyles while helping them get to know and become a continuing source of support to one another. An HMO could sponsor the same type of group.

Once the decision is made as to the parameters of the group, the next deciding factor is whether the group will be open or closed. A closed group is one for which enrollment is limited to members of the organization; an open group is one for which enrollment is open to everyone. If possible, a restorative group should be open to any older adult in the community who needs it. This proviso makes it easier to fill the group because there may not be enough appropriate, interested members within the organization. For example, in a retirement community only a handful of residents may need the support of a group at any one time. Another advantage of the open group is that it helps to integrate the group within the larger community. As an example, one of the Honolulu groups opened in the social hall of a new seniors housing project. Group members who lived in the residence met people from the community and group members from the larger community became familiar with the housing project. Thus, the open group helped the town and the housing project become integrated. Other examples are a small church attended by older adults may decide to open the group as a means of outreach to the community, or a hospital or an HMO may launch an open group as a public relations gesture.

Closed groups have their advantages as well. An organization may limit group membership if the goal of its program is to help in-house members improve supportive behaviors with one another. A large seniors housing community could launch a closed group as a way to build smaller communities within the larger one. A large church attended by many older adults may hold a restorative group that is limited to its older members.

Funding

The original Honolulu program received funding from a variety of sources: the Honolulu Chamber of Commerce, the Honolulu Medical Group, the county Area Agency on Aging, the United Way, donations from clients, and federal funding under the Older Americans Act of 1965. Some of the public sources may or may not contribute to the program—for example, federal funding has been reduced significantly since the Reagan administration—but sources are still available. The five possibilities for program funding sources are your own organization, the public sector, the philanthropic sector, the corporate sector, and fee for service from clients.

Public Sector

Each county in the United States maintains an Area Agency on Aging, created under the Older Americans Act, as amended, to allocate funds for social services grants. Title III B outlines general social services that can be funded. Title III F provides a small amount of funds for disease prevention and health promotion. Federal funds for social services are provided through block grants to the states, so the funds come through state purchase-of-service contracts. To find out more about funding opportunities in your county or state, contact the director of your county Area Agency on Aging.

Philanthropic Sector

Many charitable organizations provide funds for social services programs in the community that target older adults. Often, these organizations supplement program funds from public sources. Since the 1970s a mixture of public and private funds have been the predominant method of funding social programs and services. The United Way is one of the largest programs. The Interactive Aging Network web site (http://www.ianet.org) lists a number of the top U.S. aging funding organizations, including The Robert Wood Johnson Foundation, the Pew Charitable Trusts, the Commonwealth Fund, the Surdna Foundation, and the American Federation for Aging Research. Each organization has its own requirements for funding, such as a research goal or a category of people or needs to be served.

Corporate Sector

The Interactive Aging Network also lists corporations that provide funds for community programs. Large HMOs are corporations that could be a source of support. As the cost-effectiveness of preventive programs such as the restorative group is demonstrated, HMOs may consider sponsoring such programs in order to maintain their members' health and thus keep payouts low. As of this writing, the National Council on the Aging (NCOA) is encouraging joint demonstration projects between aging service providers and their local HMOs.

Fee for Service from Clients

Under the Older Americans Act service providers are obligated to target individuals who are economically or socially disadvantaged. Programs are not permitted to charge fees, but they are mandated to ask participants for contributions. The Honolulu program requests donations on a sliding scale, according to income level. The client response to a sliding-scale donation system has been good (monthly range in 1998: from $0 for low-income clients to $40 for high-income clients). Under this system annual client contributions cover around one fifth of the Honolulu program's budget. An in-house program, operating with in-house staff and facilities, could cover its costs with a fee-for-service plan.

Finding a Place to Meet

Finding a place where the restorative group can meet regularly is another essential early step in planning. Having a place to meet regularly creates consistency and security, which is important to frail older adults. An in-house program may have space available on the premises—for example, an activity room, a conference room, or a classroom. Finding a room that is available at the time of day that the group wants to meet (usually mornings) may be difficult, however. Managers of seemingly appropriate buildings must be contacted and screened to be sure that 1) they have a large room that is available on the days and times when the group will meet, 2) they express some curiosity about the group and openness to welcoming it as a part-time tenant, and 3) they are forthcoming about leasing rates or are willing to discuss discounted rates for the nonprofit restorative group program (this kind of generosity is good public relations for them). Building managers will screen you and your group as well. You should be prepared to answer questions about the program. You can then visit the buildings that pass the initial screening to determine whether they meet the following criteria.

The Ideal Building and Room

The ideal building is within two blocks of public transportation stops, offers convenient parking, has an accessible entryway for use by wheelchair-transport vans, and is wheelchair accessible. The ideal meeting space is a room that is at least 24 feet wide and 60 feet long (approximately the size of a large double classroom), large enough to accommodate 20 group members, the group leader, and approximately six helpers, all seated in a circle with enough space between the chairs so that participants can extend their arms fully during the exercise portion. If possible, arrange for a room that has adjoining space in which caregivers and visitors can gather within view of the group. The room should be somewhat soundproof and located in a reasonably quiet area of the building—preferably away from the main flow of traffic—so that members can hear one another during group discussions. Be sure that the room is available year-round if the program being created is to be held year-round. Such rooms must be chosen carefully. For example, many recreation centers hold children's summer programs. Even if a room is still available in the summer, the noise that children make may disturb or overwhelm the group. The room must be well ventilated or air-conditioned, wheelchair accessible, and located close to wheelchair-accessible rest rooms. Access to a telephone is necessary in case of an emergency. Thirty sturdy chairs and two or three long tables (folding chairs and tables are acceptable) are needed for clients, staff, visitors, and others. A kitchen should be available for group social events, and the room should contain a lockable storage cabinet (minimum size $4 \times 2 \times 6$ feet) in which to store exercise equipment.

Cost

Programs that must work within tight budgets must locate rent-free facilities. Possible rent-free facilities are senior centers, churches, and HUD–subsidized (U.S. Department of Housing and Urban Development) housing projects for older adults. If building management is savvy, then they will determine that although the group pays no rent, it pays them in free publicity because management is using the group positively as a community service/outreach.

Relationships with Management and Residents

As group leader you will interact with managers on many occasions, so it is extremely important that the resident manager, building manager, minister, or recreation director be understanding and supportive of the program. This point is illustrated by the following example: A group member becomes confused and arrives at the site by public van transportation on a day that the group does not meet. The group member is confused further by the absence of the group leader. It will be left to the site manager to handle the situation, which could go very wrong if he or she does not understand or support the program. Most managers eventually learn to feel kindly toward restorative groups because they supply information about services for older adults and often help their "troublesome" residents. One manager of a building used by the Honolulu program became so interested in the group that he entertains them with his guitar and is recording their personal histories to incorporate into a book.

Eliciting the support of the site's residents is also important, whether or not any participate in the group program. One way to obtain support is to choose new residences or communities in which feelings of territoriality have not yet taken hold. In established buildings or communities it is advisable to meet with the tenants' association to explain the program and gain its support. Some prejudice or misinformation may need to be overcome: Healthy older adults sometimes demonstrate little empathy for their frail counterparts; perhaps they feel that contact with them brings their own frailty too close, which may cause them to deny that a restorative group is needed. One way to win over these healthy older people is to recruit several of their leaders as program volunteers. In one Honolulu residence, the wife of a group member not only volunteered in the group but also paid nurturing home visits to resident group members when they were ill.

Publicizing the Restorative Group Program

Once the restorative group has been planned, the community must be made aware of its existence. Publicity helps group leaders to recruit members and to gain the support of the community. Press releases distributed to the local media are an appropriate way to reach the general public. The most effective way to reach potential clients is to contact aging network agencies and health professionals who work with older adults. The county Area Agency on Aging should be informed about the program because its information and referral service keeps older adults abreast of all community services specific to their needs. The health care professionals who are the most likely to refer clients are hospital social workers/discharge planners, case managers, home health aides, physicians (especially geriatricians), and others who actively help older adults plan long-term care. Local chapters of national social services organizations, such as the American Heart Association, the Alzheimer's Association, the American Diabetes Association, the National Osteoporosis Foundation, the National Parkinson Foundation, and the Arthritis Foundation, are additional resources for prospective clients and information (Appendix A provides a more extensive list of health care and social services organizations).

Because the concept of a restorative group is not familiar to most of the active community agencies and health professionals, verbal explanations should supplement written communications. Follow up on press releases and letters by developing a telephone or face-to-face relationship with these organizations and individuals. Some health professionals are harder than others to convince of the merit of the group. Not all physicians take the time to investigate supportive resources for their patients. In fairness to physicians, many demands are placed on their time, and in this era of managed care the situation is not likely to change. As an alternative, perhaps a nurse or an office manager could be educated by the group leader, who could then educate the physician and serve as the contact person for client follow-ups. Working to strengthen a referral process through primary care physicians is worth the effort. A researcher reports that clients referred by their physicians for mental health services yielded the highest rates of attendance at groups that are similar to restorative groups (P.M. Mosher-Ashley, personal communication, February 15, 1998). Some internists and geriatricians who were made aware of restorative groups and convinced of their benefits have referred appropriate patients to the group. One Honolulu internist joked that the restorative group is the "medicine" he most commonly prescribes to his patients.

Adding Services to Meet Emerging Needs

Caregiver Support Group

One of the Honolulu group leaders noted that while group members exercised and socialized, caregivers waited in the hallway, looking stressed and reaching out to one another to compare caregiving notes. From this observation, a support group was created to provide caregivers with ways to support one another. (This monthly caregiver group was featured in Deborah Bass's *Caring Families: Supports and Interventions* [Bass, 1990]).

Caregiver Respite Program

During the course of the first Honolulu support group, caregivers asked group leaders how they could negotiate time off from their 24-hours-a-day, 7-days-a-week caregiving duties. The Honolulu program staff began to keep an informal roster of paid companions who were willing to work for a morning or an entire day in order to provide caregivers with respite. This service was formalized as the caregiver respite program, which links family caregivers with paid care providers who provide many hours of respite.

Summer Education Series for Caregivers

Caregivers asked Honolulu group leaders for much-desired information about topics such as incontinence, medication management, dementia, and the legal aspects of caregiving. In response the Honolulu Gerontology Program organized a summer caregiver education series. Eight local experts, encompassing doctors, nurses, lawyers, and other service providers, each donate an hour to talk to caregivers. The summer caregiver education series attracts hundreds of caregivers looking for help. The most popular topic has been "Managing Demanding and Manipulative Behaviors."

Crisis and Short-Term Interventions Program

Several case management agencies were initiated in Honolulu during the 1980s, and each quickly had a waiting list. To meet the need for immediate help, group leaders in the Honolulu Gerontology Program developed a service to help older adults and their families cope with emergencies—for example, a bedridden woman whose caregiving spouse dies suddenly, a newly homeless man, a stroke-affected man who is being discharged from a nursing facility after a hip fracture and must cope alone at home, a blind widow who moved back to Hawaii from the mainland against her family's wishes, a 90-year-old woman whose increasingly paranoid behavior is putting her at risk of eviction from her apartment. The intervention program's staff of social workers, nurses, licensed practical nurses, nursing assistants, and a consulting psychologist made themselves available to assist individuals at a moment's notice.

Group Volunteer Program

As the Honolulu restorative groups grew, group leaders found that they needed help with the many aspects of facilitating a group of frail older adults. Older people needed help in entering the meeting room, some group members wanted someone of their own age to talk to, and snacks needed to be prepared for the monthly social. Group leaders observed that some of the healthier group members began to help them on an informal basis. After a while, these older adults were incorporated into a group volunteer program (see also Chapter 3). Volunteering helped older people who had been depressed to get back on the road to active living, and the program staff appreciated their assistance greatly. Other healthy older adults and younger volunteers have helped from time to time, but the most dedicated, caring volunteers have been the graduates of the restorative groups. Each group has at least two volunteers who help to enrich the group experience.

Student Practicums Program

Schools in Hawaii discovered that the restorative groups provided a marvelous laboratory for students to experience working with older adults. Group members report that they love being around young people and that they can exercise their perhaps-waning generativity needs. The students gain respect and understanding for their grandparents' generation. Twelfth graders at one Honolulu high school received academic credit for providing community service by volunteering during group sessions. Students in community college physical and occupational therapy assistant programs learn to lead exercises with older adults who are chronically ill. Both bachelor's and master's degree–level students in social work and human development receive the opportunity to practice their interpersonal and social work skills with these inspiring older men and women.

. . .

This concludes the narrative portion on restorative groups. Turn to Parts 2 and 3, which are filled with practical programming ideas, exercises, and games.

Part 2
The Exercises[1]

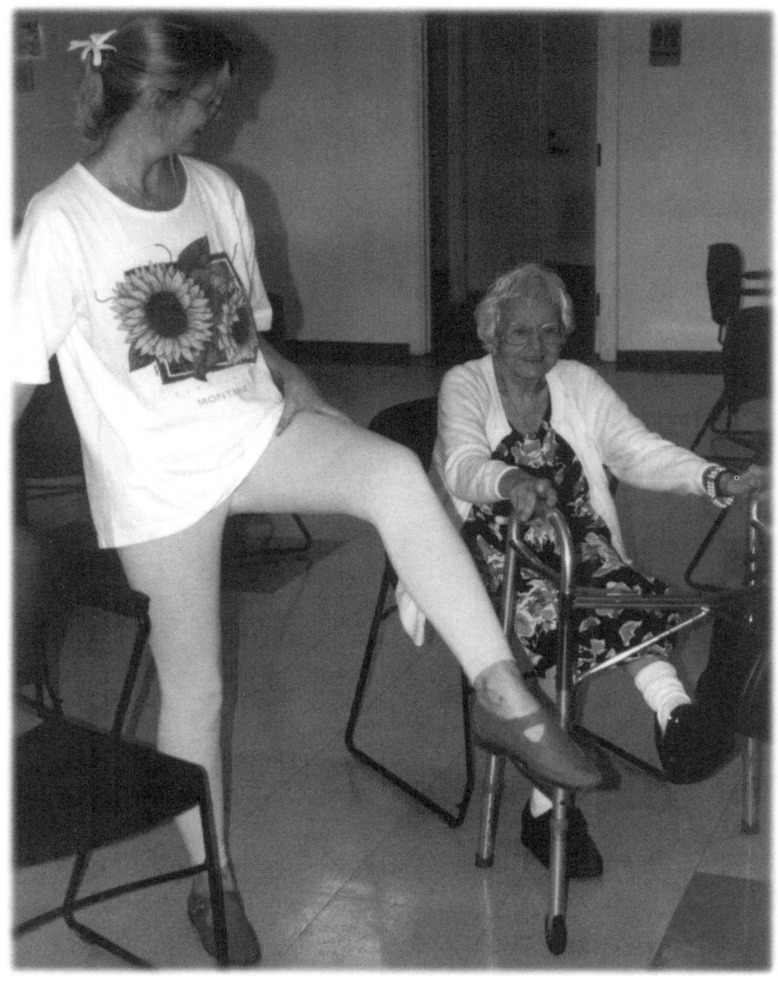

[1]The exercises were developed by Cecile Freitas Morris, L.P.T.A., who was the Honolulu Gerontology Program's exercise specialist for 10 years. Cecile has worked with older adults in nursing facilities and wellness and group programs since 1974. She is an ACE certified fitness instructor and personal trainer and is certified by the Senior Fitness Association as a long-term care fitness leader and senior fitness instructor. Cecile is employed by NovaCare, leaders in geriatric rehabilitation, and has been the instructor trainer for the Oahu YWCA and Hawaii Medical Service Association's senior fitness programs.

Chair Exercises

Begin the chair exercises by asking participants to sit comfortably using good posture: feet comfortably apart and flat on the floor, back straight, shoulders back, and head up. This is the starting position from which most of the chair exercises begin. Remind members several times during the session to resume good posture. The number of repetitions necessary for each exercise depends on the particular exercise and the group's abilities. Unless otherwise stated, six to eight repetitions of each exercise are recommended.

These chair exercises can be augmented for additional muscle strengthening and motor-skills training by adding hand weights, dowels, therabands, balls (e.g., tennis, beach, playground), beanbags, towels, and other "props." See pages 100 to 102 for exercises using weights, and pages 103 to 105 for games using props.

Forward

Neck

4–6 repetitions of each exercise

Forward. From the starting position, slowly tilt the head forward, moving the chin toward the chest. Then, slowly move the head back to the starting position. *Caution:* Do not tilt the head backward (i.e., chin toward ceiling). This warning is meant particularly for group members with arthritis of the spine or severe osteoporosis.

Turn

Turn. From the starting position, turn the head to the right and look over the right shoulder. Return to the starting position. Turn the head to the left and look over the left shoulder. Return to the starting position.

Tilt. From the starting position, gently tilt the head so that the right ear moves toward the right shoulder. Return slowly to the starting position. Tilt the head so that the left ear moves toward the left shoulder. Return slowly to the starting position.

Tilt

Shrug

Circular shrug, back/forward

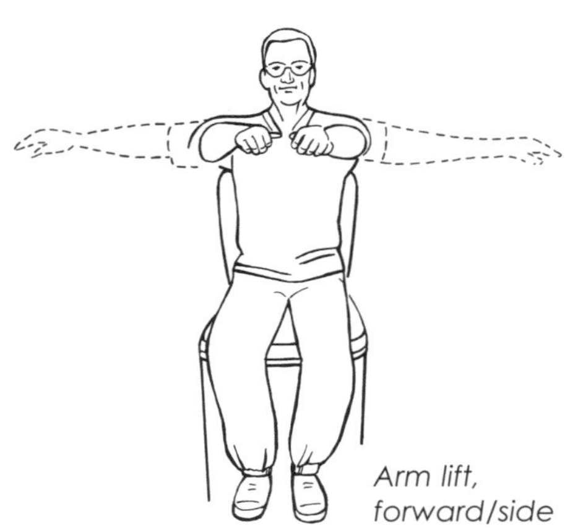

Arm lift, forward/side

Shoulders

6–8 repetitions of each exercise; these exercises can be done using one shoulder/arm at a time or both shoulders/arms at the same time

Shrug. Starting position: arms relaxed, hanging at the sides. Lift the shoulders toward the ears, then lower them gently to the starting position (do not drop the shoulders).

Circular shrug back. Starting position: arms relaxed, hanging at the sides. Using a circular motion, move the shoulders in a circular motion up and toward the back.

Circular shrug forward. Starting position: arms relaxed, hanging at the sides. Move shoulders in a circular motion up and toward the front of the body.

Arm lift forward. Starting position: arms relaxed, hanging at the sides. Lift both arms forward to shoulder height.

Arm lift to side. Starting position: arms relaxed, hanging at the sides. Keeping the arms straight at the sides (do not lock the elbows), lift both of them to shoulder height.

Internal and external rotation. Relaxing the upper arms, bend the elbows at a 90-degree angle in front of the torso. Turn the palms so that they face one another. Bring the hands together in front of the body, and then separate them slowly so that the back of the hands move away from one another and toward the back as far as is comfortable.

Arm lift to back. With both arms raised to the side at shoulder level, move the arms toward the back at about a 45-degree angle from the starting position.

Shoulder blades. Maintaining correct posture, raise arms to the side. Reach toward the front of the body and cross one arm over the other to hug yourself. Feel the shoulder blades separate. Then, uncross the arms and reach elbows toward the back, as if trying to touch the shoulder blades together.

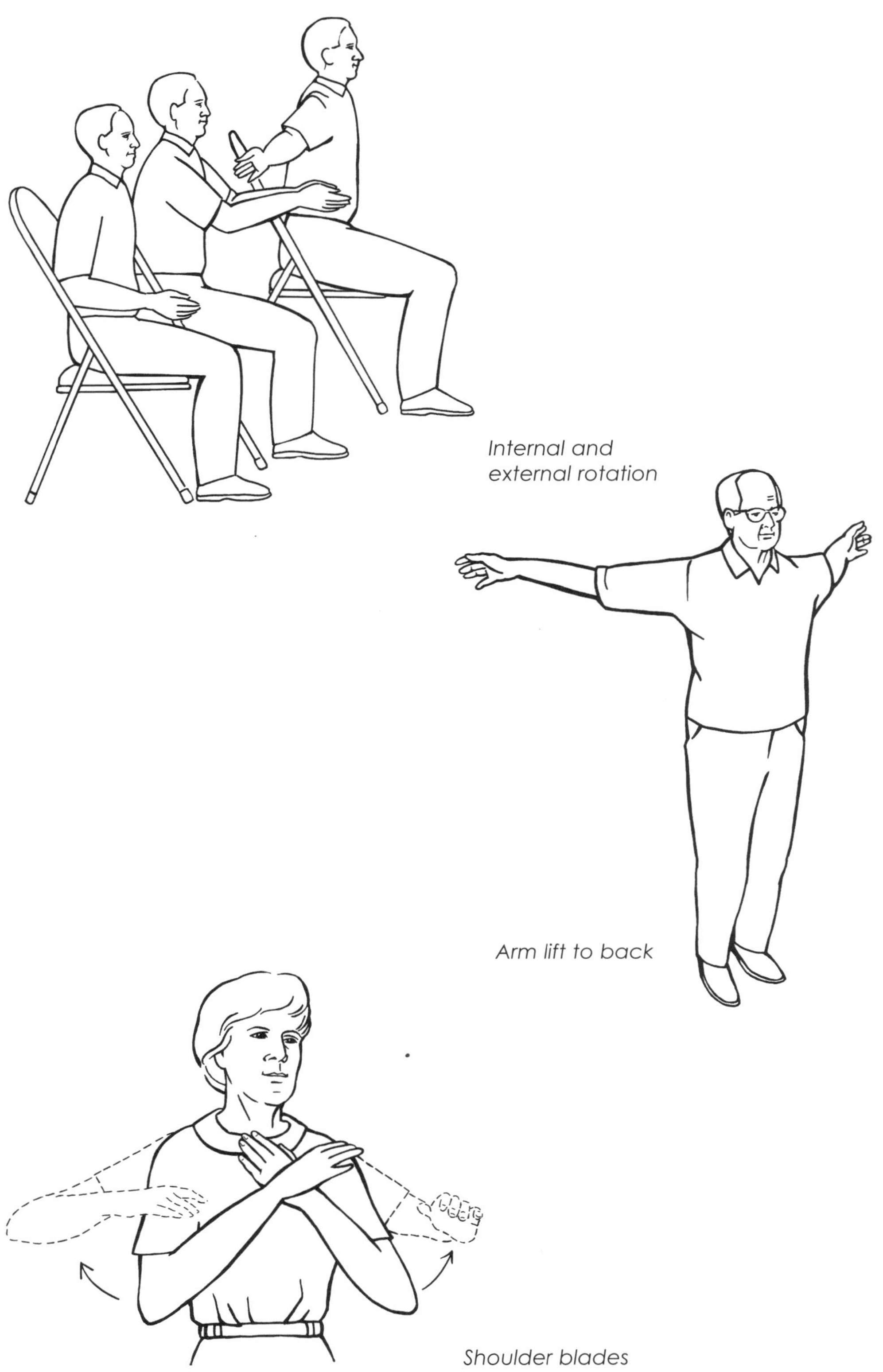

Internal and external rotation

Arm lift to back

Shoulder blades

Hand to shoulder

Elbow

6–8 repetitions of each exercise

Hand to shoulder. With the palm facing up, bend the arm so that the hand touches the shoulder on the same side. This exercise can be done using both arms at once.

Wrist

4–6 repetitions of each exercise

Flexion/extension. While holding both arms out in front with palms down, bend the wrist so that the fingers are pointed toward the ceiling, then toward the floor.

Rotation (supination and pronation). With arms straight out in front, rotate the wrists by turning the palms up and then down.

Radial and ulnar deviation. Holding the hands in front of the torso and using the wrists, move hands outward and then inward, parallel to the floor.

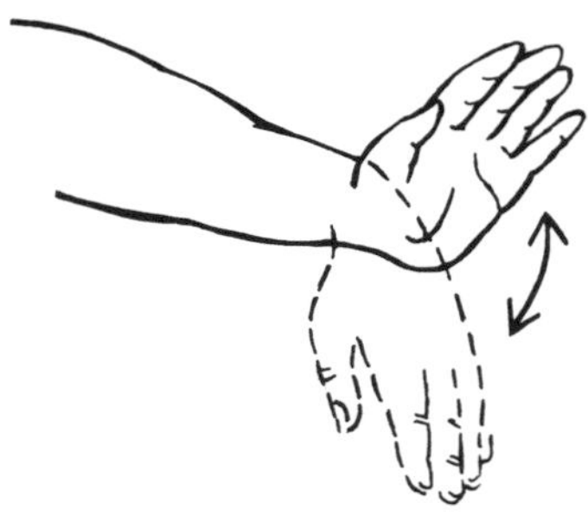

Flexion/extension

Fingers

4–6 repetitions of each exercise; hold hands in front of torso (if participant has weakness in the arms, he or she can support the elbow by using the chair armrests or, if necessary, the lap)

Open. Separate fingers slowly, then bring them together again.

Extension. Open hand as full as possible (do not hyperextend), then make a fist.

Opposition. Touch each finger to the thumb, one at a time.

Claw. Using the first and second joints of each finger, make a claw, then open the hand.

Thumb circles. Circle the thumb in both directions.

TAKE A DEEP-BREATHING BREAK.

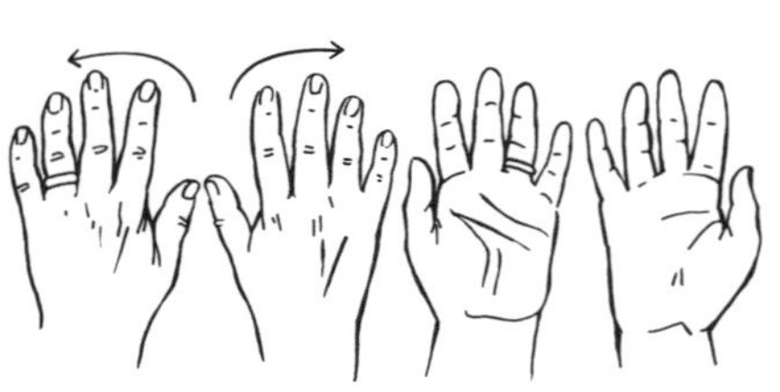

Rotation

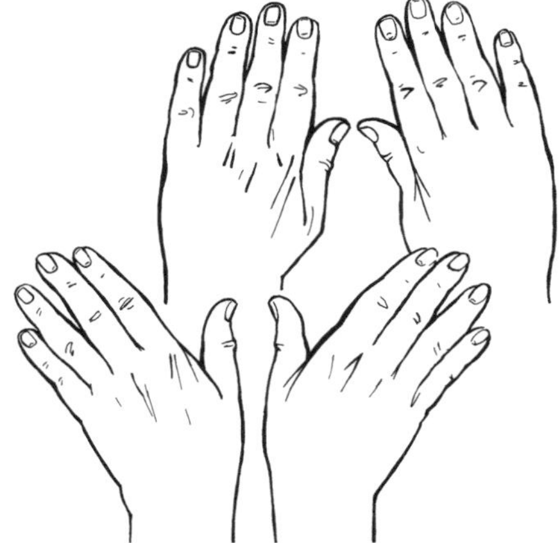

Radial and ulnar deviation

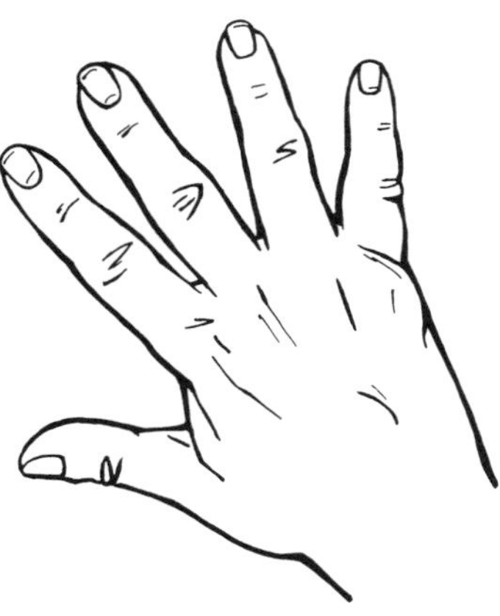

Open

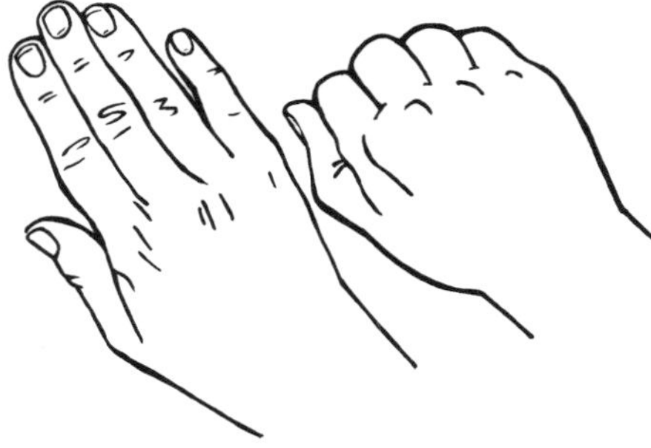

Extension

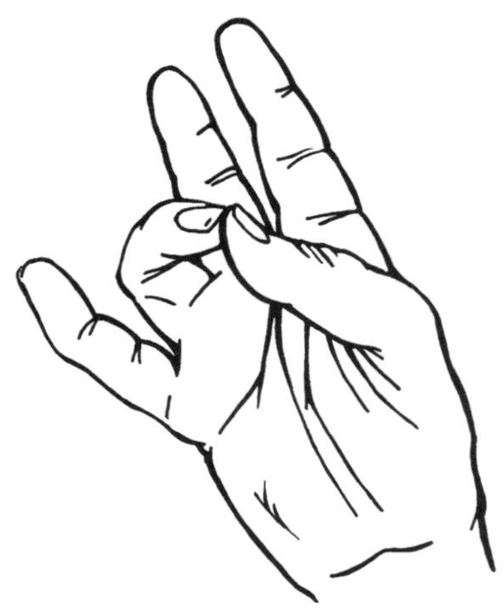

Opposition

Claw

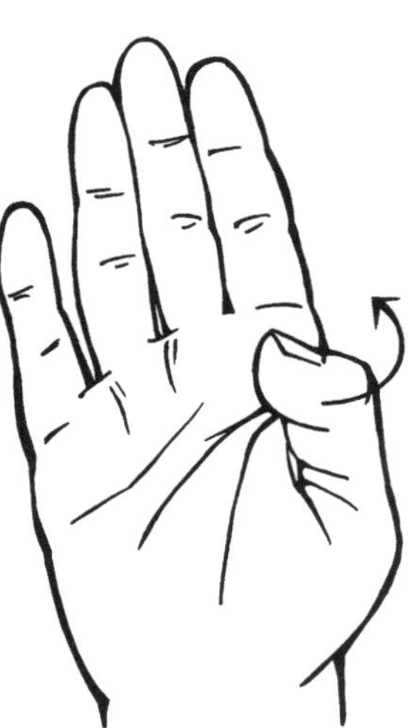

Thumb circles

Arms

4–6 repetitions of each exercise

Reach. Using one arm at a time, reach toward the ceiling.

Reach

Reach and bend. Using one arm at a time, reach toward the ceiling. Then, with the palm facing behind the body, bend the arm to touch the back of the neck.

Circle. Using one arm at a time, circle the arm up and around in a slow, backward motion, as if swimming the backstroke.

Spine

4–6 repetitions of each exercise

Forward lean. Bending from the hip, lean forward in the chair and touch the floor with the fingertips. (Lean forward as far as is comfortable; people with severe osteoporosis or arthritis should limit motion.) Return to the starting position; the hands may be placed on the thighs to assist in this action.

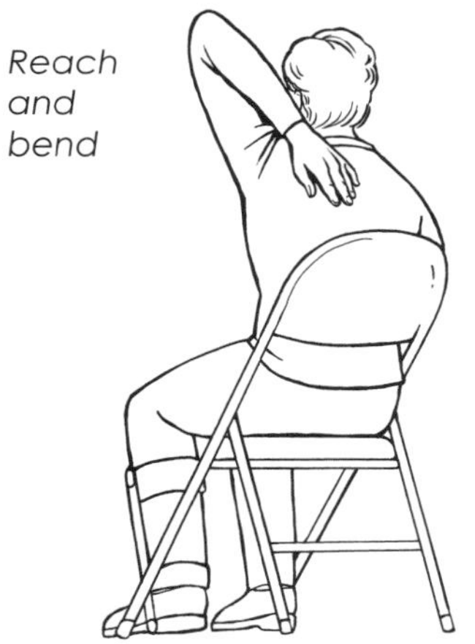

Reach and bend

Turn. Turn the torso to the right. Turn the head and look over the right shoulder, as far as is comfortable. Hold this position for 4–6 seconds; remember to breathe normally. Return to center. Turn the head and look over the left shoulder, as far as is comfortable. Hold this position for 4–6 seconds; remember to breathe normally.

Side lean. Hold onto the chair seat or the chair back with the left hand. Leading with the right arm and shoulder, lean to the right and stretch the arm toward the floor. Then, leading with the left arm and shoulder, lean to the left and stretch the arm toward the floor.

TAKE A DEEP-BREATHING BREAK.

Circle

Forward lean

Turn

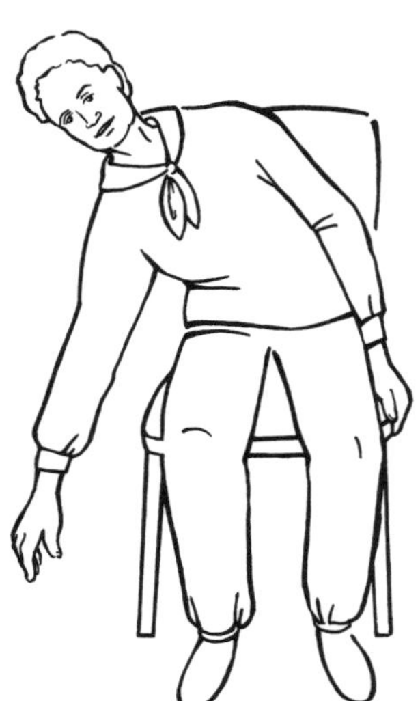

Side lean

Abdominals

Contract. Contract (i.e., squeeze) the abdominal muscles. Hold for 4–6 seconds, then release. Remember to breathe normally.

Hips and Knees

Lifts I. The body is in the starting position. Lift the left leg (knee is bent) as high as is comfortable. Gently and slowly lower the leg to the floor—do not let the leg drop to the floor. For best results, do 6–8 repetitions with one leg, then with the other leg.

Lifts II. The body is in the starting position. Straighten the left leg and then lower it to the starting position. For best results, do 6–8 repetitions with one leg, then with the other leg.

Hip rotation. (This exercise should not be done by people with severe osteoporosis or hip replacements. In addition, other group members may not be able to do the exercise. Do not urge participants to do something that they cannot.) The body is in the starting position. Raise the right foot and rest it on the left knee. Lean forward gently and then sit upright. Do 3–4 repetitions. Repeat the exercise using the left foot.

Internal hip rotation. The body is in the starting position but with thighs and feet together. Slowly separate feet to both sides; thighs remain together. Then, bring the feet together. Do 4–8 repetitions.

Prepare to stand. The body is in the starting position. Inch the buttocks, one cheek at a time, toward the front of the chair seat. Inch back to the starting position. Do 3–4 repetitions.

Lifts I

Lifts II

Hip rotation

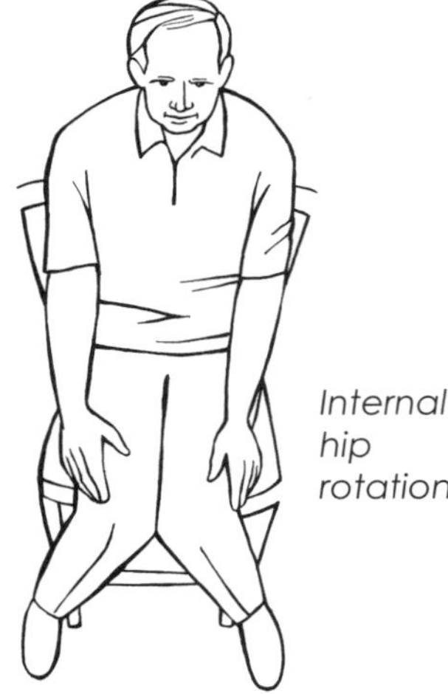
Internal hip rotation

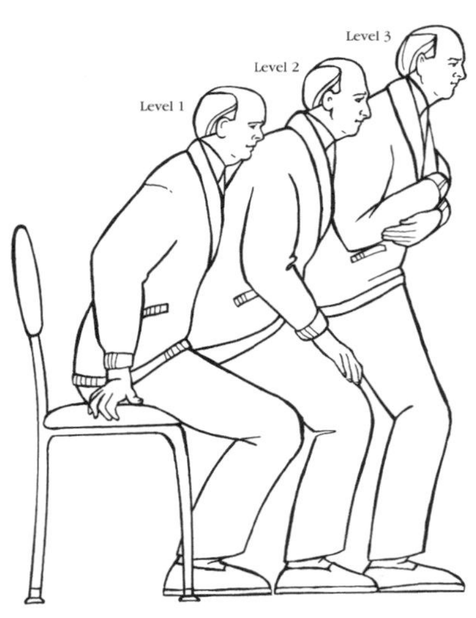

Coming to stand

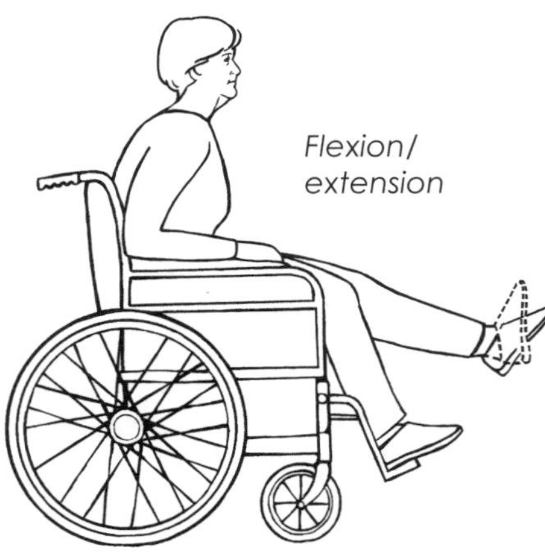
Flexion/ extension

Coming to stand. The body is in the starting position. Sit with feet apart, planted firmly on the floor. Inch the buttocks, one cheek at a time, to the front of the chair seat. Do 2–4 repetitions of each of the following levels. (*Note*: If group members have difficulty with this exercise, do the Level 1 exercise only; progress to Level 3 as they become stronger.)

Level 1 (beginner): The body is in the starting position. Place the hands on the armrests or the chair seat. Push down on the armrests or seat and lift the buttocks off the chair as if trying to stand (or stand and then sit down).

Level 2 (intermediate): With the hands on the thighs, push down on the thighs and lift the buttocks off the chair as if trying to stand (or stand and then sit down).

Level 3 (advanced): With the hands placed across the chest, try to push the buttocks off the chair as if trying to stand (or stand and then sit down).

Ankles and Feet

Flexion/extension. From the starting position, straighten and raise the right leg. Flex and point the foot 4–6 times. Repeat with the left leg and foot.

Inversion/eversion. The body is in the starting position. Try to place the soles of the feet together (inversion) and then separate them (eversion). Do 6–8 repetitions.

Toe tap. The body is in the starting position. Keep heels on the floor. Tap the toes on the floor straight ahead, to the right, and to the left (6–8 times in each direction). Then, tap the toes away from each other and toward each other (6–8 times in each direction).

Heel tap. The body is in the starting position. Keep the toes on the floor and tap the heels straight ahead, to the right, and to the left (6–8 times in each direction). Then, tap the heels away from each other and toward each other 6–8 times.

Heel/toe tap. The body is in the starting position. Rock the feet from toes to heels 6–8 times.

Toe curl. The body is in the starting position. Curl the toes and then stretch them 6–8 times.

TAKE A DEEP-BREATHING BREAK.

Inversion/eversion

STANDING EXERCISES

The starting position for the standing exercises, unless stated otherwise, is to stand facing the back of the chair for support. The legs are straight, and the feet are placed hip-width apart. As with the chair exercises, repeat each exercise 6–8 times unless otherwise stated. Use controlled and deliberate motions in doing the leg exercises; fast or jerky motions do not build strength and endurance and may lead to injury. Avoid locking the knees at any time.

Advanced members can use therabands or leg weights during the exercises. A few participants may be able to do the standing exercises without using a chair back for support. Most group members should place a chair in front of them and hold onto it for support and balance. More frail older adults need a chair placed in front and one behind them so that they can sit down quickly, if necessary. The chair placed behind does inhibit movement during some of the exercises, but it is necessary for the safety of participants whose balance is poor. A volunteer or family caregiver can help by moving the chair slightly out of the way during backward leg kicks and similar movements. Monitor participants carefully so that they do not sit down without a chair behind them.

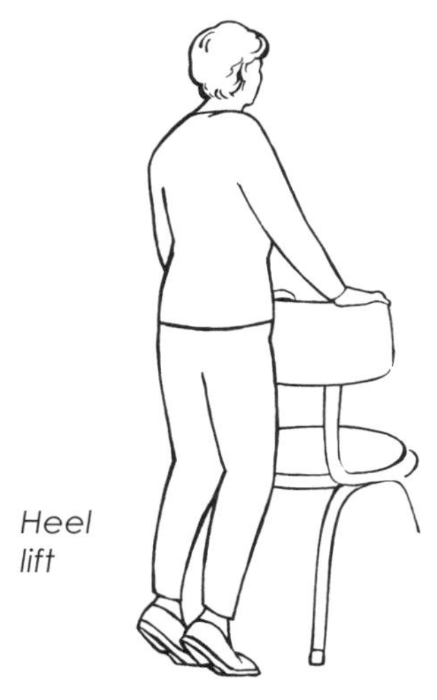

Heel lift

Heel lift. The body is in the starting position. Using the back of the chair for support, rise slowly onto the tiptoes, raising the heels off the floor.

Knee bend. The body is in the starting position. Slowly bend the knees 20–30 degrees, keeping the back straight. (Do not do deep knee bends.)

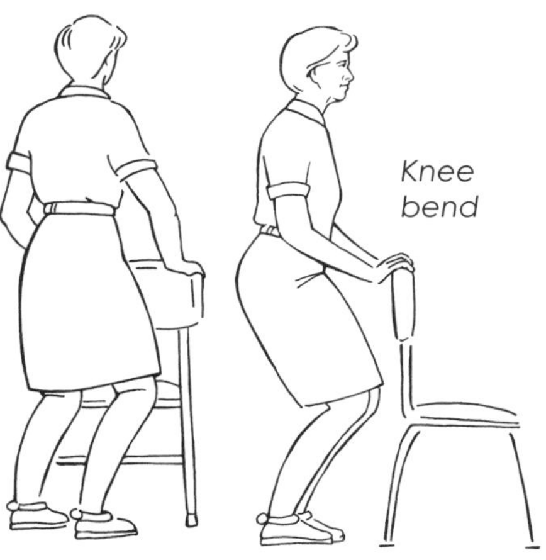

Knee bend

Heel and knee. Alternate the first two exercises: Stand on the tiptoes and return to the starting position. Then, lower the body by bending the knees. Remember to avoid locking the knees. Return to the starting position.

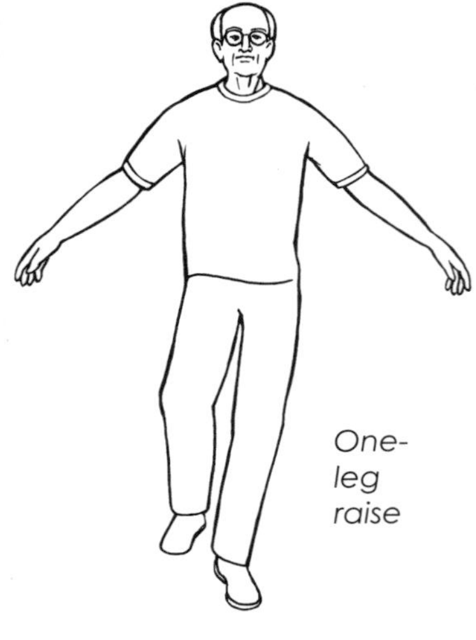
One-leg raise

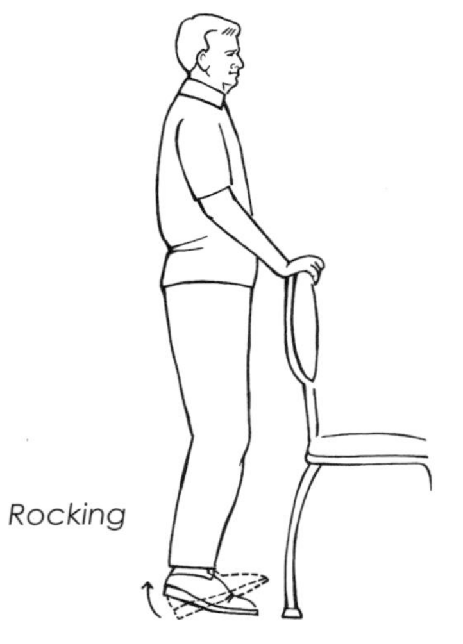
Rocking

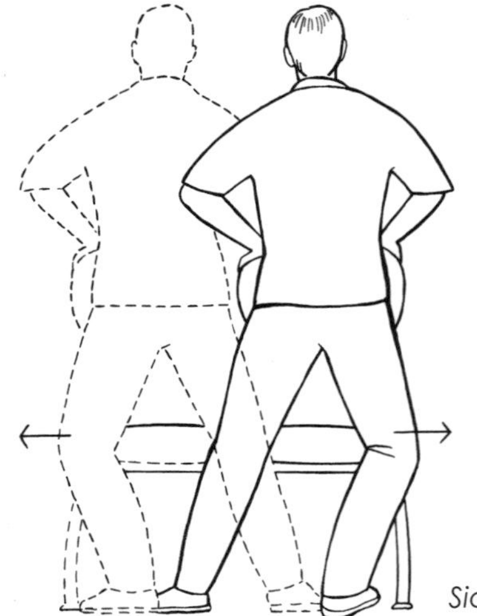
Side lunge

One-leg raise. The body is in the starting position. Bend one knee and lift the leg off the floor. Use the chair back for support if necessary. Balance on the opposite leg for 5–10 seconds and then lower the leg. Repeat on the other side.

Rocking. The body is in the starting position. Rock back and forth, from toes up to heels up.

Slow side lunge motion. Spread legs wider apart than hip width, with toes pointing out. Do simple, small, slow lunges, bending knees 20–30 degrees to the right, back to center, to the left, and back to center. Lunge slowly and deliberately, shifting the weight from side to side.

TAKE A DEEP-BREATHING BREAK.

Knee lift. From the starting position, alternate the legs: Lift the right knee and lower it; lift the left knee and lower it. The motion should be slow and controlled—avoid dropping the foot to the floor. In this exercise, height is not important, but control and balance are critical.

Side leg lift. From the starting position, face the chair. Lift the right leg to the side and lower it. Then, lift the left leg to the side and lower it.

Rear leg lift. (The chairs that are placed behind participants may be moved out of the way.) From the standing position, lift the right leg to the back and lower it. Then, lift the left leg to the back and lower it.

Heel lift. Facing the chair, stand on one leg and bend the other knee to raise the heel toward the buttocks. Repeat using the opposite leg.

TAKE A DEEP-BREATHING BREAK.

Knee lift

Side leg lift

Rear leg lift

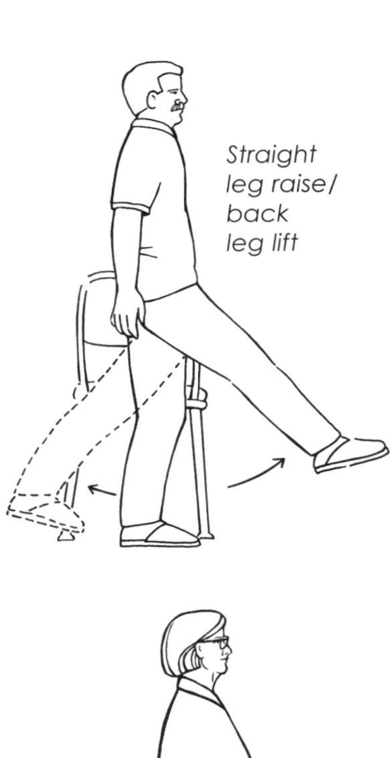

The following four exercises are done by standing at a right angle (approximately 45 degrees) to the chair back. Hold onto the chair back with the left hand. Do 4–6 repetitions of these exercises with the right leg. Then, turn around, hold the chair with the right hand, and repeat the same exercises using the left leg.

Straight leg raise. Holding onto the chair back with the left hand, raise the right, straightened leg forward, then lower it slowly to the floor. Do not lock the knee.

Side leg lift. Lift the straightened right leg to the side and lower it slowly to the floor.

Back leg lift. Lift the straightened right leg to the back and lower it slowly to the floor.

Leg swing. Gently swing the right leg forward and then backward. This exercise should be used only with advanced members who have good balance.

TAKE A DEEP-BREATHING BREAK.

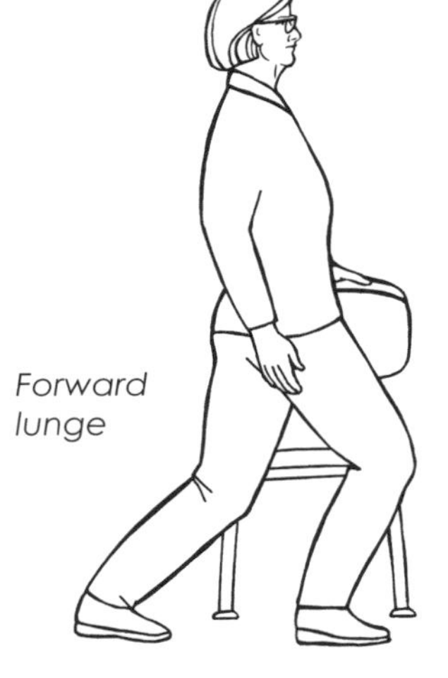

Shoulder rotation. Alternating the arms, do the backstroke slowly and in as large a circle as is possible. Do 4–6 repetitions.

One-leg stand. With the feet hip-width apart, practice releasing the chair back to work on balance. Stand on one leg for as long as is comfortable and then alternate.

Forward lunge motion. With the feet hip-width apart, hold onto chair back with the left hand. Place the right foot a small step forward and bend the knee slightly to shift weight over the right foot. Return to the starting position. Repeat motion with the left leg. Slowly alternate right and left legs 4–6 times. Focus on balance.

TAKE A DEEP-BREATHING BREAK.

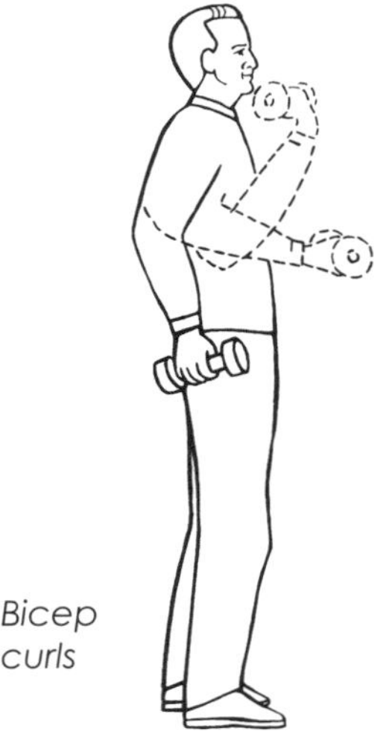

USING HAND WEIGHTS

Weight routines using 1- to 5-pound hand weights (dumbbells) increase muscular strength significantly (the weights provide the resistance against the flexed muscle, which builds strength). The exercises in this section focus on building upper-body strength. Weight routines can be performed in a seated position, and should be supervised carefully so that the participants perform them correctly. Movements should be slow and deliberate, with no jerking or dropping of limbs. Be sure that group members do not hold their breath while they are lifting weights.

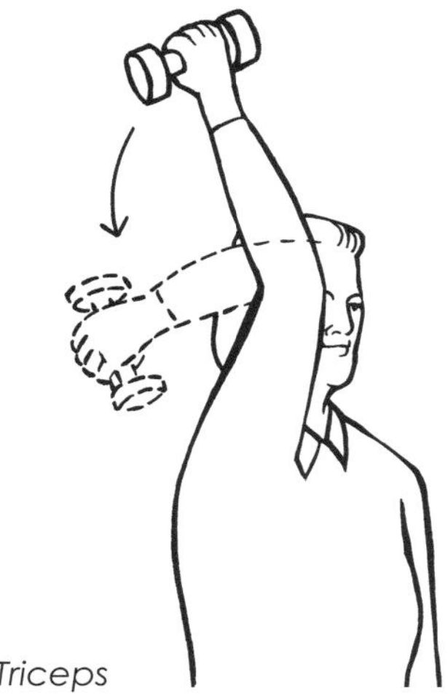
Triceps

Choosing Weight Size

Because there is a risk of injury, participants should begin lifting using 1-pound weights. Some will want to start with a heavier weight, but do not allow them to do so. When a group member reports that the weight is becoming too easy to lift and you have observed that it is, allow him or her to move to a 2-pound weight. Some individuals may progress to a heavier weight in a few days, whereas others may take weeks or may never progress beyond a small weight. Starting small and working up not only allows the muscles and joints to adjust gradually to the use of weights and resistance but it also allows group members to become aware of improving their strength. As the exercise leader, you can keep a record of each member's progress.

Working the Stroke-Affected Arm

In general, stroke-affected sides are not strong enough to be worked with weights. If in doubt, check with the client's physician.

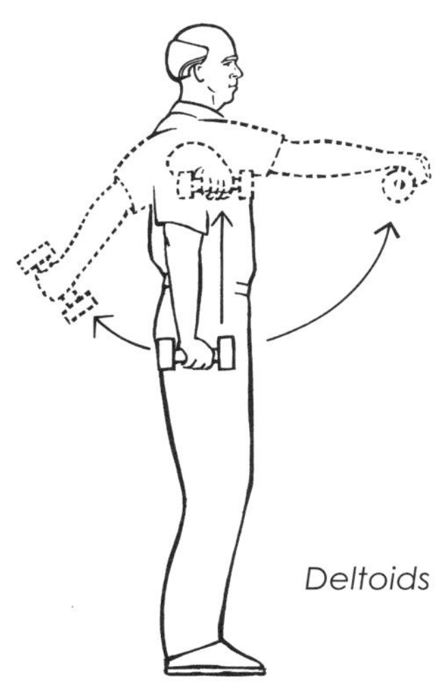
Deltoids

Exercises

4–6 repetitions of each exercise; the weight routines should be performed in a seated position (participants are sure to be tired after standing, and sitting helps them focus on the routines; stronger groups or members could do them standing)

Bicep curls. From the starting position (seated, arms resting at the sides), bend the elbow and slowly lift the weight so that the hand and weight reach the shoulder. Lower the arm slowly. This exercise can be performed using both arms simultaneously.

TAKE A DEEP-BREATHING BREAK.

Overhead press

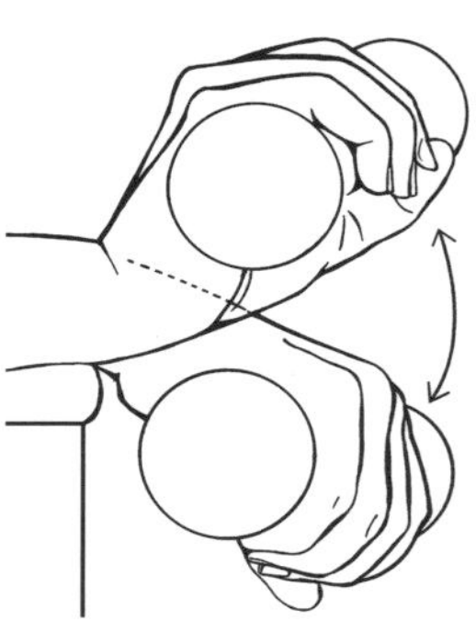

Wrist flexion/extension

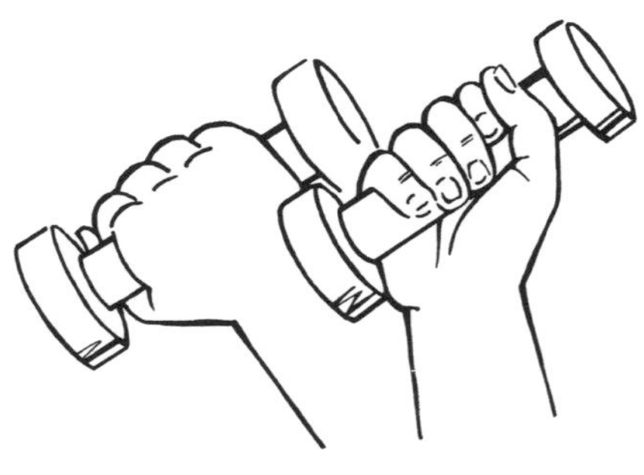

Pronation/supination

Triceps. Work one arm at a time. Lift the arm overhead, keeping the upper arm as close to the ear and as straight as possible. With the elbow pointing toward the ceiling, bend the elbow so that the hand and weight go behind the head. (Be careful not to hit the head with the weight.) Repeat using the other arm.

TAKE A DEEP-BREATHING BREAK.

Deltoids, anterior/posterior. From the starting position and keeping the arm straight (do not lock the elbow), lift the arm forward to shoulder height, then lower it slowly to the side (anterior). Do 4–6 repetitions. Next, lift the arm at the side to shoulder height, then lower it slowly to the side. Do 4–6 repetitions. Then, lift the arm toward the back to approximately a 45-degree posterior angle. Do 4–6 repetitions.

TAKE A DEEP-BREATHING BREAK.

Overhead press. From the starting position (arm hanging loosely at the sides), bend the elbow and slowly lift the weight to shoulder height. Then, straighten the arm toward the ceiling (do not lock elbows). Lower the arm to the starting position slowly and deliberately. Alternate arms. Do 4–6 repetitions. This exercise can be done using both arms simultaneously with a weight in each hand.

TAKE A DEEP-BREATHING BREAK.

Wrist flexion/extension. Place the forearm on the chair armrest or lean forward and place the forearm on the thigh. Holding the weight with the palm facing down, keep the forearm stationary and lift wrist up and then down. Return to the starting position and alternate arms.

TAKE A DEEP-BREATHING BREAK.

Pronation/supination. Place the forearm on the chair armrest or lean forward and place the forearm on the thigh. Holding the weight with the palm facing down (or just hold elbows in to the side, bending the arm forward), rotate the forearm/wrist so that the palm faces up. Return to the starting position and alternate arms.

TAKE A DEEP-BREATHING BREAK.

Games

Games provide variety and fun as well as cognitive motor skills training specifically in the areas of coordination, reaction time, and teamwork. Members remain seated for all games.

Game 1 Kickball

Objectives: Improve coordination, concentration, leg strength, and reaction time; learn members' names; increase interaction among members
Materials: One lightweight, inexpensive playground ball for every two participants
Seating: One large circle, spaced comfortably
Instructions: Round 1—Stand in the center of the circle and kick the ball on the ground to a group member. He or she stops the ball with the foot and kicks it back to you. Be sure the ball remains on the ground (a few football fans may try to punt or kick an extra point). When the skill has been learned by all participants, distribute additional balls so that everyone is involved at the same time. Round 2—When the skill has been learned, ask group members to kick a ball to another person, calling out the name of that person before the ball is kicked. Round 3—Add a few more balls and continue kicking to one another, calling out names. Round 4—Use all of the balls. Be sure that group members remain seated at all times. Your job is to chase stray balls, or you can ask young volunteers to chase them. Round 5—Pass the ball around the circle from one member to the next using gentle kicks. Stop the ball each time before kicking it again. On your command, reverse the direction (clockwise and then counterclockwise).

Game 2 Volleyball

Objectives: Improve concentration, reaction time, coordination, shoulder range of motion, and ability to reach up; practice using one another's names
Materials: One or two large beach balls
Seating: One large circle, spaced comfortably
Instructions: Round 1—Stand in the center of the circle. Call a group member's name and toss the beach ball gently to the person using a one- or two-handed volleyball pass. The participant returns it to you in the same manner. Continue moving around the circle, batting the ball to each member. (This is the practice portion, which may take more than one round of leader-initiated throws.) You can throw more than once to a member who needs more practice in order to master the technique. Round 2—Once the members have learned the gentle volleyball-passing technique, they toss the ball across the circle to one another. Round 3—Once the group members have mastered the passing technique, ask them to call the name of the person before tossing the ball to him or her. Round 4—Try to keep two balls in play simultaneously.

Game 3 Basketball

Objectives: Improve concentration, coordination, and shoulder and wrist range of motion; develop arm strength; experience feelings of cohesion with other team members
Materials: One lightweight, inexpensive playground ball for each group member; one large box or clean round wastebasket, lined with a plastic bag
Seating: One large circle, spaced comfortably
Instructions: Place the box or wastebasket in the center of the circle. Round 1—Move around the circle, handing in turn to each member a ball to try to throw in the basket. Do a round or two using a loopy shoulder pass and a round or two using a bounce pass.

Move the box a little closer for very frail group members. Applaud all efforts as well as successes. Round 2—Divide the circle into two teams (do not move the chairs). Ask a volunteer to keep score. The throws alternate between one team and the other. The team that makes the most baskets wins.

Game 4 Tennis Balls 1

Objectives: Improve eye–hand coordination, hand and finger strength, and ball-handling skills
Materials: One tennis ball for each participant; a basket or a box
Seating: One large circle
Instructions: Round 1—Squeeze a tennis ball in each hand. Hold the squeeze for a few seconds. Round 2—Bounce the tennis balls. Round 3—Throw the tennis ball up and catch it. Start with small throws a few inches high. Round 4—Place the box or basket in the middle of the room and ask participants to throw the tennis balls in it. Try first with an overhand pass, then with a bounce pass (see Game 3, Round 2).

Game 5 Tennis Balls 2

Objectives: Improve coordination, concentration, and rhythm; experience feelings of cohesion with other group members
Materials: One tennis ball for each person, plus an extra ball of a different color or type
Seating: One large circle, with chairs close together
Instructions: Round 1—Each person has one tennis ball. On your command, balls are passed around the circle to the right. (Members should pass with their right hand and receive with their left. People with hemiplegia will receive and pass with the same hand.) Some participants may need a little help to coordinate this activity, so proceed slowly at first. When you call for the group to stop, everyone should be holding one ball. Some participants will have two or more balls, creating a lot of laughs. Resume the game, but this time pass the balls to the left. (Members should receive with their right hand and pass with their left.) When members have mastered the task and the balls flow smoothly and evenly from one person to another, changes in direction can be made without pausing. Round 2—Add an extra ball of a different color. The person who ends up with the different ball is declared the winner.

Game 6 Dowels

Objectives: Improve arm strength, shoulder range of motion, hand strength, and finger dexterity; use stronger arm to assist weaker arm
Materials: 1/4- to 1/2-inch wooden dowel for each participant
Seating: One large circle, with chairs widely spaced or staggered
Instructions: Repeat each routine three or four times. Round 1—Holding the dowel in both hands, raise the arms as far as is comfortable. (Some group members may be able to raise the arms all the way, and then, with elbows pointing up, lower the forearms and hands behind the back.) Round 2—Holding the dowel overhead, lean to the right and to the left. Round 3—Holding the dowel in front of the torso, reach around to the right and to the left. Round 4—Holding the dowel like a canoe paddle, with the right hand on top and the left hand halfway down the dowel or as far as is comfortable, "paddle" to the left. Then, switch hands and "paddle" to the right. Round 5—Holding the dowel vertically in one hand, use the fingers to walk up and down the dowel. Start by holding the dowel on the bottom.

Game 7 Partner Drills

Objectives: Improve coordination and cooperation
Materials: Balls—tennis or playground
Seating: In pairs, about 3 feet apart, facing each other
Instructions: (Plan several routines of three or more parts to be carried out by each pair. The pairs must not only work together but also perform in unison. Some pairs may catch on quickly, whereas others may need more time, but the group will feel a sense of accomplishment.) Sample round: no balls—Slap the thighs twice, clap the hands twice, clap partners' hands twice, clap the hands twice, slap the thighs twice. Sample round: with balls—Partner 1 bounces the ball in front of the body twice and then bounces the ball to Partner 2. Partner 2 bounces the ball in front of the body twice and then bounces the ball to Partner 1. As group members' skills grow, plan more challenging routines.

Game 8 Row Relays

Objectives: Promote teamwork, cooperation, and interaction
Materials: Two tennis balls (easier) or two playground balls (more difficult)
Seating: Two rows or columns of chairs
Instructions: Round 1—Form two columns of teams, with all participants on both teams facing forward. The first person in each column has a ball. On command, the group member passes the ball to the person behind him or her. Each person passes the ball back until it reaches the last person, who passes it forward. The first team to return the ball to the front of the column is the winner. Repeat the relay for several trials. The team that wins the most trials wins the game. Round 2—One column faces the other column. The first person in the column passes the ball to the person next to him or her. Play continues down the row and back again to the first person. (A tennis ball is easier to handle than a playground ball for people who can use only one hand. If several people in the group have this disability, be sure to evenly assign them between the two teams.)

Game 9 I Touch You

Objectives: Promote cohesion within the group; encourage people to touch one another; increase arm strength and range of motion in the shoulders
Materials: None needed
Seating: One large circle, with chairs spaced closely so that members can hold hands or touch the shoulder of their neighbor without leaning or stretching
Instructions: (This routine is recommended as a cool-down exercise at the end of the session, and it promotes a feeling of closeness.) Holding hands, raise the arms toward the front of the body to shoulder level and then lower the arms. Repeat the movement three times. (Ensure that the person who is holding the arm or hand of a person who has had a stroke is cautious about making these movements.) Leaning forward, touch the hands to the floor (or as close to the floor as the participant is able) and sit up. Repeat the movement three times. Placing the hands on the shoulders of the neighbors, lean slightly to the right. Then, lean slightly to the left. Repeat the movement three times. Let go of the neighbors' shoulders. Shake hands with the neighbor on the right and the left and give a greeting or affirmation such as, "Thank you for coming," "Have a good day," "You did really well today," "We're getting stronger," or, "I care about you."

Recommended Readings and Videos

Additional practical information on exercises can be found in the following illustrated guides and videos, all of which are geared to frail older adults.

American Association of Retired Persons. (1987, December). *Pep up your life: A fitness book for seniors* (Booklet No. D549). Washington, DC: Author.

Arthritis and exercise: Information package. (Available from the National Institute of Arthritis and Musculoskeletal and Skin Diseases. U.S. Department of Health and Human Services, Public Health Service, Bethesda, MD 20892-3675.)

Be active: A suggested exercise program for people with Parkinson's disease. (Available from the American Parkinson's Disease Association, 60 Bay Street, Suite 401, Staten Island, NY 10301. Phone [800] 223-APDA.)

Fisher, P.P. (1995). *More than movement for fit to frail older adults: Creative activities for the body, mind, and spirit.* Baltimore: Health Professions Press.

Hurley, O. (1996). *Safe therapeutic exercise for the frail elderly: An introduction.* Albany, NY: Center for the Study of Aging.

Kamaaina Kalisthenics. (1988). [Video]. (Produced by the Hawaii Heart Association; distributed by Cecile Morris, 2447 Oriole Lane, Santa Cruz, CA 95062. Phone [831] 462–9886.)

Keep movin': An exercise program for people with Parkinson's disease. (1989). [Video]. (Distributed by the Struther's Parkinson's Center, 6701 Country Club Drive, Golden Valley, MN 55427. Phone [612] 993-5495. $20.00 plus $3.00 shipping and handling.)

More than movement: Creative activities for older adults. (1997). [Video]. (Distributed by Health Professions Press.)

Perkins-Carpenter, B. (1987). *The fun of fitness: A handbook for the senior class.* (Available from Senior Fitness Productions, 1606 Penfield Road, Rochester, NY 14625. $16.95 plus $3.00 shipping and handling.)

Perkins-Carpenter, B. (1989). *How to prevent falls: A comprehensive guide to better balance.* New York: St. Martin's Press.

Senior gym. (1994). [Video]. (Distributed by Child and Family Service, 200 North Vineyard Boulevard, Building No. B, Honolulu, HI, 96817. Phone [808] 543-8490, extension 320.) (The video focuses on healthy older adults, but shows how to adapt the exercises for people who are nonambulatory.)

The SMILE program (So much improvement with a little exercise). (1992). [Video and instruction manuals]. (Distributed by the University of Michigan School of Public Health, Department of Health Behavior and Health Education, 1420 Washington Heights, Ann Arbor, MI 48109-2029. Phone [734] 647-0212.)

Stroke survivor's workout video. (1997). [Video]. (Distributed by the American Heart Association, Stroke Connection, 7272 Greenwell Avenue, Dallas, TX 75231-4596. Phone [800] 553-6321. $13.00, stock no. 50-1117.)

Part 3
The Support Sessions

All of the handouts mentioned in the "Materials" sections of Part 3 can be found following Session 58 (p. 187). The sources for the group leader–oriented handouts, Optional Handouts, and Readings can be found in the appendixes. Many of the Age Page brochures published by the National Institute on Aging are now included on NIA's web site. NIA's home page is www.nih.gov/nia. Their email address is Niainfo@access.digex.net.

Session 1

The Mingler

Objectives: Get to know other members of the group in a nonthreatening environment, practice sharing information about oneself in a group setting, practice listening in a group setting

Materials: One copy of the reproducible handout, "The Mingler," for the group leader

Seating: One large circle

Instructions: Take the initiative and maintain control during this session, introducing the process and presenting each topic for general group response. Explain the activity in your own words (or read word for word from the following paragraph):

This exercise helps us to get to know one another better. One of the goals of this program is to build social support. Getting to know other group members is the first step to becoming a source of support to one another. Some of you may be willing to share today; others may prefer to listen. Either is fine—both sharers and listeners are appreciated. In fact, during this session, let's practice some listening skills: Let's give our full attention to each person.

Begin with a nonthreatening question from the handout, for example, "Who among us has a pet?" Group members can raise their hands to respond. A participant who is comfortable sharing personal experiences in a large group might expound on the topic by sharing an anecdote about his or her pet. This exercise is one of the least threatening to shy people because they can respond with a simple "yes" and do not need to disclose more than that. Participants may also choose not to respond; individuals who merely listen are observing that others can share in the group without being criticized. This first session is the perfect time for you to begin to work with people who monopolize conversations. Interrupt gently, thank the person for sharing, and remind him or her that everyone in the group who wants to speak should be given an opportunity to do so. You should then move to another group member. This approach models for the group members the need for everyone to share talking time.

Once the first question has been answered and discussed, move on to another question from "The Mingler" handout, such as "Who among us does crossword puzzles?" If a given topic brings no response or generates little or no enthusiasm, then move to another topic. It is fine if only a handful of the topics are covered in a half-hour. "The Mingler" can be used on another day.

Conclusion: Compliment those who shared their experiences during the discussion and praise the group for their ability to listen. Remind the group that this exercise helps them to get to know one another better and begin to learn things they have in common as well as the experiences that are unique to each individual.

Reading: American Association for Retired Persons. (1989). *Reminiscence: Finding meaning in memories.* [Training Guide No. D13404]. Washington, DC: Author.

Session 2

What Do We Have in Common?

Objectives: Experience sharing in small groups, practice self-disclosure, practice listening, feel some sense of belonging in a group in which others share common backgrounds and experiences

Materials: A pencil and a piece of paper for each group

Seating: One circle, which is then split up into groups of three to five people

Instructions: This session helps group members get to know one another and begin the bonding process. Before breaking up into small groups, explain the activity in your own words (or read word for word from the following paragraph):

Many of us share common cultures and experiences. By identifying these commonalities, we can get to know one another better. Today, we'll break up into small groups. Small groups are good because more people get to share and some people feel more comfortable sharing in this kind of a setting. The members of each group will talk among themselves and find three things they have in common. One person in each group should play the role of the secretary and take notes. At the end, each group will report on their three commonalities.

For this activity, members should form their own small groups with people in neighboring chairs. You can help if you notice that an individual is left out or seems to be confused by the assignment. Circulate among the groups, assisting each in starting the discussion process, and even lingering in a group that is having trouble with the assignment (e.g., some members may have difficulty with the term *commonalities*). The small group discussions should last approximately 10 minutes.

Conclusion: After approximately 10 minutes of sharing, reconvene the group into one circle, or, if the group has many frail members, ask the participants to turn in their chairs toward you. A representative from each small group reports on the three commonalities that were found. At the end of the sharing session, praise everyone and comment on how much the group has in common.

Reading: White, E. (1980). *Nourishing the seeds of self-esteem. A handbook of group activities for nourishing esteem in self and others.* Capitola, CA: Whitenwife Publications.

Session 3

What's in a Name?

Objectives: Continue the process of getting to know one another, practice sharing information about oneself in a group, continue to practice good listening skills, continue to feel interconnectedness through commonalities, begin life review by sharing the origin of one's name

Materials: None needed

Seating: One large circle

Instructions: Sharing information about one's roots helps group members to find and get to know others with a similar heritage and to begin to accept the heterogeneity of the group. Explain the activity in your own words (or read word for word from the following paragraph):

One way to get to know one another is to learn about each person's heritage. Our names are part of our heritage, and sharing some information about names tells us a little about ourselves. Today, I want to encourage everybody to contribute if they can by telling the group anything they want to about their name.

Ask each group member to share information about his or her first, middle, and/or last names. Any contribution is welcome, whether it is the name itself, its derivation, why the participant's parents gave him or her that name, or how the name changed over the years. The process of going around the circle and calling on each person puts a little extra pressure on shyer members to share. (If you are aware of a person who monopolizes conversations, then try to call on this person last.) Sharing can become more personal during this session, but each person should decide how much to divulge. Individuals could share simple stories of how their parents chose a particular name; they could share a more revealing story of how names changed so that the family could make a better adaptation to life in the United States; or the story may reveal sagas of divorce, remarriage, or illegitimacy. Such sharing helps shyer group members to understand that even the most self-disclosing story is received easily by the group. This activity begins the life-review process for many participants (see also Session 7).

Conclusion: Express appreciation for everyone making an effort to contribute to the discussion, and again praise the participants for listening quietly while others spoke.

Comment: Two provisos about using the going-around-the-circle technique: The first is that shy and/or nervous people tend to worry about what to say until they are called on. So that their nervous tension does not have a chance to build up, call on the most shy or nervous person first, and then skip to another shy person, moving randomly around the circle. The second proviso is that, once they have made their contribution, some people tend to tune out, doze off, or even leave. Remind the group to be good listeners and to give everyone time to talk.

Readings: Butler, R.N. (1963). The life review: An interpretation of reminiscence in the aged. *Psychiatry, 26*, 65–76. Butler, R.N. (1981). The life review: An unrecognized bonanza. *International Journal of Aging and Human Development, 12*(1), 35–38. White, E. (1980). *Nourishing the seeds of self-esteem. A handbook of group activities for nourishing esteem in self and others.* Capitola, CA: Whitenwife Publications.

Session 4
Learning Names

Objectives: Learn and practice using each member's name, build group cohesion

Materials: None needed

Seating: One large circle

Instructions: Many frail older adults become self-absorbed and find it difficult to reach out to others. A first step in reaching out to other members of the group is to learn their names. This game is designed to facilitate the process of learning everyone's name. You can plan ahead and devise a word for each person to use just in case the person and/or the group cannot think of one. Explain the activity in your own words (or read word for word from the following paragraph):

script

It's important to our development as a supportive group that enhances our well-being that we get to know one another. The first step in doing that is to know everyone's name and use it when we talk to one another. Let's play a word-association game to help us learn all of our names. Each person should describe him- or herself with a word that starts with the same letter as his or her name. Each of us will say, "My name is _______, and I am ________, or I like to _______." For example, I will say, "My name is Mary, and I am marvelous." All of you should reply, "Her name is Mary, and she is marvelous. Marvelous Mary." The names do not need to be serious. In fact, a silly name might be easier to remember—for example, "Sassy Selma." Let's try.

Start with your own name. As you move around the circle, you may find that someone has a hard time thinking of a descriptive word. Rather than fill in a word yourself, encourage the group to help. After completing the process, go around the circle again and ask whether everyone remembers his or her own descriptive name. The group can help. Once you have done that, issue a challenge: Ask whether anyone in the group can remember and name each person (using the descriptive word is not necessary). Usually, one or two people are brave enough to try.

Conclusion: Remind everyone that the purpose of the game is to learn and begin to use everyone's name as we build our restorative group.

Session 5

The Importance of Belonging

Objectives: Heighten awareness of the importance of social support, continue sharing personal stories

Materials: None needed

Seating: One large circle

Instructions: This activity is designed to heighten awareness of the importance of belonging, in families, in the community, and in this group. Explain the activity in your own words (or read word for word from the following paragraph):

script

Let's talk about times in your lives when you felt like you belonged in a group of people. I'm going to go around the circle and ask each of you what kind of group it was and how you felt about it. *[Members usually relate stories about happy times with the family at holiday gatherings, group adventures as children or teenagers, or perhaps experiences of closeness with co-workers. Be sure to ask them to tell both the story and the good feelings that went with the sense of belonging. Once the group has related some brief stories, continue.]* Now, let's talk about times in the past that you have felt excluded or isolated from people. *[Be prepared to listen to difficult stories of a mean kid treating a group member badly as a child or an act of discrimination by a teacher, employer, or social group. In my groups in Hawaii, some Japanese Americans tell stories about being interned in U.S. concentration camps during World War II.]*

Conclusion: Help everyone to agree that the feeling of belonging is far better than the feeling of being excluded. One of the roles of families throughout our lifetime is to give us a place to belong, where we are accepted just as we are. One of the purposes of the group program is to help members feel a sense of belonging to a kind of family, which is very important to their well-being. Ask members to comment on whether they feel they belong in the group. Allow them to make some concluding comments.

Optional Handouts: American Association of Retired Persons. (1991). *So many of my friends have died or moved away. . . .* [Brochure No. D13831]. Washington, DC: Author. [50 for $10.00; in Spanish, Brochure No. D14948]

Readings: Butler, R.N. (1975). *Why survive?: Being old in America.* New York: Harper & Row. Kaplan, B.H., Cassel, J.C., & Gore, S. (1977, May). Social support and health. *Medical Care, 15*(Suppl. 5), 47–58. White, E. (1980). *Nourishing the seeds of self-esteem. A handbook of group activities for nourishing esteem in self and others.* Capitola, CA: Whitenwife Publications.

Session 6
What I Like About Our Group

Objectives: Express feelings about the group experience, help a new member to feel positive about the group, reinforce feelings of belonging

Materials: None needed

Seating: One large circle

Instructions: This discussion is an excellent way to help members remember why they come to group and find that various needs are met through the group experience. (You may want to conduct this session periodically for this purpose.) Another good time to conduct this discussion is when a new member joins the group. Begin the discussion by introducing the new member and inviting him or her to say something.

script

Some people who come to group for the first time want to make a statement—maybe about the event that brought him or her to group; an explanation of who he or she is; or the expression of a lot of pent-up emotions about his or her illness, his or her family, or the hospital or facility. *[You and/or the group members can respond to the new member's introduction]* Thank you for introducing yourself, ______. I can see that you're feeling a need to get back on your feet. What I'd like to do today is have the other members introduce themselves to you and tell you why they come to this group. It may help you to understand better what the group is all about.

Ask group members one by one to give their name, tell why they come to group, and how long they have been coming.

Conclusion: After all of the introductions have been made and reasons given for coming to group, thank everyone for his or her ideas and for the support for the newcomer. Tell the newcomer that everyone looks forward to seeing him or her at the next meeting.

Comment: Group leaders repeat this exercise often, perhaps because it gives everyone, including the leader, a great morale boost about the power of the group. The responses vary: Most but not all are positive; some members may say they come because they have nothing better to do, others may say they come because the group energizes them, or someone may say she comes because her daughter forces her. One of my group's responses covered the following: the friendliness of the people, the helpfulness of the program in general, the opportunities for give and take, the exercise workout, the ability to comply with doctor's orders, the conversation, the stimulating and educational programs, the variety, the chance to get out of the house, the laughter, the occasional lunches, the feeling of belonging, and the chance to be with other people of the same age. One person said that she did not know why she came but that she kept coming back. Another said she had learned her lesson: She dropped out of the group, thinking that she did not need it. During her absence from the group, she was admitted to the hospital three times. After that, she understood the value of the exercise and the support and was back in the group to stay.

Session 7

Where It All Began—Childhood Memories

Objectives: Begin the life-review journey, share childhood memories, experience feelings of universality

Materials: A large world map and stick-on name tags for each person are helpful. If a map is not available, then you can put participants' names on the blackboard or easel/flip chart and categorize them by states, regions, or countries, depending on how heterogeneous the group is.

Seating: One circle, which is then broken up into groups of three to five people

Instructions: This exercise officially begins the life-review process for the group because the members talk about where they began their lives. Members get to know one another's life stories and find commonalities in their childhood. Introduce the activity in your own words (or read word for word from the following paragraph):

Today we're going to talk about our earliest days, childhood—where it all began. Let's start our sentimental journey. *[Pointing]* Here's a map of the world. Let's start with Lois. Lois, where were you born and where did you live for the first 10 years of your life?

Continue around the circle, asking each group member to share where he or she was born and raised. The person's name tag can be placed on the map or on the list of regions, if no map is available. When you have finished going around the circle, ask people born in the same area to form small groups to talk about what their childhood was like. (For example, in my program, at least four groups form: U.S. mainland, Asia, Hawaii, and Europe.) Ask each group to select a spokesperson to either stand and speak about the commonalities or to tell you so that you can repeat the remarks for the group. After 10–15 minutes of small-group discussion, reconvene the group by asking participants to turn their chairs toward you. Ask each spokesperson to say something about what he or she found in talking about childhood. Responses may include traveling by boat or train to a new home, not having many (or any) toys, having to work hard at an early age, having strict parents or teachers, not seeing much of their father, having to walk miles to school, and interacting with ethnic groups other than their own.

Comment: Many memories are produced by discussions of childhood. This discussion can become a series by adding other topics such as school days, friends, games we used to play, or people who lived in your house. You should be prepared for the group member who cannot remember his or her childhood or prefers not to talk about it. He or she may gain a great deal by listening to others' stories.

Readings: American Association of Retired Persons. (1989). *Reminiscence: Finding meaning in memories.* [Training Guide No. D13404]. Washington, DC: Author. American Association of Retired Persons. (1995). *The power of memories: Creative use of reminiscence.* [Brochure No. D14930]. Washington, DC: Author. Burnside, I.,

& Schmidt, M.G. (1994). *Working with older adults: Group process and techniques* (3rd ed.). Boston: Jones & Bartlett. Butler, R.N. (1963). The life review: An interpretation of reminiscence in the aged. *Psychiatry, 26,* 65–76. Butler, R.N. (1981). The life review: An unrecognized bonanza. *International Journal of Aging and Human Development, 12*(1), 35–38. Silver, M.H. (1995). Memories and meaning: Life review in old age. *Journal of Geriatric Psychiatry, 28*(1), 57–73.

Session 8

In a Word—Reminisce

Objectives: Continue the process of getting to know one another, share a risk-taking or troublemaking experience, feel the universality of common past experiences, promote bonding between pairs of men and pairs of women in the group

Materials: None needed

Seating: One large circle

Instructions: This activity involves reminiscing using a chosen word, in this case "trouble." Circulate among the pairs to monitor and assist anyone who has difficulty with the assignment. Members can say whatever they want about the word: the time they got someone into trouble, a troubled time in their childhood, and so forth. As often happens when reminiscing, some participants draw a blank until someone else starts to tell a story. Begin the process by telling a brief story, although it is better for group members to start, if they feel comfortable doing so. Explain the activity in your own words (or read word for word from the following paragraph):

For today's discussion, let's talk in pairs. Turn your chair toward the person next to you. *[Help to pair up people, being sure no one is left out. A third person can be added to a pair if the group comprises an odd number or if there are communication problems because of language barriers, aphasia, and so forth. When the pairs are settled, continue.]* Let's reminisce about the past by using a keyword: "trouble." You can say whatever you want about the word "trouble." Close your eyes for a minute or so and see what memories you come up with about trouble. *[Pause for a minute.]* Now, open your eyes and share with one another. *[Be sure each person gets a chance to talk.]*

Move from pair to pair to ensure that everyone is participating. After approximately 5 minutes, remind the pairs that each person should tell a story about "trouble," so that the partner who has been listening has a chance to talk.

Conclusion: After approximately 20 minutes, thank everyone in the group for participating, and ask members to share anything they would like about their stories. Some people may have brought up sensitive issues that they would prefer not to share in the larger circle. Be sure to remind them that it is not necessary to share in the larger circle.

Comment: This activity can be repeated using any word. Some possibilities are "friend," "funeral," "pet," "accident," "reward," "fear," "challenge," and "accomplishment." The advantage of this activity is that it allows people to delve into their memories and select the experience that is most meaningful to them. By not placing parameters, descriptors, or modifiers on the word, each person makes his or her own association with the word.

Readings: American Association of Retired Persons. (1989). *Reminiscence: Finding meaning in memories.* [Training Guide No. D13404]. Washington, DC: Author. Burnside, I., & Schmidt, M.G. (1994). *Working with older adults: Group process and techniques* (3rd ed.). Boston: Jones & Bartlett. Butler, R.N. (1963). The life review: An interpretation of reminiscence in the aged. *Psychiatry, 26*, 65–76. Butler, R.N. (1981). The life review: An unrecognized bonanza. *International Journal of Aging and Human Development, 12*(1), 35–38. Silver, M.H. (1995). Memories and meaning: Life review in old age. *Journal of Geriatric Psychiatry, 28*(1), 57–73.

Session 9

The Working Life

Objectives: Continue the life-review process, share experiences in the world of work, experience feelings of universality surrounding discussion of the years spent working

Materials: One copy of the reproducible handout, "Talking About Work," for each participant

Seating: Two groups: one for men, one for women (if there are a sufficient number of women who worked outside the home, it is possible to create two groups for the women: one for those who worked outside the home and one for those who did not)

Instructions: This session focuses on the participants' working years. Experiences vary: For many adults, work was the center of their lives, finding nothing in life as meaningful, whereas others may have had less gratifying experiences with work. Introduce the topic in your own words (or read word for word from the following paragraph):

Let's talk about our work lives today. What kind of memories does the word "work" bring up for you? Was it the best time of your life? The worst? What was your first job? What was your worst job? What was the best job? Did you have a mean boss or a wonderful boss? Or were you the boss? If you didn't work outside the home, how did you or do you feel about that? Was your work taking care of the house, raising the children? Why did you retire? Let's divide into groups—the women in one group and the men in another. I'll give each of you a handout to help you get started talking about your work.

Circulate and spend some time listening to each group, reminding group members to give everyone a chance to share and helping the group through any awkward periods. After approximately 15 minutes of sharing, ask someone from each group to report on what they talked about.

Conclusion: It is not always necessary to summarize each group's discussion because this decreases the time that participants can spend sharing experiences. You may want to skip the summary and conclude by saying:

It seems as though you have many stories to tell about work. I hope this session has helped you get to know one another a little better and perhaps find someone you have something special in common with. This is all part of our journey of life review. Why don't you continue your discussions after group?

Readings: Same as Session 8

Session 10

The Best Years of Our Lives

Objectives: Continue to learn to share in a small group setting, think about good and bad periods in life, share stories with group members who have lived through similar experiences, continue the life-review process

Materials: One copy of the reproducible handout, "Best Years Ballot," and a pencil for each participant, and a pad of paper for the "secretary" of each small group

Seating: One circle, which is then split up into groups

Instructions: This activity is fun and permits participants to identify with others who enjoyed the same period of their lives. Give each person a ballot and a pencil. Explain the activity in your own words (or read word for word from the following paragraph):

script

All of you have come a long way on life's journey, a journey of 60 or more years. One of the tasks of growing old is to review this journey by looking back on the many events, people, and places in it and the things we have done or have not done. The purpose of reviewing our lives is to put them in perspective and understand and accept them, even with their ups and downs. What I would like you to do now is to close your eyes and think for a few moments about which of the following periods of your life was best for you: Birth to age 20, 21–40, 41–60, 61–80, or 81–100. It may be hard to choose only one age group, but do it anyway. On my signal, open your eyes and choose one period by circling it on your ballot. This is a secret ballot. Don't look to see what your neighbor picked.

When everyone has selected an age group, ask members to split up into small groups. Participants who picked ages 0–20 should gather in one group, those who selected ages 21–40 should gather in another group, and so on. Their assignment in the small groups is to talk about why that particular period was best for each of them. Ask each group to choose a "secretary" to take notes during the discussion. For example, in the ages 0–20 group, the reasons given may be that as children they had no responsibilities; that they loved school; or that their families, although poor, stayed together. Circulate among the groups to ensure that the participants are cooperating, to answer any questions, and so forth.

Conclusion: After 10–15 minutes of sharing, re-form the large circle or ask members to turn their chairs toward you, and ask each group to share a highlight or two from its discussion. Remind participants that this activity stimulates thinking about their life journeys and helps them to perceive commonalities among the group members. It also helps them to understand that they have differences as well, and that the differences are just as valuable as the things that they have in common.

Comment: I have found that each time this session is conducted, there are fairly balanced numbers in each small group, and that most people decide rather quickly which time period was best for them. I have also found it encouraging that, usually, several group members pick their current age, even if it's 81–100—this helps younger members to believe that the future can be good.

Readings: Same as Session 8

Session 11
Show and/or Tell

Objectives: Continue the life-review process, use visual props to enhance sharing

Materials: At the session prior to this one (not necessarily Session 10), ask group members to bring family pictures or souvenirs; send a reminder note home with them

Seating: One large circle (a table can be used)

Instructions: What parent can forget the task of helping children choose an object to take to school for "show and tell"? Now it is the parents' turn to bring something from home to show to the group. It can be a favorite old picture, a souvenir from their travels, an award, or a favorite household artifact. Ensuring compliance with show and tell is somewhat problematic for older adults, however. Personal cameras were not as ubiquitous in their early years as they are today, so some are hard-pressed to find pictures of themselves as young people. Others report that pictures and souvenirs have been lost, stored away, or forgotten. Searching the house for the right object or picture takes the kind of energy that some frail older adults may not possess. Also, for some group members, remembering to bring a show-and-tell item is difficult. Despite these barriers, a show-and-tell session can be fun and rewarding. If only a handful of people remember to bring something, then they will have more time to share the information. Explain the activity in your own words (or read word for word from the following paragraph):

script

Today's session is "Show & Tell." How many remembered to bring a picture or souvenir they would like to tell us about? So that this session doesn't get too noisy and out of control, let's have each person tell about his or her picture or object but hold onto it for the time being. During the last 10 minutes we'll pass around the objects for everyone to see. The last 10 minutes is very informal and everyone can talk together. During the presentations, however, let's give each speaker our full attention.

Be sure to reward the participants who remembered to bring something by calling on them first. Their souvenirs or pictures may stimulate memories and comments from members who did not bring anything. Be sure to allow enough time for those who did.

Conclusion: Thank the participants who remembered to bring something in and suggest that at the next show-and-tell session, others bring something, too.

Comment: Often, this exercise produces interesting new information about members, such as a special talent for crafts or evidence of special interests and experiences. Take care when objects are being passed around so that these precious items do not become lost or damaged. I recall one show-and-tell session in which a woman took off her huge diamond ring and passed it around the circle. I watched it nervously for fear it would disappear in the confusion.

Session 12

Being Assertive

Objectives: Learn about assertive communication, share problems caused by lack of assertive communication, practice assertive communication

Materials: One copy of the reproducible handout, "3 Ways to Communicate," for each participant

Seating: One large circle, then split up into small groups to prepare skits

Instructions: To communicate assertively is to learn to deal with other people in a way that respects your rights and theirs. Assertive communication helps older people to maintain control, self-esteem, and dignity, despite their losses, and to interact well with their families, friends, and health care personnel. Distribute the handout and explain the activity in your own words (or read word for word from the following paragraph):

script

Let's explore three ways of talking with other people. Take a look at your handout. Let's imagine that you're ill and standing in line at the pharmacy when someone cuts in front of you. There are three ways you could handle this: 1) You could say nothing and let the rude person go first. The result of doing that is that you'd probably feel angry and resentful. That's passive communication. 2) You could yell angrily, "Hey! I was here first! Who do you think you are?" That's aggressive communication. Neither passive nor aggressive communication is effective. The best way to communicate is the third way of communicating, assertive communication. Using assertive communication respects your right to be in line first by explaining that you were, in fact, in line first: "Excuse me, I believe I'm before you in line. I've been waiting 5 minutes and you just came." How would you have handled this situation? [*Allow a few minutes for participants to react.*] Let's have some fun by dividing into two groups to practice these communication styles.

Form two groups: Group 1 role-plays the three types of responses to a request from an irresponsible adult daughter who asks to borrow $500 and does not indicate when or whether she will pay it back. Group 2 role-plays the three types of responses to a doctor who casually dismisses a patient's complaint of knee pain by saying, "What do you expect at your age?" Each group practices its skit for 5–10 minutes, then performs it for the other group. After each skit, group members can guess who played which type of communicator and which type of communication was the most effective.

Conclusion: Thank the performers and ask whether they enjoyed role-playing and learned something new. If the group appears interested, then this subject could be pursued in more depth through other activities, by inviting a psychologist to speak to the group on the subject, or both.

Optional Handouts: Choose from the exercises in *Assertiveness: A practical approach* (see Readings).

Readings: Alberti, R.E., & Emmons, M.L. (1995). *Your perfect right: A guide to assertive living* (7th ed.). San Luis Obispo, CA: Impact Publishers. Holland, S., & Ward, C. (1990). *Assertiveness: A practical approach.* Beachwood, OH: Wellness Reproductions. ($36.95)

Session 13

Solving Problems

Objectives: Share problems encountered by members, learn an effective problem-solving technique

Materials: A blank piece of paper and a pencil for each participant; blackboard and chalk; after the session, distribute the reproducible handout, "5 Steps to Solving Problems," to each participant to take home to work on his or her own problems

Seating: At one large table

Instructions: Older adults have many problems to solve as they try to cope with change and loss. This activity teaches a simple but effective process for solving problems. Give each group member a pencil and a blank piece of paper and explain the activity in your own words (or read word for word from the following paragraph):

script

Today, we are going to practice a problem-solving technique. By learning this simple technique, we can learn to analyze a problem and look for the best solution to it. People who have learned this technique say they are happier with their ability to solve problems. The technique has five steps: Step 1 is to state the problem. Think for a minute about a problem you have—any kind of problem. Choose a problem you'd be willing to share with the group. Write down a few words about the problem on your blank piece of paper. *[Give everyone a few minutes to write in his or her own words what the problem is. Circulate among the group members in case anyone needs help with the task. Then, ask several people to share what they wrote and list the problems on the blackboard. From this list, select a problem to work on. Try to pick one that applies to other members as well—"I don't see enough of my children," "I can't get out to do my shopping," "I can't see to read," or "I can't walk in my neighborhood."]*

Step 2 is to identify the details of the problem. This step is important because in listing the details, participants may think of possible solutions. *[Ask the group member to tell all of the details about the problem that she can think of. For example, if you and the group select "I don't see enough of my children," the details of the problem could be that the adult children have children of their own, both parents work, the grandchildren go to school, and on weekends they all participate in sports activities. The speaker is afraid to be a burden, so does not ask them to visit her or go to their home, and the speaker's daughter is not organized.]*

Step 3 is to list possible solutions. *[Ask group members to brainstorm and suggest several possible solutions. Try not to criticize any of the solutions at this point.]*

Step 4 is to pick the solution that is the most appropriate for both parties. *[For example, the speaker could call her daughter to suggest a regular meeting time: "I really want to see you because I love you, but I don't want to pester you about it all the time. Could we meet for lunch, say, every Wednesday? I could take the Handi-van downtown and meet you." If Wednesday is not convenient, then try another day.]*

Step 5 is to put into action the most appropriate solution. *[Ask the speaker to think about trying the solution and reporting back to the group once she has done so. Because the speaker is required to use the assertive communication technique (Session 12), she may need to role-play and practice in the group before trying it with her daughter. In many cases, adult children do not intend to be neglectful of their parents, but they do get caught up in their own lives. The daughter may appreciate her mother's taking the initiative to make better visiting arrangements.]*

Conclusion: Thank everyone for participating, particularly the group member who spoke about her problem.

Comment: The problem detailed above is one shared by many older adults. Working on a sample problem helps group members to learn to think their own problems through calmly and find a solution. This session is quite lengthy, so you may want to divide it into two sessions. During the first session, you can complete Step 1; during the second session, you can carry out Steps 2–4 or 5. This technique gives you a chance to think the problem through in order to facilitate the process during Steps 2–4.

Readings: D'Zurilla, T.J. (1990). Problem solving training for effective stress management and prevention. *Journal of Cognitive Psychotherapy, 4*, 327–354. Watson, D.L., & Tharp, R.G. (1996). *Self-directed behavior: Self-modification for personal adjustment*. Pacific Grove, CA: Brooks/Cole.

Session 14

Making Good Decisions

Objectives: Learn a basic decision-making technique, share problems about which a decision needs to be made

Materials: Blackboard and chalk or easel/flip chart and markers, and one copy of the reproducible handout, "Making Good Decisions," for each participant

Seating: One large circle

Instructions: This activity teaches a decision-making technique that can be used in considering matters of concern to an older adult, such as: Shall I have surgery? Shall I move closer to my children? Shall I give up driving? Shall I join a senior club? In this session the sample problem of deciding where to live is used. (For more on this topic, see Session 44, "Where Shall I Live?") Introduce the activity in your own words (or read word for word from the following paragraph):

script

Carefully thought-out decisions create better results. Often, people make decisions without too much thought. They may make a decision based on just one factor without thoroughly studying all factors. Making good decisions involves using a model, even though we may not be aware that's what it is. This model comprises looking at 1) the advantages and disadvantages of the decision, 2) the short- and long-term effects of the decision, and 3) the impact of the decision on self and on others. Let's practice this decision-making model using the case of Linda, 84, whose stroke affected her ability to live independently in her home. She doesn't want to move to a nursing facility, but she wonders if she should. Let's help Linda decide what to do by using our decision-making model. *[Write the following title and six headings on the blackboard: Should I Stay in My Own Home? Advantages, Disadvantages, Short-Term Impact, Long-Term Impact, Impact on Self, Impact on Others. Ask group members to list verbally several descriptors under each heading; write them on the board as they do so. Some examples follow.]*

Advantages

My home is familiar and comfortable. I like it.

Taking care of myself helps me stay independent.

Living in my own house is cheaper than moving to a nursing facility.

Going to a nursing facility feels like the end of my life.

Disadvantages

I need help at home, but help is hard to find and isn't always reliable.

I don't think I can handle the details of hiring outside help.

I may become socially isolated.

I may not get enough exercise.

Short-Term Impact
It's easier to stay where I am because moving is hard.

Long-Term Impact
I might need more help in the future.

Impact on Self
Staying home is okay for me.

Impact on Others
If I stay at home, will it put pressure on my family to help me? I don't want to be a burden.
Will they worry about me being home alone?
If I move, will they be willing to help me move?
I wonder how they feel about it.

Once you have listed the group's descriptors, discuss as a group what Linda should do and agree on a decision that she can make.

Conclusion: Thank everyone for participating and for all of their great ideas. Distribute the reproducible handout, "Making Good Decisions." Tell group members to take it home and use it when they need to make a decision.

Comment: Using the model to work through the decision-making process helps participants think about new possibilities. For example, in one of my groups, a participant wanted to make a decision about whether to leave all of her money to the niece who helped her most. After discussion in the group using the decision-making model, she realized that, in the long run, the impact of her decision could be to create bad feelings and strife among other members of her family. The woman decided to leave other family members money as well.

Because this session is lengthy, you could continue this session on another day. On the second day, group members could sit at tables and use the handout to work on a decision they are trying to make or might have to make in the future.

Readings: Janis, I.L., & Mann, L. (1977). *Decision-making*. New York: Free Press. Watson, D.L. (1992). *Psychology*. Pacific Grove, CA: Brooks/Cole.

Session 15

Grieving Losses

Objectives: Learn about the grieving process, share experiences of grief over past losses

Materials: One copy of the reproducible handout, "Grief Worksheet," and a pencil for each participant

Seating: At tables

Instructions: Grief is a natural response to and a process for coping with loss. Most older adults have experienced loss and grief many times in their lives. During this session, they have a chance to share their experiences with grief. Introduce the activity in your own words (or read word for word from the following paragraph):

script

> Today, I would like for the group to share some of our experiences with grief. Over the years, most of us have lost a loved one, a pet, a job, our health, or our home, which caused us great sadness and for which we needed to grieve. Each of you has a "Grief Worksheet." Take a few minutes *[2–5 minutes]* to describe a loss that you have experienced. *[When everyone has finished writing, review with the group the remainder of the worksheet, which describes Elisabeth Kubler-Ross's five stages of grief. As you review each stage, ask group members if they recall the feelings they experienced at that stage, and be sure to explain that people slip in and out of the stages and that they may not experience the stages in the order in which they are listed. Also mention that anyone who feels "stuck" in grief after a "reasonable" period of time should seek professional help, but remember that what is reasonable for one person may be too long for another. For example, the profound losses of aging (e.g., stroke, serious chronic illness) may take several years to grieve. I have observed clients in the group program who are depressed grieve a loss for several years before they come to the final stage of grief, acceptance.]*

Conclusion: Try to end on a positive note by reserving a few minutes at the end of the session to ask group members how they managed to get through their grief.

Optional Handouts: American Association of Retired Persons. (1991). *I wonder who else can help: Questions and answers about counseling needs and resources.* [Brochure No. D13832]. Washington, DC: Author. [50 for $10.00; in Spanish, Brochure No. D14946] American Association for Retired Persons. (1995). *On being alone: Guide for widowed persons.* [Brochure No. D150]. Washington, DC: Author. American Association of Retired Persons. (1991). *So many of my friends have died or moved away. . . .* [Brochure No. D13831]. Washington, DC: Author. [50 for $10.00; in Spanish, Brochure No. D14948] American Association of Retired Persons. (1991). *If only I knew what to say or do: Ideas for helping a friend in crisis.* [Brochure No. D13830]. Washington, DC: Author. [50 for $10.00] *Asking for help.* [Journeyworks No. 5016]. *Coping with change: How to manage the stress of change.* [No. 1252 ZFFM]. San Bruno, CA: Krames Communications. ($1.35) *Going through bereavement: When* *a loved one dies*. [No. 45914A-10-96]. South Deerfield, MA: Channing L. Bete Co. *Moving through grief and loss*. [Journeyworks No. 5014-J9]. [50 for $15.00] *Moving through grief and loss: Understanding the many losses we all face*. [No. 1275 ZFFM]. South Deerfield, MA: Krames Communications. ($1.10)

Readings: Goodall, A., Drage, T., & Bell, G. (1994). *The bereavement and loss training manual*. [W-BER]. Beachwood, OH: Wellness Reproductions. ($139.95) Gordon, S. (1985). *When living hurts*. New York: Dell Publishing. Kubler-Ross, E. (1969). *On death and dying*. New York: Macmillan.

Session 16

Coping with the Holiday Blues

Objectives: Realize that feeling sad or depressed during holidays is common, share reasons for sadness during holidays, share ideas on how to cope with sadness during holidays

Materials: One copy of the reproducible handout, "Tips for Cheering Up During the Holidays," to be distributed to each participant at the end of the session

Seating: One large circle

Instructions: Holidays can be difficult for older people who are alone or have experienced significant life changes (i.e., "it's not like the good old days"). This activity helps group members to realize that others feel sad or depressed and that these feelings are acceptable. You will ask three questions during the session; it is very important to ask them in order and not allow participants to jump ahead. (This tactic prevents people who are in denial from interrupting others' expressions of sadness with their tales of "marvelous" coping techniques.) The three questions are

1. What do we mean by "the holiday blues"? *(Undoubtedly, members will provide good descriptions of feeling sad or depressed during holidays.)*
2. What causes us to feel sad or depressed during holidays? *(Participants will supply a variety of answers, such as "I can't be with my loved ones," "The good old days are gone," "I don't have any money for gifts," "I have too many grandchildren to shop for," "I can't get out to shop," "I don't have the energy to bake, shop, or decorate," or, "The holidays are too commercial these days." After the causes have been explored thoroughly, move to Question 3.)*
3. What coping mechanisms can we use to fight the holiday blues? *(Solicit as many ideas as possible from group members, then distribute the reproducible handout "Tips for Cheering Up During the Holidays" and review it as a group.)*

Conclusion: Thank everyone for sharing their experiences and their ideas, and emphasize that we all have similar feelings; even young adults look back with nostalgia on memories of the holidays of their childhood.

Reading: Clements, C.B. (1994). *The arts/fitness quality of life activities program: Creative ideas for working with older adults in group settings*. Baltimore: Health Professions Press.

Session 17

What Keeps Me Going?

Objectives: Share coping techniques, learn new ways to cope and enjoy life

Materials: None needed, although comments can be listed on a blackboard or flip chart

Seating: One large circle

Instructions: This session helps members to identify the basic values that enable them to face each day even when "the going gets tough." Members may identify and take pride in their strengths and gain by hearing about what motivates their peers. Introduce the activity in your own words (or read word for word from the following paragraph):

script

Does anyone ever wake up in the morning and think, "Why bother? Why should I get up and struggle through another day?" I think we all have days like that. As we get older and our losses mount, maybe we have even more days like that. When we have that kind of a day, what gets us out of bed? What basic values, activities, or other motivating force helps us to carry on? Each of us is different, so we may answer this question in many different ways. Let's close our eyes for a few moments to collect our thoughts about what keeps us going. *[Group members should close their eyes for a minute or so.]* Okay. What gets us going in the morning? *[You should ask everybody, starting with group members who are eager to speak. You may hear a variety of responses such as "my garden," "the sunrise," "thoughts of my spouse or children," "morning chores," "I need to go to the bathroom," "I'm determined to get well," or "my spiritual beliefs." Some participants may deny that they cannot get up in the morning, that they never have such gloomy moments. Tell them how lucky (and perhaps unusual) they are.]*

Conclusion: Thank everyone for sharing their feelings, and point out that the variety of answers shows that there are many reasons to value our time on earth and that there is a lot of wisdom in the group.

Session 18

Being an Older Adult Is . . .

Objectives: Identify one's own feelings about being older, share feelings with other members of the group about getting older

Materials: One copy of the reproducible handout, "Being an Older Adult Is . . . ," for each participant

Seating: At one large table

Instructions: This session allows participants to express how it feels to be an older adult in creative ways. Explain the activity in your own words (or read word for word from the following paragraph):

Let's talk about how it feels to be an older person. I want everyone to think about it for a few minutes, then write or draw something on your handout that expresses how you feel about it. Remember, each of us is different and all of your feelings are acceptable. *[Some members may start writing or drawing immediately, whereas others may sit, staring at a blank page. You and the volunteers should circulate among the group members and work with those who need help getting started, even having them dictate their comments to you. As with other exercises, this activity produces a range of reactions, from very positive to extremely negative. When it seems as though most people have written something on their handout, ask if anyone would like to share what he or she wrote.]*

Conclusion: Conclude by asking if anyone wants to share what he or she gained by thinking and writing.

Optional Handout: *100 great things about growing older.* [Journeyworks No. 5021-J9]. [50 for $15.00]

Session 19

People Who Have Influenced Me

Objectives: Become aware of people who have influenced your life for the better, become aware of people whose lives you have influenced

Materials: None needed

Seating: One large circle

Instructions: The influence exerted by others on ourselves plays a role in the development and maintenance of our self-esteem. People we have admired through the years influence us for the better. We, in turn, influence others, sometimes without knowing it. This activity helps group members to become aware of the role of people's influence in our lives. Begin by reading pages 76 and 77 of Robert Fulghum's *All I Really Need to Know I Learned in Kindergarten: Uncommon Thoughts on Common Things*. Fulghum shares his sense of grief when his barber of many years retired without letting him know. In conclusion, he writes, "Without realizing it, we fill important places in each other's lives." Explain the activity in your own words (or read word for word from the following paragraph):

script

Think of someone who has filled an important place in your life, someone who has been an important role model, friend, mentor, or inspiration. Let's close our eyes for a moment and think of someone who has been a good influence on us. *[After a minute or two, ask members to open their eyes and share stories of their important influence.]*

After several members have shared, ask members to close their eyes again and think of someone they have influenced. Caution members that this may be more difficult because, like Robert Fulghum's barber, we may not be aware that we are influencing others. At least one person will think of a story. In one of my groups, a member spoke of a hiking partner whose consciousness she helped raise about the wonders of nature and how, as a result, they are still friends.

Conclusion: Conclude by asking the participants to take these thoughts home and continue to think about people they have influenced. We all have influenced others, and with thought, perhaps we can remember them.

Comment: In one group discussion I conducted, this topic provided opportunities for participants to realize the power of the group. One man spoke lovingly about a group member who had died the previous year. This story was touching and presented an opportunity to show how a person's influence lives on. Another participant told of the loving care shown him by his caseworker in the group program.

Readings: Fulghum, R. (1988). *All I really need to know I learned in kindergarten: Uncommon thoughts on common things.* New York: Ivy Books. White, E. (1980). *Nourishing the seeds of self-esteem. A handbook of group activities for nourishing esteem in self and others.* Capitola, CA: Whitenwife Publications.

Session 20

A Balance in Caring

Objectives: Learn how caring relates to the maintenance of self-esteem, think about the "three kinds of caring" (see handout)

Materials: Blackboard and chalk or easel/flip chart and markers; one copy of the reproducible handout, "3 Kinds of Caring," for each participant

Seating: One large, open circle in which you place the blackboard or easel or flip chart

Instructions: This activity heightens group members' awareness of the role of caring in the maintenance of well-being and self-esteem. Draw on the board the three faces from the handout and introduce the activity in your own words (or read word for word from the following paragraph):

Let's talk about caring today. Earl White has said, "To express and accept affection, to experience being cared for and caring for others, is to esteem our own humanity" (White, 1980, p. 111). Caring involves accepting care from others, caring for ourselves, and caring for others. A balance of all three keeps us balanced. If we always give and do not take, we become depleted. If we always receive and do not give, we feel useless and beholden. If we always care only for ourselves without involving others, we become isolated. As we age, there's a danger that our lives can become unbalanced. How can we keep that from happening? Let's brainstorm ways that each of us can bring our caring into balance, and I'll write them on the board [easel/flip chart].

The following are some examples that can help you guide the group:

Caregiver. Take time for yourself; allow and encourage the care receiver to help as much as possible and to show appreciation. If the care receiver cannot or will not co-operate, then the caregiver should get being-cared-for needs met by others. The caregiver should ask others to help and specify needs.

Care receiver. Remain as independent as possible. Spend good-quality alone time. Smile at, nurture, and show appreciation to your caregiver. Nurture a grandchild, pet, or another group member.

Isolated person. Join a group of some kind. Reach out to others who can help you meet both caring-for-others and being-cared-for needs.

Reading: White, E. (1980). *Nourishing the seeds of self-esteem. A handbook of group activities for nourishing esteem in self and others.* Capitola, CA: Whitenwife Publications.

Session 21
Appreciation

Objectives: Become aware of the importance of appreciation in the maintenance of self-esteem, practice appreciating and being appreciated

Materials: Checklist of names of group members, with an appreciative comment about each one (prepare ahead of time, but do not distribute to the group)

Seating: One large circle

Instructions: When our lives become difficult, we often become self-absorbed and forget to appreciate the good parts of our lives and the good people in them. This session reminds us to maintain these good social skills. Introduce the activity in your own words (or read word for word from the following paragraph):

Being appreciated and showing appreciation to others are important to good self-esteem. Talking about this subject in the group reminds us to show our appreciation and to accept being appreciated by others. Can someone tell us something you appreciate about another person in the group?

As group members contribute appreciative comments about others, check off each person's name. Continue to elicit comments from the participants, trying to prompt a positive comment about each person in the group. Draw on your own list to make appreciative comments about anyone who was missed by the group members. With a little thought and creativity, positive words can be found for everyone, for example, "dedicated group attendance," "a nice smile," "very friendly," "helpful," "sharp dresser," "asks good questions," "works hard at exercise," "tries his or her best."

Conclusion: Express your appreciation to all of the group members for their comments and for participating in the group. Ask members to go home and actively appreciate someone or something in their lives.

Reading: White, E. (1980). *Nourishing the seeds of self-esteem. A handbook of group activities for nourishing esteem in self and others*. Capitola, CA: Whitenwife Publications.

Session 22

"Old People"

Objectives: Heighten awareness of stereotypes about older adults

Materials: Blackboard and chalk or easel/flip chart and markers; a pencil and one copy of the reproducible handout, "Old Person," for each participant

Seating: At one large table

Instructions: Older adults should be aware of stereotypes about aging and older people so that they can help to dispel them. College students, for example, use twice as many negative words as positive words to describe older people, but this negativity is not limited to young people. Many individuals hold simplistic views about being old and older adults. There are even some older adults who do not like other older people. This session helps group members to see whether older adults believe these stereotypes about themselves. Introduce the activity in your own words (or read word for word from the following paragraph):

Today, I have a special assignment for you. I'm going to say something, and you're going to write three words that come to mind on your handout. Don't look at anyone else's paper—I want independent reactions. *[Distribute the handout.]* The phrase is "old person." Write three words that come to mind.

Circulate among the participants to see if anyone needs assistance with the assignment. When all group members have completed the task, collect the handouts and begin listing the words on the blackboard or easel/flip chart under three headings: Positive, Negative, Neutral. Place words such as "kind" under the Positive heading, words like "crotchety" under the Negative heading, and words like "grandparent" under the Neutral heading; write words that do not fit into any of these categories under the heading Other. Once you have listed all of the words, discuss them. For example: Do the words fall mainly into the Positive or Negative category? What kinds of words does the Neutral category contain?

Conclusion: Give the group feedback about their views of themselves. Are they positive views of people with rich experiences, wisdom, and talent, or are they allowing themselves to be as unidimensional as society sometimes stereotypes them?

Readings: Panek, P.E. (1984). A classroom technique for demonstrating negative attitudes toward the aging. *Teaching of Psychology, 3*, 173–174. Watson, D.L. (1992). *Psychology* (p. 411). Pacific Grove, CA: Brooks/Cole.

Session 23

Objectives: Dispel some of the myths about aging and older adults, share thoughts on these myths

Materials: One copy of the reproducible handout, "What's Your Aging IQ?," for each participant and a pencil for you to record the group's answers

Seating: One large circle

Instructions: Aging is a challenge that is made more difficult when erroneous ideas about it are perpetuated. This session is designed to dispel some of the myths about aging and older people and to share the group's thoughts about these myths. Introduce the activity in your own words (or read word for word from the following paragraph):

Let's take a quiz to see how much we know about aging. Don't worry, you won't be graded, and we'll do it as a group. I'll ask the questions, and you answer "true" or "false" with a show of hands. Once you've answered, we'll see what the experts say, and I'll ask you what your experiences have been. You can take a copy of the quiz home to try with your family.

Conclusion: Distribute copies of the quiz to group members, reminding them to share it with their family members and friends as an opportunity to dispel myths about aging.

Optional Handout: American Association of Retired Persons. (Published annually). *A profile of older Americans*. Washington, DC: Author.

Readings: National Institute on Aging. (1993). *In search of the secrets of aging*. [Brochure No. 93-2756]. Gaithersburg, MD: Author. Williams, M.E. (1995). *The American Geriatrics Society's complete guide to aging & health*. New York: Harmony Books.

Session 24

"Seniors" and "Teeners"

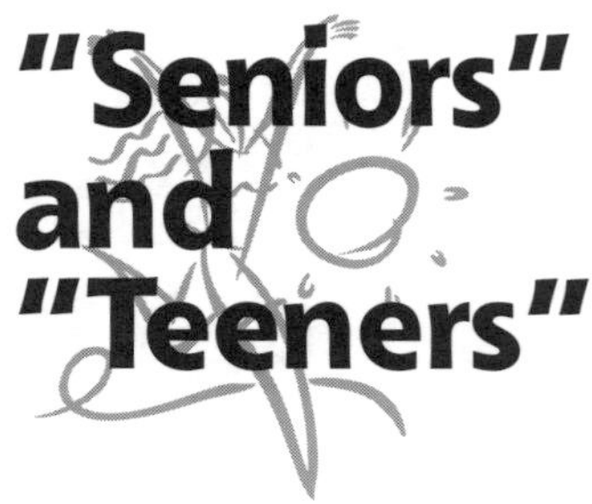

Objectives: Understand the concept of ageism, promote intergenerational understanding

Materials: Blackboard and chalk or easel/flip chart and markers

Seating: Semicircle facing blackboard or easel/flip chart

Instructions: An editorial in *Newsweek* magazine (September 5, 1994, p. 15) featured the thoughts of an 88-year-old woman who said that she feels much the way she did as a teenager. Her views form the basis for a discussion that helps you to heighten the group's awareness of ageism and society's tendency to exclude certain groups. Introduce the activity in your own words (or read word for word from the following paragraph):

How many of you were teenagers? *[Expect laughter.]* Close your eyes for a moment and think what it was like to be a teenager and what it's like for you now as "seniors."

On the blackboard or easel/flip chart, write "Seniors" at the top left and "Teeners" at the top right, and draw a line down the middle. Ask the group to tell you about some changes in, problems with, or complaints heard by and about older adults. (You can add some from the list below.) Then, ask them to show you how similar words apply to teenagers. If group members have trouble coming up with ideas, then use items from the list below to prompt them.

Seniors	**Teeners**
Changes in our bodies	Bodies changing
Money problems	Always broke
Lots of free time	Too much free time
Unemployed—no one wants to hire us	Unemployed—no real role in society
Kids expect us to baby-sit	Parents want chores done
We want our own lives	Want their own lives
Nobody listens to us	Nobody listens to them
Sensitive or irritable, moody	Sensitive or irritable, moody
Kids always telling us what to do	Parents always telling them what to do
Having to live with kids	Having to live with parents

script

Ageism is treating people a certain way just because they are a particular age. Ageism happens both to older adults and to teenagers. Often, people are prejudiced against older adults (e.g., "they're too slow," "they're so forgetful," "they're too wrinkled") and against teenagers (e.g., "they drive too fast," "they're smart-alecky," "they dress like bums"). Sometimes the greatest perpetrators are the older adults or teens themselves, who internalize the negative attitudes they're exposed to. Accepting these stereotypes gives us convenient excuses for not moving forward in our lives. What do you think about what I've just said? *[Listen to group members' comments.]*

Conclusion: Ask group members to rethink their prejudices toward themselves and toward teenagers. How can they be friendly or helpful to teenagers, who face many of the same problems as they do?

Comment: The goal of this session is to promote better understanding of older people, teenagers, and ageism. However, the meeting could go in a different direction and become a gripe session about teenagers. If it does, then let group members air their complaints, but try to conclude the session by suggesting more positive ways of thinking about the issue. Try a second session using a problem-solving technique: "How can we help to promote a better image of 'seniors and teeners'?," or, "What can we, as older adults and grandparents, do to help teenagers through the rough years?"

Session 25

Losses and Gains of Aging

Objectives: Become aware of the changes associated with aging, find comfort in knowing that change is normal

Materials: Blackboard and chalk or easel/flip chart and markers

Seating: One large circle

Instructions: Becoming aware of the very real changes that occur with aging helps group members to grow comfortable with the process of aging and to experience feelings of universality—that they are not alone, that others are going through similar changes. Once they begin to grow comfortable with aging, coping with the changes becomes easier. Introduce the activity in your own words (or read word for word from the following paragraph):

We all experience changes as we age. Some of these changes are positive, some are negative, and some are neutral. Talking about these changes helps us to realize that we are not alone, that others are facing change as well—some the same, some different. Once we accept that change is normal and inevitable, we can cope with it better. Let's brainstorm a list of some of these changes. We'll start with the changes that feel like losses.

Write Losses on the top left side of the blackboard or easel/flip chart. Ask the group members to list losses they have experienced personally. If they have a hard time thinking of losses or resist revealing them, then you can use items from the following list, which I compiled from some of the comments made during my groups' sessions:

General

Importance (one man said that at 40, he had a wife, children, and a business; now, he had none of these)
Independence in transportation
Family closeness
Money and financial resources
Freedom in dietary choices
Spouse, friends, other relatives
Social contacts
Motivation to organize
Ambition, or outlets for using ambition
Interest in or opportunity for sex and intimacy

Physical

Energy
Vision
Normal blood pressure
Mental capacity/memory
Hearing
Appetite
Strength
Hair
Teeth
Agility
Normal joint range of motion
Ability to sleep soundly
Adequate bladder capacity

When you have listed all of the losses, write Gains on the right side of the blackboard or flip chart and ask members to list the gains of the aging process. Although this may be a much shorter list, there are some important areas that can be covered: "lots of free time" (i.e., time to "stop and smell the roses" and do the things they could not do while working), "understanding and wisdom," "empathy with people who are less fortunate than we are," "gratitude for what I still have," "no more burden to make a living," "grandchildren," and "relating to my children as adult friends."

Conclusion: If time permits, then ask participants how they can cope with and compensate for these losses. One coping mechanism that should be discussed is acceptance of things that we cannot change (as in the famous "serenity prayer": "Grant me the serenity to accept the things I cannot change, the courage to change the things I can, and the wisdom to know the difference"). If you have run out of time, then the group can agree to focus on coping and compensation ideas during a future session. See also Session 27 on developing a healthful lifestyle.

Optional Handout: *100 great things about growing older.* [Journeyworks No. 5021-J9]. [50 for $15.00]

Reading: Williams, M.E. (1995). *The American Geriatrics Society's complete guide to aging & health.* New York: Harmony Books.

Session 26

What's Happening to My Memory?

Objectives: Learn about "normal" versus pathological memory loss, share personal experiences with memory loss, practice tips for dealing with memory loss

Materials: Blackboard and chalk or easel/flip chart and markers; one copy of the reproducible handout, "My Memory Improvement Plan," for each participant

Seating: At tables

Instructions: Sharing thoughts on memory loss helps to dispel the common fear that a little forgetfulness means the beginning of a dementing illness. Introduce the activity in your own words (or read word for word from the following paragraph):

Changes in memory may make us concerned and fearful, and we may ask ourselves, "Why do I keep forgetting things?" The fear, spoken or unspoken, is that forgetting may mean you have a dementing disease, such as Alzheimer's. Sometimes memory loss does mean the onset of a medical problem, which may or may not be treatable, but for most people, changes in memory are normal and represent what is called "normal senescent forgetfulness," a slowing down of the parts of the brain that store memory. A doctor should be consulted if the loss is pronounced. Let's talk about what kinds of things you forget and see if we can come up with some ideas to help you.

Distribute copies of "My Memory Improvement Plan" to each group member. Read, or have various members read, each of the items. Then, ask members to describe the kinds of things they forget. As the participants call out items, make a list on the blackboard or easel/flip chart. The following list was compiled by one of my groups: "turn off the stove"; "remove the laundry from the washer"; "leave on time for an appointment"; "pack all of the necessary items for a trip"; "pay bills"; "remove food from the freezer"; "serve all the items planned when entertaining"; "names and addresses of all the grandchildren, friends, and acquaintances"; "whether medications have been taken"; and "whether Medicare or insurance reimbursements have been received." When you think that there are enough items listed on the board, review each one, asking group members to contribute ideas on how to improve their ability to remember. You can contribute ideas based on your own experiences as well. Some ideas are "set a timer" (for stove, washer, and appointments), "organize a system for bill paying and insurance reimbursement," "make a list of travel items," "make a list of dishes to be served," "write down and use the names of grandchildren often," and "use a reminder system for medications."

Conclusion: During the last 10 minutes of the session, ask each person to write on the worksheet a memory problem he or she experiences and possible solutions. Circulate among the tables, offering assistance to people who need it. Tell members that they can take the handout home so that they can identify other problems and solutions, and ask them to practice the solutions. Plan another session in approximately 1 month to ask if they have experienced improvement in their memory.

Comment: If participants show a great deal of interest in this topic, then you can plan additional sessions. An excellent resource for planning sessions on memory is the guidebook by Garfunkel and Landau (see below), who outline a series of six group sessions on memory. A psychologist who is interested in memory problems could be asked to teach more specific skills for memory improvement. To schedule a speaker on disease-related memory loss, contact your local chapter of the Alzheimer's Association.

Optional Handouts: Alzheimer's Disease Education and Referral Center. (1995). *Alzheimer's disease.* [Fact Sheet No. Z-12]. Silver Spring, MD: Author. Alzheimer's Disease Education and Research Center. (1993). *Multi-infarct dementia.* [Fact Sheet No. 93-3433]. Silver Spring, MD: Author. American Association of Retired Persons. (1991). *Now where did I put my keys? A self-help guide for understanding and improving memory.* [Brochure No. D13829]. Washington, DC: Author. [50 for $10.00; in Spanish, Brochure No. D14949]

Readings: Crowley, S. (1996, April). Aging brain's staying power: Studies show healthy brains stronger longer. *AARP Bulletin, 37,* 4. Garfunkel, F., & Landau, G. (1981). *A memory retention course for the aged: Guide for facilitators.* [NCOA Publication No. 4160]. Washington, DC: National Council on the Aging. [$4.00] National Institute on Aging. (1993, May). *In search of the secrets of aging.* [Brochure No. 93-2756]. Gaithersburg, MD: Author. Williams, M.E. (1995). *The American Geriatrics Society's complete guide to aging & health* (pp. 34–40, 135–158). New York: Harmony Books.

Session 27

What Is a Healthful Lifestyle?

Objectives: Heighten awareness of the many facets of a healthful lifestyle, share ways to practice a healthful lifestyle

Materials: Blackboard and chalk or easel/flip chart and markers

Seating: One large circle

Instructions: Brainstorming the elements of a healthful lifestyle helps older adults realize that there are many steps they can take to improve their well-being. Introduce this activity in your own words (or read word for word from the following paragraph):

Today's topic is achieving a healthful lifestyle. Let's see how many factors we can think of that contribute to good health and well-being. Be as specific and as clear as you possibly can. I'm going to write your ideas on the board [easel/flip chart].

In helping participants to be specific, you should encourage them to break down the idea into parts. For example, if someone says "eat good food," the specific parts might be "eat less fatty foods," "do not add as much salt to food as usual," "eat more vegetables," and so forth. You also may clarify or revise some suggestions. For example, if someone says "lose weight," you should point out that some people may need to gain weight, so perhaps he or she should rephrase "lose weight" to say "maintain ideal weight." The group may need your assistance to discuss psychosocial factors such as socializing or thinking positively. If group members run out of ideas, then add some from the following list, which was compiled from the input provided by several of my groups: eat in moderation; eat less salt; eat less fat; eat less sugar; maintain ideal weight; take multivitamins (after checking with physician); eat lots of fruits, vegetables, and grains; exercise regularly; go for walks, if possible; do range-of-motion exercises; do stretching exercises; have supportive friends and, hopefully, family; socialize with friends and family; be nice to friends and family; be forgiving of friends and family; maintain some interests or hobbies; be accepting of life's changes; take risks, try new interests; read; keep up on world events; believe in something; don't watch too much television; appreciate nature; enjoy music and art; find ways to express creativity; see your doctor regularly; be assertive with your doctor and ask questions; take medications as prescribed; report medication side effects to doctor; follow (or question) doctor's orders; be aware of your body's signals; be aware of your feelings; be assertive with everyone; don't smoke at all or drink much alcohol.

Conclusion: Thank everyone for contributing, and remind the group of how many actions we *can* take to improve our lives. If time permits, then ask participants which of the practices are difficult to maintain and lead a discussion on one of the practices or tell the group members you would like to have a speaker come to talk about areas of particular interest to them. Any of the optional handouts can be used to complement this session, or if the discussion reveals a particular interest in one area (e.g., sleep problems), a session can be planned using the appropriate handout (e.g., "A Good Night's Sleep").

Optional Handouts: American Optometric Association. (1991). *Rites of sight: Protecting your eyes for a lifetime of good vision.* St. Louis: Author. *I won't smoke today because. . . .* [Journeyworks No. 5019-J9]. [50 for $15.00] *It's never too late to quit,* [Journeyworks No. 5020]. [50 for $15.00] *I walk because. . . .* Journeyworks No. 5022. [50 for $15.00] National Institute on Aging. (1992). *Age Page: A good night's sleep.* Gaithersburg, MD: Author. National Institute on Aging. (1995). *Age Page: Aging and your eyes.* Gaithersburg, MD: Author. National Institute on Aging. (1995). *Age Page: Don't take it easy—exercise!* Gaithersburg, MD: Author. National Institute on Aging. (1995). *Age Page: Hearing and older people.* Gaithersburg, MD: Author. National Institute on Aging. (1995). *Age Page: Hormone replacement therapy: Should you take it?* Gaithersburg, MD: Author. National Institute on Aging. (1996). *Age Page: Skin care and aging.* Gaithersburg, MD: Author. National Institute on Aging. (1994). *Age Page: Shots for safety.* Gaithersburg, MD: Author. National Institute on Aging. (1991). *Age Page: Smoking: It's never too late to stop.* Gaithersburg, MD: Author. National Institute on Aging. (1994). *Age Page: Taking care of your teeth and mouth.* Gaithersburg, MD: Author. *What everyone should know about wellness.* (1991). [Brochure No. 12674F-1-88]. South Deerfield, MA: Channing L. Bete Co.

Readings: American Association of Retired Persons. (1990). *Have you heard? Hearing loss and aging.* [Brochure No. D12219]. Washington, DC: Author. [50 for $14.00] American Association of Retired Persons. (1996, February). *Health promotion.* [Brochure No. D15706]. Washington, DC: Author. American Association of Retired Persons. (1996). *Healthy questions: How to talk to and select physicians, pharmacists, dentists, and vision care specialists.* [Brochure No. D12094]. Washington, DC: Author. American Institute for Preventive Medicine. (1997). *HealthyLife® seniors.* Self-care guide. Farmington Hills, MI: Author. [$5.95]

Session 28

Healthful Eating Wheel of Fortune

Objectives: Reinforce learning about good nutrition, provide mental stimulation, have fun

Materials: Blackboard and chalk or easel/flip chart and markers

Seating: Large semicircle around the blackboard or easel/flip chart

Instructions: "Healthful Eating Wheel of Fortune" is a game that can be played after staging a formal talk on the subject of nutrition (see "Comment" below for ideas on speakers). The purpose of the game is to reinforce learning about good eating habits by focusing on individual actions that one can take to make better food choices. The popular television game show "Wheel of Fortune" provides the basis for this game, which is adapted according to the group's abilities. Introduce this activity in your own words (or read word for word from the following paragraph):

script

The purpose of the Healthful Eating Wheel of Fortune game is to help us remember to make good food choices. I'll write a phrase on the blackboard [easel/flip chart], using blanks instead of the letters. We'll go around the circle, giving everyone a chance to guess a letter to put in the blanks. If you guess correctly, all the blanks with that letter will be filled. If the letter you guess is not correct, the next person can try another letter. Remember that on the TV show, contestants can't guess vowels, so we'll do it that way, too. *[Depending on the cognitive abilities of your group, you can make the game easier by allowing participants to guess vowels.]*

Choose a phrase (e.g., "poached eggs instead of fried eggs"), then write on the board a blank to represent each letter:

_ instead of _

Call on a group member to begin guessing. If he or she chooses a correct letter, then put it in the appropriate blank(s). If it is not a correct letter, then list it separately. Anyone can guess the phrase when they think that they know it. Other suggested phrases are "Angel food cake instead of devil's food cake"; "Pretzels instead of potato chips"; "Baked or broiled fish instead of fried fish"; "Soup and salad instead of hamburger and fries"; "Frozen yogurt instead of ice cream"; "Tuna packed in water instead of tuna packed in oil"; "English muffin instead of a doughnut"; "Skim milk instead of whole milk"; and "Bake, broil, boil, steam, poach, or microwave instead of fry."

Conclusion: You can end the game when the scheduled meeting time is up. Remind the group that this game is for fun, learning, and mental stimulation. Encourage people to play the game on television and to do crossword puzzles and other games that help them keep their minds sharp.

Comment: *Warning*—Most participants love this game, but some have difficulty with it, either because they have never played; are not adept at word games; or are illiterate, aphasic, or do not speak English well enough to spell the words. An adaptation that you can make to simplify the game is to put all of the letters in a bag and ask each person to pull out a letter that he or she can guess. If anyone has trouble reading the letter, then call it out for him or her. You can make the game more competitive by forming two teams and keeping score of which team guesses each phrase first. For speakers or films on nutrition, contact the local health department, a university extension service, the education department of a local hospital, the group dining program of the county Area Agency on Aging, or the local chapters of the American Heart Association and the American Diabetes Association.

Optional Handouts: *About fiber in your diet.* (1989). [Brochure No. 37606B-12-89]. South Deerfield, MA: Channing L. Bete Co. American Association of Retired Persons. (1994). *Healthy eating for a healthy life.* [Brochure No. D15565]. Washington, DC: Author. [50 for $30.00] *What you should know about good nutrition in the later years.* (1983). [Brochure No. 01373]. South Deerfield, MA: Channing L. Bete Co.

Readings: American Association of Retired Persons. (1994). *Healthy eating for a healthy life.* [Brochure No. D15565]. Washington, DC: Author. National Council on the Aging. (1987). *Eating well to stay well.* [NCOA Publication No. 4181]. Washington, DC: Author. ($2.95) Center for Science in the Public Interest. (1996, April). *Nutrition Action Newsletter.* Washington, DC: Author.

Session 29

What Do I Know About High Blood Pressure?

Objectives: Review basic facts about hypertension, assess group members' knowledge of and interest in the topic, share experiences in preventing or managing hypertension

Materials: One copy of the reproducible handout, "What Do I Know About High Blood Pressure?," for each participant (hand it out after the session)

Seating: One large circle

Instructions: This activity can be used to introduce the subject of hypertension, to assess members' knowledge of and interest in hypertension, or to reinforce a previous presentation by an invited speaker. Introduce the activity in your own words (or read word for word from the following paragraph):

Blood pressure has a tendency to rise as we get older, and nearly half of all people over age 65 have mildly elevated blood pressure. When we allow our blood pressure to get too high, we put ourselves at risk for stroke and heart disease. We need to know about high blood pressure—how to prevent it and how to manage it. Today's quiz will help. I'll read each question and let you guess the answer. Please share your personal experiences if you want.

Read each question and have group members guess the answer. Then read the correct answer and ask the participants to share their reactions or experiences.

Conclusion: Ask whether group members would like more information on high blood pressure. Encourage participants to take the quiz home to review and share with their families.

Comment: Suggested sources for speakers on the topic of hypertension are physicians, nurses, or representatives from the local American Heart Association or county health department.

Optional Handouts: American Heart Association. (1995). *About high blood pressure: Control, risk, lifestyle, weight.* [Brochure No. 50-1079]. Dallas, TX: Author. American Heart Association. (1995). *High blood pressure: The silent stalker for stroke (brain attack).* [Brochure No. 50-1081]. Dallas, TX: Author. National Council on the Aging. *Keeping the pressure down.* [NCOA Publication No. 2046]. Washington, DC: Author. ($45, kit with manual & 20 handouts)

Reading: Williams, M.E. (1995). *The American Geriatrics Society's complete guide to aging & health.* New York: Harmony Books.

Session 30

What Do I Know About Diabetes?

Objectives: Learn the risk factors for diabetes, share personal experiences with diabetes, assess members' interest in and knowledge of diabetes

Materials: One copy of the reproducible handout, "What Do I Know About Diabetes?," and a pencil for each participant

Seating: One large circle

Instructions: This quiz helps group members to think about diabetes, and it helps you to assess their interest in and knowledge of the topic. Encourage members who are diabetic to share their experiences. Introduce this activity in your own words (or read word for word from the following paragraph):

Diabetes is a serious disease that affects nearly 18.4% of Americans over age 65. Some people have diabetes and don't know that they do. This test helps us learn about diabetes and its treatment. Take the quiz home with you and show it to your family. Ask your doctor whether you are at risk for diabetes.

Either read each statement or ask various group members to read each statement, and let members guess whether it is true or false. Then, read the answers on the back of the quiz and ask participants to comment. Encourage diabetic group members to share their experiences with the disease. You may find that there is much to discuss and that you need to control the dialog to be able to complete the quiz.

Conclusion: Thank everyone for participating and express your hope that the group has become more aware of diabetes and its treatment. Allow about 10 minutes at the end of the session to distribute an American Diabetes Association diabetes risk test and ask members to complete it, or distribute the test for members to take at home and then share the results with their physicians. These risk tests vary by region: Ask for one that is geared toward older adults and the ethnic populations in your group.

Optional Handouts: National Institute on Aging. (1991). *Age Page: Dealing with diabetes*. Gaithersburg, MD: Author. *Type II diabetes*. [Brochure No. 1472-ZFFM]. San Bruno, CA: Krames Communications. [$1.40; in Spanish, Brochure No. 1480-ZFFM] *What everyone should know about diabetes*. (1988). [Brochure No. 11611-12-87]. South Deerfield, MA: Channing L. Bete Co.

Reading: Williams, M.E. (1995). *The American Geriatrics Society's complete guide to aging & health*. New York: Harmony Books.

Session 31

What Do I Know About Osteoporosis?

Objectives: Heighten awareness of osteoporosis, share personal experiences with osteoporosis, assess knowledge of and interest in osteoporosis

Materials: One copy of the reproducible handout, "Osteoporosis: The Silent Bone Thinner" (hand it out after the session)

Seating: At one large table

Instructions: Approximately 25 million adults—women *and men*—have osteoporosis, which is the progressive loss of bone mass that results in weakened bones and a high risk for fractures. Awareness of this "silent disease" may lead older adults to seek ways to maximize bone strength and minimize bone tissue loss. Introduce this activity in your own words (or read word for word from the following paragraph):

Let's see how much we know about osteoporosis. I'll ask questions from the Age Page I'm going to hand out at the end of the session. You guess the answers and share with the group your own experiences with osteoporosis and broken bones.

You should become familiar with details in the Age Page, and then ask such questions as the following: What is osteoporosis? Who can get it? How is it diagnosed? How is it prevented? How is it treated? Allow participants to share their knowledge and then share facts from the Age Page or read each section.

Conclusion: Ask members whether they have learned anything new about osteoporosis. Offer to talk to individuals who want more information or a referral for help after class.

Optional Handouts: *A woman's guide to osteoporosis*. [Brochure No. 1179-ZFFM]. San Bruno, CA: Krames Communications. [$1.35; in Spanish, Brochure No. 1719-ZFFM National Osteoporosis Foundation web site: http://www.nof.org/ *Ten ways to lower your risk of osteoporosis*. [Journeyworks No. 5075-J9]. [50 for $15.00]

Readings: Williams, M.E. (1995). *The American Geriatrics Society's complete guide to aging & health* (pp. 262–267). New York: Harmony Books.

Session 32

Coping with Pain

Objectives: Allow members to express their "aches and pains," feel universality in understanding that others have similar "aches and pains," share techniques for coping with pain

Materials: Blackboard and chalk or easel/flip chart and markers; one copy of the reproducible handout, "Taking Charge of My Pain," for each participant

Seating: One large semicircle facing the blackboard or easel/flip chart

Instructions: Many older adults report frequent or chronic pain related to arthritis, injuries, stroke, and so forth. They may find comfort in knowing that they are not alone in trying to cope with pain. They may also learn from one another ways to cope with and manage pain. Introduce this activity in your own words (or read word for word from the following paragraph):

script

Many older people report that pain is a part of their daily lives. Maybe it would be helpful to talk about the kinds of pain we have and what we do about them. Let's go around the circle and each person can tell where they have pain, how often they have it, and what causes it.

Start the discussion by disclosing any pain you experience or ask for a volunteer from the group who is willing to talk about his or her pain. Your self-disclosure will make people feel more comfortable about sharing this information because, at home, family members may discourage loved ones from discussing their pain (e.g., "Oh, here she goes again with the aches and pains! We've heard enough!"). Write across the top of the blackboard [easel/flip chart] three columns: Area of Pain, Frequency of Pain, and Cause of Pain. Once you or the group member has self-disclosed (e.g., about arthritis in the knees that seems to flare up under stress), write "knee" as area of pain, "occasionally, when stressed" as frequency, and "not known" as cause. Go around the circle, asking group members to self-disclose. Add their contributions to the lists. When another person also says "knee," mark a slash next to "knee" to indicate a second person, and then fill in their frequency and cause. By the time all group members have been polled, you may notice certain trends. In one of my groups I found that a large number of people reported shoulder pain; daily frequency; presumable cause, arthritis. After all of the members self-disclose and trends have been noted, ask participants what they do about their pain (you do not need to go around the circle again; just make the discussion a general one). In the group that reported a great deal of shoulder pain, participants mentioned that their shoulder pain had decreased since they began doing the range-of-motion and strength-building exercises in the group (see Part 2). In fact, nearly all of the long-term members reported a decrease in pain since joining the group. Newer members loved hearing this because it gave them encouragement.

Conclusion: Summarize the findings about pain and how group members manage theirs. Review the handout, "Taking Charge of My Pain," which mentions the development of a pain management plan. This plan may include working with a doctor or pain clinic, doing physical or occupational therapy, exercising, relaxing, going to leisure counseling, and taking medications, which should be limited to the least amount necessary. You can list on the back of the handout local sources of medical help. Some communities have pain control clinics that help individuals control their pain more effectively.

Optional Handouts: *About living with chronic pain.* (1992). [Brochure No. 15107D-12-91]. South Deerfield, MA: Channing L. Bete Co. Arthritis Foundation. (1993). *Arthritis: Do you know?* [Brochure No. 5786/1-93]. Atlanta: Author. Arthritis Foundation web site: http://www.arthritis.org/ *Managing your chronic pain.* [Brochure No. 1309 ZFFM]. San Bruno, CA: Krames Communications. [$1.35] National Institute on Aging. (1996). *Age Page: Arthritis advice.* Gaithersburg, MD: Author.

Readings: Chronic pain. Its many impacts on older Americans and their families. (1991, November/ December). *Perspective on Aging,* 6–13. Williams, M.E. (1995). *The American Geriatrics Society's complete guide to aging & health.* New York: Harmony Books.

Session 33
Managing My Medications

Objectives: Help members become aware of good medication management, share ideas and experiences with medications, role-play a visit to a doctor and a pharmacist

Materials: Script for role play, "A Successful Doctor's Visit"

Seating: Start with one large circle, then adjust to a semicircle if participants want to perform before the group

Instructions: The topic of medication management is extremely important but complex. You may want to devote several sessions to the topic and invite both physicians and pharmacists to talk with your group members. The goal of this session is to introduce the idea that each person must take a partnership approach with his or her doctor in the use of medication. The role-play activity helps members to practice the skills necessary for taking responsibility for their medications and asking pertinent questions of their doctor and pharmacist. Introduce this activity in your own words (or read word for word from the following paragraph):

script

> Medication management is one of the most important subjects we cover during our sessions. You need to take an active part in knowing and monitoring the medications you're on. The many drugs available today can help us to live longer, healthier, and happier lives, but those of us who take a lot of medications run a higher risk of adverse reactions, overdoses, and illnesses caused by these medications. The average person over age 65 takes 2 or 3 prescriptions every day, 14 prescriptions every year. The more medications you use, the more likely you are to have problems, so it's important to learn about the drugs and to monitor your use of them carefully. If your memory isn't what it used to be and you need help to do that, tell your doctor and your family so that they can help you. Let's role-play to help us practice talking with the doctor and the pharmacist about the drugs they give us.

Ask for volunteers to read the four roles in the skit (doctor, Mrs. Delaney, clerk, and pharmacist). Give members a few minutes to read over their parts, and then have them read to the group (with or without going to the front of the room, depending on whether the group likes to perform).

Conclusion: If time permits, then another group of four people can role-play. Ask members for their reactions to the skit. They may say that it is hard to ask the doctor all of those questions and take up so much of his or her time. Suggest that they take along the "A Successful Doctor's Visit" handout to help them remember the answers and to write them down. (In addition, you may want to review the "Being Assertive" session.) Also suggest that practicing at home helps them to feel more comfortable in the doctor's office, and if they are still unclear about the medicine when they get home, then tell them they should call the doctor's office and ask the nurse to find the answers for them.

Comment: This session can be used as an introduction to the topic of medication management. Physicians and pharmacists can be invited to address the group on specific issues relating to managing medications. I arranged to have pharmacy students from a local university talk to my groups. The students discussed medications during one session, and during a second session, the group members brought all of their medicines to the meeting in a brown bag so that they could be reviewed individually by the students. Group members found these sessions helpful for increasing their awareness about their medications, and the experience gave the pharmacy students excellent practice in communicating with older adults.

Optional Handouts: *How to manage your medications.* [Scriptographic Booklet No. 1423D-2-86]. South Deerfield, MA: Channing L. Bete Co. National Institute on Aging. (1995). *Age Page: Medicines: Use them safely.* Gaithersburg, MD: Author. *Understanding your prescription.* (1983). [Scriptographic Booklet No. 1259B-9-82. South Deerfield, MA: Channing L. Bete Co.

Readings: American Association of Retired Persons. (1992). *AARP pharmacy service prescription handbook* (2nd ed.). New York: HarperCollins. Silverman, H.M. (Ed.). (1996). *The pill book.* New York: Bantam Books. Watterson, K. (1988). *The safe medicine book.* New York: Ballantine Books. Wolfe, S.M. et al. (1993). *Worst pills, best pills II: The older adult's guide to avoiding drug-induced death or illness.* New York: Pantheon.

Session 34

Discussing Medications

Objectives: Discuss various problems related to the use of medications, continue learning about the safe use of medications, involve more group members in the process

Materials: 23 problem cards with problem on front and suggestions on back (see handouts section at the back of the book)

Seating: One large circle

Instructions: This activity involves everyone in discussing the many issues related to the use of medicines by older adults. Introduce this activity in your own words (or read word for word from the following paragraph):

Medicines can be helpful to us for our various medical problems, but it's important that we know as much as possible about using them safely. Today, I'm going to distribute cards that have sample problems written on them. Each person can read the problem, and as a group we'll talk about how to handle that problem. On the back of each card is a brief suggestion about how you might deal with it.

Distribute the cards to those who are willing to participate (some people may demur because of problems with seeing, reading, or speaking). You could give these individuals a card anyway and ask a volunteer to stand by to read the card. When the person reads the problem, allow group members to voice their opinions before he or she reads the answer.

Conclusion: Ask group members if any questions have come up for them as a result of participating in the activity. If so, then a speaker (e.g., physician, pharmacist, nurse) should be invited to speak to the group.

Comment: This activity can be repeated many times because guessing the answers to each question and the subsequent discussion take a lot of time—you are unlikely to cover all of the questions in one session.

Handouts and Readings: Same as Session 33.

Session 35

Do I Have the Right Doctor?

Objectives: Share information about group members' primary physicians, evaluate the primary physicians' ability to provide good care

Materials: One copy of the reproducible handout, "Do I Have the Right Doctor," for each participant

Seating: One large circle

Instructions: Many people are intimidated by physicians or are awed by them, which discourages them from asking questions, challenging the doctor's authority, and/or taking responsibility for their own health care. Introduce this activity in your own words (or read word for word from the following paragraph):

script

Older people have many special health needs that should be attended to by a doctor. How do you feel about your doctor? Do you have a doctor who cares about you and helps you to participate in your own health care? Or do you have a doctor who says, "Just do what I say," or tells you your problems come simply from getting old. Let's talk about that. Turn to your neighbor and chat for a few minutes about what your doctor is like and whether you like him or her. *[After 5 minutes or so, bring the group back to order, distribute the handout, and ask members to comment on what they found when they chatted about their doctors.]* This questionnaire can help you evaluate your present doctor or select a new one who can best meet your needs. You can take the list home with you to think about some of these issues and talk them over with your family. Let's discuss this checklist for evaluating a physician.

Conclusion: Express your hope that this opportunity to share has helped members to realize that their doctor is either wonderful or not, and some may want to consider looking for a doctor with whom they feel more comfortable.

Optional Handouts: American Association of Retired Persons. (1996). *Healthy questions: How to talk to and select physicians, pharmacists, dentists, and vision care specialists.* [Brochure No. D12094]. Washington, DC: Author. [package of 50 for $16.00] *Asking questions.* [Brochure No. 1190]. San Bruno, CA: Krames Communications. National Institute on Aging. (1990). *Age Page: Hospital hints.* Gaithersburg, MD: Author. National Institute on Aging. (1996). *Age Page: Talking with your doctor: A guide for older people.* Gaithersburg, MD: Author.

Readings: Williams, M.E. (1995). *The American Geriatrics Society's complete guide to aging & health* (pp. 53–58). New York: Harmony Books.

Session 36

Symptoms We Shouldn't Ignore

Objectives: Become aware of some emotional problems that can affect older adults, become able to recognize symptoms of poor or failing mental health

Materials: Blackboard and chalk or easel/flip chart and markers, one copy of the reproducible handout, "Symptoms I Shouldn't Ignore," for each participant

Seating: One large semicircle facing blackboard

Instructions: Before the session begins, write these words in large letters on the blackboard or easel/flip chart: stress, anxiety, insomnia, depression, paranoia, alcohol abuse, medication problems, financial abuse, abuse and neglect, addiction. Introduce this activity in your own words (or read word for word from the following paragraph):

script

Someone I know used to say "aging is not for sissies." It's true. The many losses and changes you face are hard on your mental health, so it's important to be alert to potential mental health problems because those caught early can be treated most easily. This quiz introduces you to some of the symptoms that might indicate you need outside help. *[Distribute handout.]* If any of these stories sounds familiar to you, please talk to me, a trusted friend, or a member of your family.

Read each question or ask one of the group members to read aloud. After each question is read, ask members if they can guess the answer from the list of words on the board. Some of these words may not be familiar to certain group members. If someone in the group does not know one of the words, then read the definition on the back of the quiz. After each item, ask whether the group members have questions or comments.

Conclusion: Praise the participants for their attention during the session, and add that, as a group, we need to talk about difficult problems if we are to take charge of our lives, and we need to address any of these problems as early as possible. Offer to stay after the meeting to counsel privately with anyone or to take calls at the office. Suggest that members take the quiz home and share it with their families.

Comment: Be prepared for some members to approach you after the meeting about some of the warning signs, either for themselves or for someone they know. You can counsel them or refer them to the appropriate resources in your community for help.

Optional Handouts: *A guide to managing stress.* [Brochure No. 1108-ZFFM]. San Bruno, CA: Krames Communications. [$1.35] *About alcohol abuse and older people.* (1993). [Brochure No. 14423F-6-93]. South Deerfield, MA: Channing L. Bete Co. American Association of Retired Persons. (1995). *Alcohol, medications and older adults: How to get help.* [Brochure No. D15939]. Washington, DC: Author. [50 for $5.00] American Association of Retired Persons. (1993). *Backgrounder: Stress in later life.* [Brochure No. D14219]. Washington, DC: Author. [50 for $5.00] American Association of Retired Persons. (1991). *I wonder who else can help: Questions and answers about counseling needs and resources.* [Brochure No. D13832]. Washington, DC: Author. [50 for

$10.00; in Spanish, Brochure No. D14946] American Association of Retired Persons. (1991). *If only I knew what to say or do: Ideas for helping a friend in crisis.* [Brochure No. D13830]. Washington, DC: Author. American Association of Retired Persons. (1995). *If you're over 65 and feeling depressed.* [Brochure No. D14862]. Washington, DC: Author. American Association of Retired Persons. (1991). *Is drinking becoming a problem?* [Brochure No. D14365]. Washington, DC: Author. [50 for $10.00] *Dealing with depression.* [Journeyworks No. 5013]. [50 for $15.00] National Institute on Aging. (1995). *Age Page: Aging and alcohol abuse.* Gaithersburg, MD: Author. *Overcoming chemical dependency.* [Brochure No. 1186]. San Bruno, CA: Krames Communications. *Relief from stress.* [Journeyworks No. 5015]. [50 for $15.00] *Stress and the older person.* (1992). [Brochure No. 13870B-6-92]. South Deerfield, MA: Channing L. Bete Co.

Readings: Billig, N. (1987). *To be old and sad: Understanding depression in the elderly.* Lexington, KY: Lexington Books. Busse, E.W., & Blazer, D.G. (1980). *The handbook of geriatric psychiatry.* New York: Van Nostrand Reinhold. Butler, R.N., & Lewis, M.I. (1982). *Aging and mental health.* St. Louis: Mosby. Williams, M.E. (1995). *The American Geriatrics Society's complete guide to aging & health* (pp. 187–212, 460–466). New York: Harmony Books.

Session 37

When I'm Depressed

Objectives: Share experiences with feelings of depression, share coping techniques for preventing and alleviating depression

Materials: Blackboard and chalk or easel/flip chart and markers; one copy of the reproducible handout, "Symptoms of Depression," for each participant

Seating: One large circle

Instructions: The social losses and chronic conditions that are experienced by most of the group members put them at risk for depression. Understanding more about this mental health problem helps group members to cope with it. Introduce this activity in your own words (or read word for word from the following paragraph):

script

Today's discussion focuses on the most common disturbance of mood, especially among older adults: depression. We all have times when we feel depressed, or blue. Most depression is a temporary mood that, in general, lifts after a short time or after a period of adjustment to a traumatic or sad event in our lives. However, when that mood persists for more than 2 weeks and is accompanied by other symptoms, it's called clinical depression. [*Distribute the handout "Symptoms of Depression" and read the symptoms to the group.*] An estimated 20% of older adults suffer from clinical depression, and among the members of a group like this, that number could be higher. We, our families, and our doctors often fail to recognize that we are depressed and in need of treatment. Fortunately, depression is easily treatable. Medication, counseling, exercise, and social support are some of the methods that can help a person to recover from depression. Would anyone like to tell the group about a time when he or she was depressed? *[Allow members to share, but do not pressure anyone to do so. If no one seems willing to volunteer, then you may wish to share your own experiences (if any) with depression in order to break the ice.]*

As group members share their experiences, be careful not to evaluate their stories and do not allow other members to do so—active listening is the most powerful means of support in this instance. Encourage people to describe what helped them pull out of their depression. If members are not willing to share, then move on to reviewing the handout. Remember to end on a positive note by asking the group to brainstorm some of the things they do to ward off depression. Write at the top of the blackboard or easel/flip chart "Things I do when I feel blue," and ask participants to contribute their ideas. Some of the ideas contributed by my groups include walk on the beach, call a friend, do a puzzle, and sing or listen to music.

Conclusion: Thank those who have shared their stories, and encourage members to speak with you, their doctor, a psychiatrist, psychologist, or social worker if they think they are depressed. Remind them again that depression is not a character weakness but a real physical malady that can and should be treated.

Optional Handouts: American Association of Retired Persons. (1989). *I wonder who else can help: Questions and answers about counseling needs and resources.* [Brochure No. D13832]. Washington, DC: Author. American Association of Retired Persons. (1995). *If you're over 65 and feeling depressed.* [Brochure No. D14862]. Washington, DC: Author. *An older couple deals with depression: Bill and May's story.* [Brochure No. 44404A-4-96]. South Deerfield, MA: Channing L. Bete Co. *Asking for help.* [Journeyworks No. 5016]. *Dealing with depression.* [Journeyworks No. 5013]. *What everyone should know about depression.* (1992). [Brochure No. 12229B-6-90]. South Deerfield, MA: Channing L. Bete Co.

Readings: Billig, N. (1987). *To be old and sad. Understanding depression in the elderly.* Lexington, KY: Lexington Books. Butler, R.N., & Lewis, M.I. (1982). *Aging and mental health.* St. Louis: Mosby. American Association for Retired Persons. (1996). *Perspectives in Health Promotion and Aging, 11*(2). Mosher-Ashley, P.M., & Barrett, P.W. (1997). *A life worth living: Practical strategies for reducing depression in older adults.* Baltimore: Health Professions Press. Robinson, R.G., Lipsey, J.R., & Price, T.R. (1984, July). Depression, an often overlooked sequela of stroke. *Geriatric Medicine Today, 3,* 71. Scogin, F., & McElreath, L. (1994). Efficacy of psychosocial treatments for geriatric depression: A quantitative review. *Journal of Counseling and Clinical Psychology 62*(1), 69–74. Williams, M.E. (1995). *The American Geriatrics Society's complete guide to aging & health.* New York: Harmony Books.

Session 38

A Safe Home Is No Accident

Objectives: Be reminded of the need for home safety, think about the safety features of specific areas in your home

Materials: One copy of the reproducible handout, "A Safe Home Is No Accident," for each participant

Seating: One large circle

Instructions: More than 20,000 Americans die every year in accidents in the home, and about 3 million more are injured, some permanently. Many of these deaths and injuries could have been prevented. This activity reminds group members of the importance of home safety. Introduce this activity in your own words (or read word for word from the following paragraph):

Our objective for today's session is to think about home safety. I'm going to pass out a home safety checklist that covers every room of your house. Let's go over the checklist together. Perhaps you can spot some problems in your own home, and together we can think of ways to solve some potentially dangerous situations.

Review the checklist point by point, encouraging participants to share any comments, suggestions, and experiences.

Conclusion: Ask members to take the checklist home to share with family members and to do a careful survey of their home. Offer to find information and resources for group members who have problems they need to solve.

Optional Handouts: *About accident prevention and older people.* (1986). [Brochure No. 13490-1-86]. South Deerfield, MA: Channing L. Bete Co. American Association of Retired Persons. (1995). *Crime prevention.* [Brochure No. D15869]. Washington, DC: Author. *Safeness.* [Brochure No. 1185]. San Bruno, CA: Krames Communications. U.S. Consumer Product Safety Commission. (1987). *Safety for older consumers: Home safety checklist.* Washington, DC: Author.

Reading: Bonder, B.R., & Wagner, M.B. (1994). *Functional performance in older adults* (pp. 225–239). Philadelphia: F.A. Davis.

Session 39

Preventing Falls

Objectives: Share experiences with falls, learn about risk factors for falls, learn ways to prevent falls

Materials: One copy of the reproducible handout, "All About Falls" (see Optional Handouts below) for each participant

Seating: One large circle

Instructions: Introduce this activity in your own words (or read word for word from the following paragraph):

Falls are a major problem for older adults. Raise your hand if you have fallen in the past year or so. *[Pause for members to raise their hands.]* How many of you have fractured a bone as a result of a fall? *[Pause for members to raise their hands.]* How many worry about falling? *[Pause for members to raise their hands.]* Let's see what we can learn about falls by taking a quiz. *[Note: Do not distribute the quiz "All About Falls" until after the session.]*

Read each of the questions and informally canvass group members for the answers before reading the correct answer. Encourage discussion and the sharing of experiences concerning each of the points.

Conclusion: Distribute a copy of the "All About Falls" quiz to each participant to take home.

Optional Handout: *Accident prevention and older people.* [Brochure No. 13490.] South Deerfield, MA: Channing L. Bete Co.

Readings: American Association of Retired Persons. (1993). *Developing fall prevention programs for older adults: A guide for program planners and volunteer facilitators.* [Brochure No. D15236]. Washington, DC: Author. Perkins-Carpenter, B. (1989). *How to prevent falls: A comprehensive guide to better balance.* New York: St. Martin's Press. Tideiksaar, R. (1987). Fall prevention in the home. *Topics in Geriatric Rehabilitation, 3,* 57. Tideiksaar, R. (1998). *Falls in older persons: Prevention and management (2nd ed.).* Baltimore: Health Professions Press. Tinetti, M.E., Baker, D.I., McAvay, G., Claus, E.B., Garrett, P., Gottschalk, M., Koch, M.L., Trainor, K., & Horwitz, R.I. (1994). A multifactorial intervention to reduce the risk of falling among elderly people living in the community. *New England Journal of Medicine, 331*(13), 821–827. U.S. Department of Health and Human Services. (1991). *Physical frailty: A reducible barrier to independence for older Americans. Report to Congress* (NIA/NIH Publication No. 91-397). Washington, DC: U.S. Government Printing Office.

Session 40

Getting Help in an Emergency

Objectives: Think about responding to an emergency, prepare emergency list

Materials: One copy of the reproducible handout, "Getting Help in an Emergency," for each participant

Seating: At tables

Instructions: Many older adults, especially those who are frail and/or live alone, worry about what would happen if they had a medical emergency. How would they get help? Despite their fears, many are reluctant to take the steps necessary to prepare for such an event. This session helps group members to begin considering some alternatives. Introduce this activity in your own words (or read word for word from the following paragraph):

How many of you think about what would happen if you fell at home and couldn't get up, or if you had a stroke or heart attack and no one was around to help you? What would you do? I know it's hard to even think about such possibilities, but we really need to because these things do happen and we should be prepared. Have any of you had such an experience, and if so, what happened?

Go around the circle, asking each person about his or her experience in this area and whether he or she has a plan in place to obtain emergency help. (You may find that one, maybe more, of the group members has a story that illustrates the need to be prepared.)

Conclusion: Review the reproducible handout as a group, eliciting comments and questions about each item. Suggest that members take it home to share with their family and to enlist their help in preparing an emergency plan.

Comment: Expect some group members to be in denial about this topic and to exhibit resistance to the idea of having such a plan. This session at least starts people thinking about a plan. You can invite speakers from the sponsors of emergency response systems to speak to the group.

Optional Handout: American Association of Retired Persons. (1992). *Product report: PERS (Personal emergency response systems).* [Brochure No. D12905]. Washington, DC: Author.

Session 41

What Help Will I Need?

Objectives: Think about the kinds of help you need now or may need in the future, learn about the categories of services that are available

Materials: Blackboard and chalk or easel/flip chart and markers; one copy of the reproducible handout, "Services for Older Adults," to be distributed to each participant after the brainstorming portion of the session

Seating: At tables

Instructions: This exercise helps members to think about the kind of help they need now or may need for the future and how they can obtain it. Introduce the activity in your own words (or read word for word from the following paragraph):

We are likely to remain independent if we can get the help we need when we need it. Let's talk a little about what you think you need now or expect you might need in the future. I'll go around the circle so that we can get each person's ideas. We can learn from one another. We are all different in our needs, so during this stage, please don't comment on or criticize what others say.

Ask someone to volunteer to kick off the discussion. Admitting to the need for help is difficult for many older people, who see the need for help as a weakness, so you need to give permission to the members to admit to having needs. Do this by praising the contribution of the first person who volunteers and by disallowing criticism. For example, if Ruth admits to needing help with grocery shopping, do not allow Marie to say, "Walk to the store, Ruth. It's good for you." Write the list of needs on the blackboard or easel/flip chart. After this part of the exercise has been completed, distribute and discuss the list of services. Ask participants to check off the services that they need or anticipate needing in the future. Have them list on the back of the paper any help that is needed that is not covered on the front. (The reason for separating the brainstorming portion from the list-completing portion is because there are many more needs than those listed, and you do not want the group members' thinking to be limited by the items in the list.)

Conclusion: Thank the group members for their participation and explain that this is just an introduction to services. Conclude by saying,

We will talk more about services in future sessions. I'm going to invite representatives from various agencies to talk to the group so that we can become familiar with what services are available. That'll help us to find them when we need them.

Optional Handout: American Association of Retired Persons. (1991). *Making wise decisions for long-term care.* [Brochure No. D12435]. Washington, DC: Author.

Reading: *Aging with confidence.* (1994). Syracuse, NY: Signal Hill Publications. ($6.95)

Session 42

Name that Service!

Objectives: Share experiences with use of community services, continue to learn about these services

Materials: One copy of the reproducible handout, "Name that Service!," and a pencil for each participant

Seating: At two or more tables, with at least one member who serves as the "team secretary"

Instructions: Learning about community services takes time and reinforcement because there are numerous services, and many people do not pay attention to them until they need them. This session continues the process of learning about services. The quiz can be used following Session 41 and after members have heard presentations by representatives from various community services. It can be adapted to reflect your community's resources. Introduce this activity in your own words (or read word for word from the following paragraph):

We are learning that our community has many services available to help older people lead independent and satisfying lives. You may already be using some of these services, or you may want to use them one day. I'm going to begin by asking you what community services you have already used.

You can help if you are familiar with who has used which service. For example, you may know that Emily attends adult day programs twice a week, so you can prompt Emily to talk about it. You may know that a few participants use the local group dining program. After the members have shared their experiences, distribute the quiz to the teams, asking each team to discuss their answers before guessing the correct one.

Conclusion: When all teams have finished or have nearly finished the quiz, review it as a group.

Comment: Although this quiz may be difficult for some group members, it gives you a better idea of what members already know and to what areas they need to be exposed.

Session 43

Developing an Independent Spirit

Objectives: Share positive behaviors used to maintain independence; learn new, positive behaviors for independent aging

Materials: Blackboard and chalk or easel/ flip chart and markers; one copy of the reproducible handout, "Tips for Independent Living," for each participant

Seating: One large semicircle

Instructions: The process of developing an independent spirit begins with group members' brainstorming ideas, which you will list on the blackboard or easel/flip chart. Do not discuss the merits of each point as it is listed. Introduce this activity in your own words (or read word for word from the following paragraph):

As we get older, most of us want to remain as independent as possible. There must be some things we can do to develop an independent spirit and to lead an independent life. Let's share some of our thoughts. After we do that, I'll hand out a list of tips for safeguarding our futures and we'll go over it.

Ask for a volunteer to write the ideas on the board or flip chart. When approximately 10 ideas have been listed, talk briefly about each point. You may need to rephrase some of the items. For example, someone may say, "Don't bother your children." That statement can be qualified by saying instead, "I understand your not wanting to be a burden to your children, but you and they want to care about one another." You could rephrase in this way, "Don't pester your children with unnecessary requests, but do establish a good relationship with them, and communicate your wishes and needs clearly." Someone else may say, "Do everything yourself. Don't ask for outside help." That can be qualified by saying instead, "Do as much as you are able, but ask for outside help from the right sources when it's needed. A little help can go a long way toward maintaining your independence."

Conclusion: Distribute the handout, "Safeguarding Your Future," and ask members to take turns reading and commenting on each point.

Optional Handout: American Association of Retired Persons. (1997). *Staying in charge: 25 tips to help you remain independent in your home and community*. [Booklet No. D15937]. Washington, DC: Author.

Readings: *Aging with confidence*. (1994). Syracuse, NY: Signal Hill Publications. ($6.95) American Association of Retired Persons. (1992). *Tomorrow's choices: Preparing now for future legal, financial and health care decisions*. [Booklet No. D13479]. Washington, DC: Author. American Association of Retired Persons. (1995). *Perspectives in Health Promotion and Aging, 10*(4). American Society on Aging. (1993, Fall). Self-care and older adults. *Generations*.

Session 44

Objectives: Share concerns regarding housing (present or future), learn about housing options, increase sense of independence and choice

Materials: Blackboard and chalk or easel/flip chart and markers; one copy of the reproducible handout, "Housing Options," for each participant

Seating: One large circle

Instructions: Housing issues create a great deal of anxiety for many older adults. As they become more frail and less able to meet the demands of home maintenance, they worry whether they should move. Their adult children may put pressure on them the first time they leave a stove burner on or fall. One alert 79-year-old expressed this fear to one of my groups: "My children are just waiting for me to make one mistake so they can insist I sell the house and move closer to them. So, I must be very careful. It keeps me on my toes." Sometimes, a move to another type of housing is a good idea. One older couple was pressured by their daughter to move from the rowhouse that they had occupied for 60 years to a retirement community. They resisted for a long time but finally gave in. Much to their surprise, they love living there. Now in their 90s, they are very active in the community. Introduce this activity in your own words (or read word for word from the following paragraph):

EDUCATION

script

Let's talk about where we live and whether we plan to keep living there. Some of you still live in the home where you raised your children. Some live in apartments of various kinds: condominium, senior housing, or retirement community. Some live in a board and care home. Some of you live alone, others live with family or a caregiver. There are advantages and disadvantages to each style of living, and all of us have different needs and preferences. It might be useful to share information about our own housing situations. I'm going to go around the circle. Please tell the group where you live, whether you live alone or with others, how you feel about your current home, whether you think about moving, and why or why not.

Call on each member to share. Each person should share what is important, whether it be a fierce determination to remain in his or her home, resentment at having moved from far away to be near adult children, loneliness at having been "put" into a senior apartment, and so forth. Members will recognize common situations among people in the group. Some may get ideas for a future move. If time permits, then list on the blackboard or easel/flip chart some of the advantages and disadvantages of each type of housing as described by the members and from the ideas below:

Advantages	**Disadvantages**
Stay in own home	Loneliness
Familiarity	Too many chores
Independence	House needs repairs
I know my neighbors	It's too noisy

Move to children's home	
People with whom to socialize	Personality conflicts
Help is handy	
Seniors apartment alone	
Independence	Loneliness
Inexpensive (seniors housing)	Expensive (private home)
Board and care home	
Help with personal care	Live with new people
People with whom to socialize	Expensive

Comment: This topic may require you to hold more than one session and invite speakers from various housing programs: seniors public housing, a retirement community, a board and care home, a nursing facility, and a financial institution that offers reverse mortgages that help people stay in their homes.

Optional Handouts: American Association of Retired Persons. (1988). *A home away from home: Consumer information on board and care homes.* [Brochure No. D12446]. Washington, DC: Author. American Association of Retired Persons. (1997). *The do-able renewable home.* [Brochure No. D12470]. Washington, DC: Author. [50 for $22.50] American Association of Retired Persons. (1997). *Homemade money: Consumers' guide to home equity conversion.* [Brochure No. D12894]. Washington, DC: Author. [50 for $27.00] American Association of Retired Persons. (1996). *Selecting retirement housing.* [Brochure No. D13680]. Washington, DC: Author. [50 for $17.50] *Long-term care insurance.* Senior Focus reproducibles. Emeryville, CA: Parlay International.

Reading: U.S. Department of Health and Human Services. (1991). *Guide to choosing a nursing home.* (HCFA Publication No. 02174). Washington, DC: U.S. Government Printing Office.

Session 45

Learning About Life Care Planning

Objectives: Learn about some basic documents needed for life care planning, become aware of the advisability to complete certain documents

Materials: Reproducible handout, "Learning About Life Care Planning," and a pencil for each participant

Seating: At tables

Instructions: Planning future legal, financial, and health care decisions is a complex subject. Your goal for this session is to raise group members' awareness of the various areas that need attention. It is suggested that an attorney or other knowledgeable speaker carry out this activity after the group has heard presentations on these subjects. It may be that in some groups with very frail members, these matters are handled by a caregiver rather than by the group member. In this case you may want to direct your educational efforts toward family members. You need to be somewhat comfortable with the concepts and terminology associated with life care planning. To become more comfortable, read the American Association of Retired Persons' brochure "Tomorrow's Choices: Preparing Now for Future Legal, Financial and Health Care Decisions" (Brochure No. D13479, 1992). Introduce this activity in your own words (or read word for word from the following paragraph):

script

The goal of this program is to help you remain self-sufficient and content for the rest of your lives. I hope that you will always be able to stay in charge of your lives and live independently. All of us need to plan, however, for the possibility that someday we could be incapacitated and unable to make decisions. Also, we can make plans to protect our survivors when we are gone. Today's quiz, which we'll take together, teaches us some of the terms we need to know to carry out sound planning for legal, financial, and health care decisions.

Distribute the quiz to group members. Read each question, ask participants to guess the answer, and solicit comments and questions. Group members can write the correct answers on the quiz. The group's comfort level with this quiz helps to determine whether there is a need to invite additional speakers for specific teaching.

Conclusion: Thank the members for taking part in the quiz. Ask whether there are areas they would like to learn more about, and ask whether they would like to have an attorney come in to talk about and help them prepare a living will and a durable power of attorney for health care.

Comment: In my experience I have found that most groups choose to ask an attorney to speak to the group about these documents. The attorney can return on another day to help individuals who want to sign them. Care must be taken, however, not to pressure members to complete them.

Optional Handouts: American Association of Retired Persons. (1989). *A consumer's guide to probate.* [Brochure No. D13822]. Washington, DC: Author. American Association of Retired Persons. (1997). *Before you* *buy: A guide to long-term care insurance.* [Brochure No. D12893]. Washington, DC: Author. American Association of Retired Persons. (1996). *Finance.* [Brochure No. D15809]. Washington, DC: Author. American Association of Retired Persons. (1996). *Medical treatment: Decide in advance.* [Brochure No. D15632]. Washington, DC: Author. National Institute on Aging. (1992). *Age Page: Getting your affairs in order.* Gaithersburg, MD: Author.

Readings: American Association of Retired Persons. (1992). *A matter of choice: Planning ahead for health care decisions.* [Brochure No. D12776]. Washington, DC: Author. American Association of Retired Persons. (1992). *Domestic mistreatment of the elderly: Towards prevention.* [Booklet No. D12810]. Washington, DC: Author. American Association of Retired Persons. (1997). *Staying at home: A guide to long-term care and housing.* [Brochure No. D14986]. [50 for $20.00] American Association of Retired Persons. (1992). *Tomorrow's choices: Preparing now for future legal, financial and health care decisions.* [AARP Booklet No. D13479]. Washington, DC: Author. Nelson, T.C. (1984). *It's your choice: Practical guide to planning a funeral.* Washington, DC: American Association of Retired Persons. Schneider, I., & Huber, E. (1989). *Financial planning for long-term care.* New York: Human Sciences Press. Soled, A.J. (1988). *Essential guide to wills, estates, trusts, and death taxes.* Washington, DC: American Association of Retired Persons.

Session 46

Let's Have a Party

Objectives: Promote informal interaction and bonding, encourage members' contribution to the group's activities

Materials: Vary, depending on plans

Seating: At tables

Instructions: A monthly birthday party provides a change of pace and an opportunity to give special recognition to people on their birthdays. Another benefit of this social event is that it provides members with an opportunity to socialize informally, to get to know one another better and begin to gravitate toward those with similar interests or concerns. Socializing adds another dimension to the group experience.

Keep the socials simple initially, or you may acquire the additional title of hostess! Work with the energy of the group: Ask volunteers to bring a box of cookies, a bunch of grapes, or juice. Some volunteers or caregivers love to help to plan, set up, and clean up from socials. Try to involve members in the planning—for example, do they want cake and ice cream? Remember, however, that practicing a healthful lifestyle is a program goal, so angel food cake and frozen yogurt are better choices than are cake and ice cream. Members need to be discouraged from bringing sweets. It is easier to bring candy or doughnuts, but minimizing these foods is recommended. In addition: Do they want to give birthday cards? Do they want to pay for cards? If these costs have not been budgeted for, then either you or the group members will shoulder the costs. Some groups establish a petty cash fund for birthday cards, paper products, juice, and so forth. One of my groups held a monthly luncheon for which a local deli fixed turkey sandwiches for a special rate of $3.00 each. This group requests the same menu each month. Another group prefers to hold their social every other month and orders a catered lunch for about $6.00 each. Other groups have held pot luck socials or fruit-cup socials, to which each person brings a piece of fruit. Volunteers cut up the fruit, which can be served with angel food cake, yogurt, or frozen yogurt. A caregiver in one group brought a feast for 25 people, but this kind of generosity is unusual.

Social outings or field trips away from the regular group meeting place can be planned occasionally. Group members become very excited about outings because they provide a change of pace and another way for members to bond. Outings require advance planning and extra logistical tasks. Planning an outside luncheon for a group of very frail older adults is challenging and time-consuming. Lining up transportation for people with mobility impairments may be difficult as is arranging special menus to meet the special needs of diabetics, people with swallowing difficulties, and so forth. The additional cost is difficult for some group members to absorb. Look for a sponsor or "scholarship" money for low-income members. Save the outing for a special occasion (e.g., a summer picnic, a Christmas luncheon).

Session 47

Sing Along with Me

Objectives: Reminisce with music, allow group members with musical ability to shine

Materials: Song sheets and musical accompaniment

Seating: Semicircle

Instructions: Nearly everyone enjoys an old-fashioned sing-along, accompanied by someone who plays guitar, ukulele, or piano. Lucky is the group leader who can do it herself and the group that counts among its members individuals with musical talent. If your group is not as lucky, then you must obtain outside help. Many singing groups at senior centers and recreation departments may be able to help; the key is to find a leader who will not simply entertain the group but who can involve the members in singing and choosing songs. Try to find music that is printed in large type on song sheets or posters.

Comment: Often, sing-alongs are pleasing to people who are aphasic (they can sing even when they cannot talk).

Session 48
Bingo

Objectives: Provide mental stimulation, excitement, and fun

Materials: Bingo set with at least 2 dozen, preferably large-print, cards (some groups prefer the sliding door–type card, which is easier for people affected by stroke); blackboard and chalk or easel/flip chart and markers

Seating: At tables

Instructions: This simple game of chance is loved by most groups. Research indicates that playing bingo may help older people to maintain some vital cognitive abilities (Freiburg, P. [1995, December]. A calculated gamble: The benefits of bingo. *American Psychological Association Monitor*). Some members may refuse to play—you must respect their choice. For some of the more frail members, bingo is one activity they can really participate in, and it provides them with mental stimulation and enjoyment. Some members have difficulty hearing during group discussions or seeing when playing other games, but with a little help, they can play bingo. A volunteer should write the numbers on the board for participants with hearing impairments. Large-print cards are available for group members with impaired vision. Volunteers assist individuals who cannot pick out the numbers, but they must not be too helpful—the best volunteer helps only when help is needed and can sense when it is not. Some members just need more time to play their markers because they do not see the correct choices as quickly. Some members cannot make the correct choices and need the volunteer to make it for them.

Members are asked to bring a small prize to group on bingo day (e.g., a can of food, white elephant items, a bar of soap). Line up several extra prizes so that everyone wins one. This game is an adapted version of the real bingo: The cards are not cleared after each round. Rather, the game is halted for a moment while the winner selects a prize. Play then continues with the same partially covered card. Only one "bingo!" per person should be allowed. If time remains after everyone has gotten one "bingo!" then play blackout bingo. In blackout bingo, the winner is the first person to have all of the numbers covered.

Session 49

Objectives: Provide mental stimulation, have fun; be mildly competitive for extra excitement

Materials: A pencil and a game grid for each participant

Seating: Divide group into two to four teams, preferably seated at separate tables

Instructions: This word game can be played in many ways, so it can be used often. By playing in teams, more people are given a chance to participate, yet no one is pressured to perform. Set a mildly competitive tone for games so that there is some excitement, but the stakes never seem too high. Introduce the game in your own words (or read word for word from the following paragraph):

Let's have some fun with a word game. We'll set up four teams: Each team will sit at a separate table and will need a secretary who can record words for the team.

You may want to pick the four secretaries first to be team captains, just to be sure that each team has someone able and willing to write down the words. Then, ask group members to count off: 1, 2, 3, 4. The 1s go to one table, the 2s to another table, and so forth. When everyone is seated, distribute the game grid and explain:

Written across the top of the grid is the word *group*. Listed down the side are four categories: round things, kitchen things, boys' names, and fruits. Your task is to think of as many words as you can for each category for each letter. We'll do one letter at a time. Let's start with the letter G. Write down as many round things, kitchen things, boys' names, and fruits as you can think of that start with the letter G. I'll give you around 3 minutes. After that, we'll move on to the letters R, O, U, and P.

Everyone in each group feeds words that begin with G to the secretary. After 3 minutes, stop the game and ask to read the words that each group found. The team with the most words wins the first round. Repeat the process for each letter.

Conclusion: At the end of the game, compute the results to see which team won the most rounds. The teams should be fairly well balanced and the results close. If not, then you may want to downplay or skip the final tally.

Comment: This game is quite popular and helps to stimulate thinking. You can point out that although the group is playing the game mostly for fun, members should be aware of the benefits of keeping the mind active. You can vary the game by using words other than "group" (e.g., try "friend," "cope"). The game can be played without using a grid or a word; you can pick various letters, which can be assigned arbitrarily or picked out of a bag that contains all of the letters of the alphabet. For groups of very frail older adults, this version may be more manageable because members need cope with only one letter at a time rather than possibly being confused by looking at the grid.

	G	R	O	U	P
Round things					
Kitchen things					
Boys' names					
Fruit					

Session 50

The Memory Game

Objectives: Practice observation skills, increase confidence in your memory by using a cooperative approach

Materials: A large paper bag with 15 common objects (e.g., a stapler, a pencil, eyeglasses, a paper cup, a paper clip, a brush, a comb, a note pad, a toothbrush, an eraser, a magnifying glass, a ruler, a key, soap, a tea towel); a piece of paper and a pencil for each team

Seating: Sitting in one large circle, members count off to form two teams; ask Team 1 to sit at one large table and Team 2 to sit at another large table across the room

Instructions: The Memory Game provides some mild competition, and both groups probably will remember all or nearly all of the objects. In any case they will be surprised at their ability to recall. Form the two teams and ask them to sit at their respective tables. Introduce this activity in your own words (or read word for word from the following paragraph):

Let's have some fun while we practice our observation skills. Each team will have 1 minute *[2 minutes for slower groups]* to look at the objects in the bag. Then, I'll close the bag and the group must try to recall all of the items and write them down. I'll give each team a few minutes to talk about the task and organize their strategy. Team 1 goes first, then Team 2. Don't talk out loud or the other team will hear you. Take as much time as you need to make your list.

Place the bag of objects on Team 1's table. Dump the objects out, and then time the group for 1 minute. As soon as time is up, put the objects back in the bag and repeat the activity for Team 2.

Conclusion: When both teams have exhausted their memories, ask them to read their lists. Observe which team has the most correct answers.

Session 51

Famous Couples

Objectives: Have fun, reminisce, stimulate memory recall

Materials: One copy of the reproducible handout, "Famous Couples" (left column only), and a pencil for each participant (you can add other names, including local personalities or a couple from the group)

Seating: Two groups: one for the women, one for the men

Instructions: The Famous Couples Game stimulates memories and enjoyment. A good time to play this game is around Valentine's Day, but any time is fine. Introduce this activity in your own words (or read word for word from the following paragraph):

script

Today we'll divide into two teams—one for the men and one for the women. We'll see who our romantics are! I'll pass out a list of names of men in a famous couple, but the list will be missing the name of the female partner. Your job is to come up with the name of the partner. The team that gets the most right answers wins. There is no time limit on this game, so don't worry if you get sidetracked reminiscing. You can work until 5 minutes before the end of the session, and we'll see if both teams have identified all of the couples. Then we'll know you're equally romantic. *[Distribute the quiz.]*

Conclusion: It does not matter who wins. The goal is to have some fun and engage in remembering some famous couples. Thank everyone for participating.

Session 52

Home-Grown Charades

Objectives: Mental stimulation, group interaction, fun

Materials: A paper bag full of skit topics (e.g., brushing teeth, having dental work done, working in the garden, watching television, drinking a soda, eating corn on the cob, driving a car, baking a cake, playing baseball, fishing, rowing a boat, getting a shot at the doctor's, taking pills, eating ice cream on a hot summer day, paying bills, milking a cow, riding a horse, operating a wheelchair); write these topics on slips of paper

Seating: Two groups—divide the room down the middle

Instructions: Home-Grown Charades is an adapted version of the game all of us have played using book, movie, and song titles. The topics are practical and easy for people to act out and to guess. The fun is in hamming it up and laughing, having fun with friends. Introduce this activity in your own words (or read word for word from the following paragraph):

How many of you have played the game charades? Well, the game we're playing today is an easy version of charades. Let's have the left side of the room be one team and the right side be the other. Team 1 picks a topic that they act out for Team 2, which tries to guess the topic. You can have one actor or several for a topic. The only rule is that you can't talk while you're acting. Then, Team 2 acts out a topic for Team 1, and Team 1 guesses the answer. *[Try to involve everyone in the acting.]*

Conclusion: Thank all of the actors for being brave enough to take part in playing charades.

Session 53

Fun with Skits

Objectives: Have fun, encourage interaction among group members

Materials: One copy of the reproducible handout, "Fun with Skits," for each participant (the skits included here come from my groups; others are available through Bi-Folkal Productions [see Appendix A])

Seating: Semicircle

Instructions: Maybe you have wanted two group members to get to know one another. These skits give you a chance to do a little "matchmaking" because you assign the partners for each skit. Use some care and you can involve nearly every member of the group. These very simple, silly skits can be read by group members without any rehearsal. Assign the skits before the group meeting because this encourages participants to work together on a small project. A few of the skits have small parts for individuals who are not able to handle more than a small role. Each skit can be assigned more than once. Ask group members to call one another the day before the next session to practice. (Make sure in advance that everyone agrees to receiving a telephone call at home and that everyone has one another's telephone number.)

Session 54

Spelling Bee

Objectives: Reminiscing about spelling bees in school, mental stimulation, competitive fun

Materials: List of words and a dictionary in case someone needs a definition (suggest using fairly easy words, at least to start, so that everyone can be successful); note pads and pencils; several cards with "pass" written on them

Seating: One large circle

Instructions: An old-fashioned spelling bee may bring back memories for some of the group members and can provide mental stimulation and fun. (I discovered that a member of one of my groups had won the national spelling bee in the early 1950s.) Not everyone may want to participate. Those who do not want to participate can be helpers or observers: One helper is needed to pass out stickers for each word spelled correctly. Another helper is needed to select and read the words and then judge correct spellings. Introduce the game in your own words (or read word for word from the following paragraph):

How many of you participated in a spelling bee when you were in school? Can you share some memories? Was it fun? Were you good at it? *[Pause for members' comments]* Maybe we have some ringers in the group. Let's have our own spelling bee today. Remember—it's just for fun. We need participants, helpers, and observers. How many are brave enough to be contestants? *[Give each contestant a pad and pencil.]* How many want to be observers only? *[Give each observer a colorful card that has the word "pass" written on it to hold up when his or her turn comes.]*

Ask one of the observers to be the helper who presents a sticker to each person each time he or she spells a word correctly. The reader pronounces the word and gives a definition if necessary. The participant can spell the word aloud or write it on the note pad first. If the participant spells the word correctly, then he or she receives a sticker. If the word is misspelled, then the next person is given a chance to spell the same word. If he or she spells it correctly, then the sticker is awarded. The game continues for an even number of rounds. At the end of the spelling bee, the person with the most stickers wins.

Conclusion: Praise those who were brave enough to participate. Ask the group observers to give everyone a hand.

Comment: The spelling bee was a great success in one of my groups, which was a rather verbal group of older adults. Members and staff were delighted with the group's performance. Although many of the members were timid initially about participating, they felt quite proud of themselves at the end. Choosing fairly easy words (e.g., choice, cinema, circle, concern, concert) helped members to feel good about their abilities. The experience proved disappointing only for one person with dementia, which affected her ability to spell. After two unsuccessful rounds, she decided to become an observer. At the end of the spelling bee, she was awarded a special card with a large heart sticker, which made her feel good. After the group session I talked with her about her memory loss. The woman with dementia was concerned about her cognitive loss because she loved to read. Knowing this enabled me to listen to her concerns and suggest that she keep trying. I praised her bravery for participating. As the group leader, you must be aware of group members' limitations and find a way to adapt activities to their abilities and remaining strengths or find a useful role for them.

Session 55

Sedentary Scavenger Hunt

Objectives: Promote teamwork, enjoy competition, use creativity and knowledge

Materials: List of 15 Sedentary Scavenger Hunt items (reproducible handout) for each person and a pencil for each team "secretary"

Seating: Teams of around five people each

Instructions: Sedentary Scavenger Hunt is based on the scavenger hunt game we played as children, with a twist: Participants never leave their chairs. The items (add some of your own if you wish) are in the members' possession or in their thoughts. Introduce the game in your own words (or read word for word from the following paragraph):

script

Today, we're going on a sedentary scavenger hunt. The game we played as children sent you all over the neighborhood in search of items. In this game the only rule is that you must remain seated. Each team has the same list of items to find. Let's split up into teams of around five people each. Then, each team will choose a secretary who can describe the item or write the answer on the list for his or her team. The first team to find all of the items wins. If no team finds all of them, then the team with the most items wins.

Session 56
Three-Letter Words

Objectives: Mental stimulation and fun

Materials: Answer sheet (reproducible handout)

Seating: Teams at small tables

Instructions: Three-Letter Words is an easy but challenging word game to play with small teams. Introduce the game in your own words (or read word for word from the following paragraph):

How well do you know your body parts? Today we'll form teams of three or four members each and play a simple word game. Each team should choose a secretary who can write down your answers, and everyone should try to help think of the answers. As your team completes the 10 items, raise your hands, and I'll check your answers. The other teams should keep working until, hopefully, we all finish.

Distribute the 10-item list to each person. Signal when the teams should begin working, and then signal when time is up. When all teams have finished or time is up, congratulate the winning team.

Comment: One of the problems you may experience with playing word games is that a few group members may be really good at them. This is nice because they receive praise and attention for their talents. Sometimes, however, they may try to dominate their teams so that no one else believes that they can participate. One way to handle this is to ask the "ringers" to be team secretaries; secretaries cannot give answers but write the answers for the team. Also, some volunteers cannot resist trying to provide all of the answers instead of encouraging members to contribute. Speak with volunteers ahead of time about their role.

Session 57

Word Scramble

Objectives: Mental stimulation and fun

Materials: Five copies of the "Name the States" handout

Seating: Three or four small teams

Instructions: In Word Scramble group members try to unscramble the names of some of the states of the United States. A few people may be very good at unscrambling words, and they will enjoy the chance to shine. Introduce the game in your own words (or read word for word from the following paragraph):

I have a list of scrambled state names. Let's see if we can unscramble the letters to form the name of the state. We'll work in small teams.

After you have formed the teams, ask each team to choose a secretary/spokesperson. Distribute the list *[folded]* to each person on each team. When all of the lists are distributed, the game can begin. When one team thinks it has all of the states unscrambled, the secretary brings it to the front for you to check. The other teams should continue working. Encourage all teams to finish.

Comment: You can make up other games by scrambling the names of flowers, presidents, countries, cars, and so forth.

Session 58
Trivia

Objectives: Provide mental stimulation, including word recall; promote reminiscing

Materials: Trivia question and answer cards (for sources for trivia questions and answers, see Resources below); blackboard and chalk or easel/flip chart and markers

Seating: One large group

Instructions: Games of trivia are fun and mentally stimulating, and depending on the subject matter, they can lead to productive reminiscing. Each person holds one or two cards and reads a question aloud. Anyone can answer the question. Introduce the game in your own words (or read word for word from the following paragraph):

Let's test our knowledge of trivia. I'll distribute two cards to each person, which I'll need back at the end of the game. Let's take turns reading the questions and guessing the answers. If the topic brings up a special memory for you, please be sure to share it with the rest of the group. *[You can control the intellectual level of the game by choosing cards that fit the desired degree of difficulty and by suggesting that the members choose from their cards the easiest question.]*

Distribute two cards to each person. Some group members may refuse because of vision or reading problems, which is fine. Once you have distributed all of the cards, ask for a volunteer to read a question. Participants then try to guess the answer. If one or two people begin to dominate by answering all of the questions, then change your approach by going around the circle and giving each person an opportunity to answer. Remember to encourage group members to reminisce.

Conclusion: Thank everyone for participating and collect the cards.

Comment: To make the game somewhat competitive but less reminiscence-based, divide the group into two teams. Ask one person on each team to act as the secretary/spokesperson and one person to keep score and list the scores on the blackboard. Team 1 reads a question to Team 2. The teammates confer and come up with an answer. Only the secretary/spokesperson can answer for the team. If the team answers incorrectly, then they can try again. If their answer is correct the first time, then they receive five points; three points are given for guessing correctly the second time; and one point is awarded for the third try. If Team 2 does not answer correctly on the third try, then Team 1 reads the answer and no points are given. Then, Team 2 repeats the process for Team 1 with a new question.

Resources: The following are good sources of questions/answers for trivia games: 1) create your own; 2) the original Trivial Pursuit or its many spin-offs (many cities have created versions that focus on local lore; the junior version of the game may be easier for some groups); 3) "Eldertrivia," a series of interesting and challenging trivia questions in several volumes (available through United Seniors Health Cooperative; for the address, see Appendix A); 4) "Reminiscing, the Game for People Over 30," a nostalgic journey through the events, fads, clothing, music, radio and television shows, and movies from the years 1939–1989 (available through Wellness Reproductions, Inc.; for the address, see Appendix A).

The Mingler

Who among us...

has a pet?

does crossword puzzles?

watches sports on TV?

feels happy today?

sings in the shower?

sleeps well?

goes for a walk every day?

does needlework?

speaks more than one language?

likes to go to Las Vegas?

enjoys gardening?

takes naps?

reads mysteries?

watches the news on TV?

eats cereal for breakfast?

watches birds?

loves the snow?

eats ice cream often?

has a favorite meal?

Talking About Work

Why I never worked outside the home

My first job   My best job   My worst job

My last job   Why I stopped working

Why I'm still working   Why I miss work

Why I don't miss work

_ _ _ _ _ _ _ _ _ _ _ _ _ _ *cut here* _ _ _ _ _ _ _ _ _ _ _ _ _

Talking About Work

Why I never worked outside the home

My first job   My best job   My worst job

My last job   Why I stopped working

Why I'm still working   Why I miss work

Why I don't miss work

Best Years Ballot

Circle the period of your life that you think was the best.

0–20 years old   21–40 years old

41–60 years old   61–80 years old   81–100 years old

_ _ _ _ _ _ _ _ _ _ _ _ _ _ _ _ *cut here* _ _ _ _ _ _ _ _ _ _ _ _ _

Best Years Ballot

Circle the period of your life that you think was the best.

0–20 years old   21–40 years old

41–60 years old   61–80 years old   81–100 years old

_ _ _ _ _ _ _ _ _ _ _ _ _ _ _ _ *cut here* _ _ _ _ _ _ _ _ _ _ _ _ _

Best Years Ballot

Circle the period of your life that you think was the best.

0–20 years old   21–40 years old

41–60 years old   61–80 years old   81–100 years old

3 Ways to Communicate

Imagine that you're in line at the pharmacy. You're sick and in pain and want to get home quickly. Suddenly, someone cuts in front of you in line. How do you react? What do you say?

1. **Passive:** Say nothing. Let him go first.

2. **Aggressive:** Yell and scream: "Hey, I was here first! Who do you think you are cutting in?!"

3. **Assertive:** "Excuse me. I believe I'm in front of you. I've been waiting 5 minutes and you just got here."

5 Steps to Solving Problems

Step 1. Identify the problem.

Step 2. List details about the problem.

Step 3. List possible solutions to the problem.

Step 4. Pick the most appropriate solution to the problem.

Step 5. Try the solution—put it into practice and check yourself periodically to be sure you're doing it.

Making Good Decisions

Complete each box and then weigh the results.

Should I ______________________________?

Advantages

Disadvantages

Short-term impact

Long-term impact

Impact on myself

Impact on others

Shall I decide to ______________________________

______________________________?

Grief Worksheet

One loss I have experienced is ______________________________

____

____

____

____

____

____

____

What Stage of Grief Am I In?

1. Shock & denial. No, this isn't happening to me.
2. Anger. Why is this happening to me? What have I done to deserve it?
3. Bargaining. Let me get better and I'll do whatever my doctor says.
4. Depression. My loss makes me so sad. Life will never be the same.
5. Acceptance. My life will never be quite the same, but I can go on and find good things in it.

Tips for Cheering Up During the Holidays

Realize that it's normal to feel sadness, and allow yourself to feel sad sometimes.

Enjoy your wonderful memories. Share them with someone.

Reach out to others in small ways: a card, a telephone call, a gift or poem.

Watch very little TV because, often, TV shows portray characters as being part of a happy, intact family.

Pay homage to a deceased loved one through an imaginary conversation or a visit to his or her grave.

Be among people at the mall, at church, in the group, at home or at a friend's home, and so forth.

Add your ideas below.

____

____

____

____

____

____

____

Being an Older Adult Is…

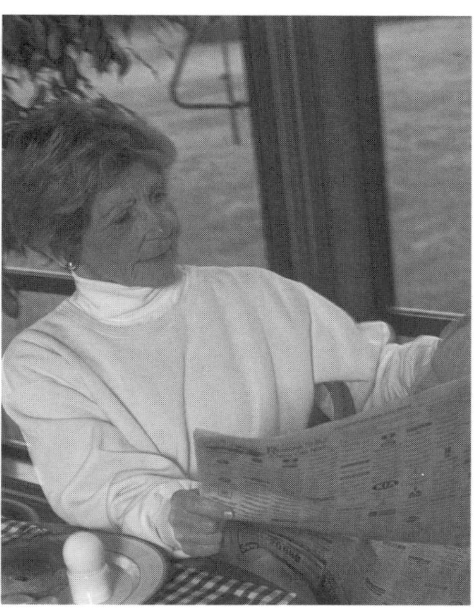

3 Kinds of Caring

I care for others by...

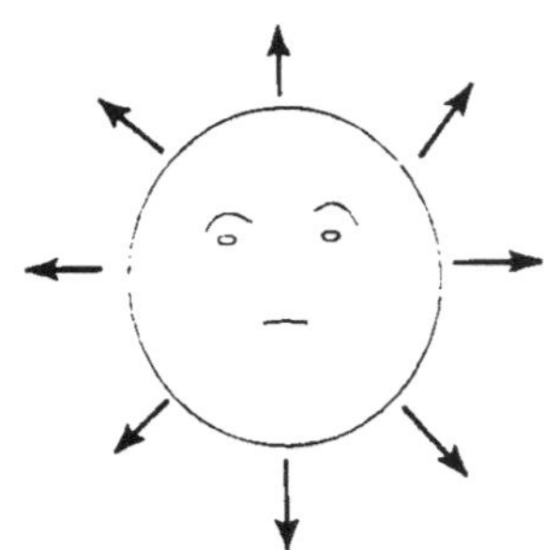

Others care for me by...

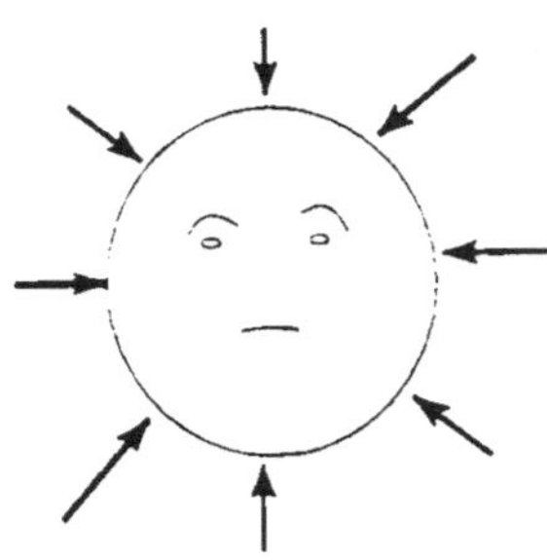

I care for myself by...

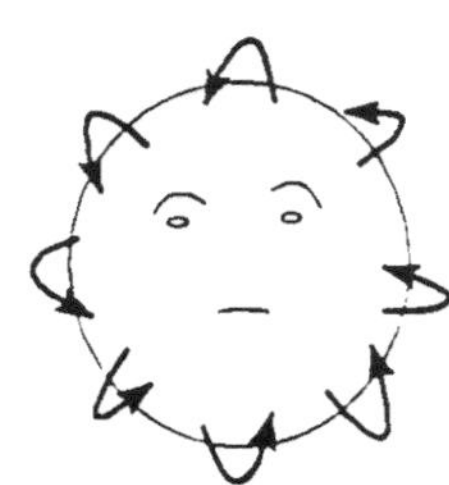

Old Person

1.

2.

3.

_ _ _ _ _ _ _ _ _ _ _ _ _ _ _ _ _ *cut here* _ _ _ _ _ _ _ _ _ _ _ _ _ _ _ _ _

Old Person

1.

2.

3.

_ _ _ _ _ _ _ _ _ _ _ _ _ _ _ _ _ *cut here* _ _ _ _ _ _ _ _ _ _ _ _ _ _ _ _ _

Old Person

1.

2.

3.

What's Your Aging IQ?

True or false?

1. "Baby boomers" are the fastest growing segment of the U.S. population.
2. Families don't bother with their older relatives.
3. Everyone becomes confused or forgetful if they live long enough.
4. You can be too old to exercise.
5. Heart disease is a much bigger problem for older men than for older women.
6. The older you get, the less you sleep.
7. People should watch their weight as they age.
8. Most older people are depressed. Why shouldn't they be?
9. There's no point in screening older people for cancer because they can't be treated.
10. Older people take more medications than younger people do.

From National Institute on Aging. (1991). *What's your aging IQ?* (Brochure No. 281-837/40019). Gaithersburg, MD: Author.

Answers

1. FALSE. There are more than 3 million Americans over the age of 85. That number is expected to quadruple by the year 2040, when there will be more than 12 million people in that age group. The fastest growing age group in the United States is people age 85 and older.
2. FALSE. Most older people live near their children and see them often. Many live with their spouses. An estimated 80% of older men and 60% of older women live in family settings. Only 5% of older adults live in nursing facilities.
3. FALSE. Alzheimer's disease or other conditions that result in irreversible brain damage can cause confusion and serious forgetfulness in old age, but at least 100 other conditions can cause people to exhibit the same symptoms. A minor head injury, high fever, poor nutrition, adverse drug reactions, and depression also can lead to confusion. These conditions are treatable, however, and the confusion they cause can be eliminated.
4. FALSE. Exercise at any age can help strengthen the heart and lungs, lower blood pressure, improve muscle strength, and, if carefully chosen, lessen bone tissue loss. See a physician before beginning an exercise program.
5. FALSE. The risk of heart disease increases dramatically for women after menopause. By age 65, both men and women have a one in three chance of exhibiting symptoms, but risks can be reduced significantly by following a healthful diet and by exercising.
6. FALSE. In later life it's the quality of sleep that declines, not total sleeping time. Researchers have found that, as people age, sleep tends to become increasingly fragmented. A number of reports suggest that older people are less likely than younger people to stay awake throughout the day and that older people tend to take more naps than do younger people.
7. TRUE. Most people gain weight as they age. Because of changes in the body and decreases in physical activity, older people usually require a fewer number of calories. Still, a balanced diet is important. Older people require essential nutrients as do younger adults. You should be concerned about your weight if you have experienced an involuntary gain or loss of 10 pounds in the past 6 months.
8. FALSE. Most older people are not depressed. When it does occur, depression is treatable throughout the life cycle using a variety of approaches, such as family support, psychotherapy, or antidepressant medications. A physician can determine whether the depression is caused by medication that an older person might be taking, physical illness, stress, or other factors.
9. FALSE. Many older people can survive cancer, especially if it is detected early. Over half of all cancers occur in people age 65 and older, which means that screening for cancer in this age group is especially important.
10. TRUE. Often, older people have a combination of conditions, all of which require drugs. They consume 25% of all medications and can have many more problems with adverse reactions. Check with your doctor to make sure all of your medications and dosages are appropriate.

My Memory Improvement Plan

To maintain my memory and prevent memory loss, I will

1. Correct any problems I'm experiencing with hearing and vision.
2. Talk to my doctor about keeping medications to a minimum.
3. Take care of my health.
4. Exercise daily.
5. Use my mind every day by reading, doing crossword puzzles, talking with friends, etc.

Use the space below to record a problem and the solutions you've thought of.

Problem:

Solutions:

1.

2.

Use the space below to record a problem and the solutions you've thought of.

Problem:

Solutions:

1.

2.

What Do I Know About High Blood Pressure?

Test your knowledge of high blood pressure with the following questions. Circle each answer either true or false. The answers are given on the back of this sheet.

1. There is nothing you can do to prevent high blood pressure. T F
2. If your mother or father has or had high blood pressure, you'll get it, too. T F
3. Young adults don't develop high blood pressure.

   T F
4. High blood pressure has no symptoms. T F
5. Stress causes high blood pressure. T F
6. High blood pressure is not life threatening. T F
7. Blood pressure is high when it's at or over 140/90 mmHg. T F
8. If you're overweight, you're two to six times more likely to develop high blood pressure. T F
9. You have to exercise vigorously every day to improve your blood pressure and heart health. T F
10. Americans consume two to three times more salt and sodium than their bodies need. T F
11. Drinking alcohol lowers blood pressure. T F
12. High blood pressure can't be cured. T F

How well did you do? Check your answers on the back.

High Blood Pressure Quiz Answers

1. FALSE. High blood pressure, or hypertension, can be prevented in four steps: maintain a healthful weight (your doctor can tell you what that is for you); become physically active; limit your salt and sodium use; and, if you drink alcoholic beverages, do so in moderation.

2. FALSE. You are more likely to develop high blood pressure if it runs in your family, but that doesn't mean you will develop it. In addition, your likelihood of developing high blood pressure is greater if you're older and/or African American. High blood pressure isn't an inevitable part of aging and everyone can take steps to prevent the disease (see Answer 1).

3. FALSE. About 15% of people ages 18–39 are among the 50 million Americans with high blood pressure. Once you develop high blood pressure, you have it for the rest of your life, so start now to prevent it.

4. TRUE. High blood pressure usually has no symptoms. In fact, it is often called "the silent killer." You can have high blood pressure and feel fine. That's why it's important to have your blood pressure checked—it's a simple test.

5. FALSE. Stress does make blood pressure rise, but only temporarily. Ups and downs in blood pressure are normal (e.g., run for a bus and your pressure rises; sleep and it drops). Blood pressure becomes dangerous when it's always high. So, what causes high blood pressure? In most cases, there is no single cause.

6. FALSE. High blood pressure is the main cause of stroke and a factor in the development of heart disease and kidney failure.

7. TRUE. Still, even blood pressure slightly under 140/90 mmHg can increase your risk of heart disease or stroke.

8. TRUE. As weight increases, so does blood pressure. It's important to maintain a healthful weight. If you need to reduce, then try to lose $^1/_2$ to 1 pound a week. Choose foods that are low in fat, especially saturated fat, because fat is high in calories. Even if you're at an appropriate weight, the most healthful way to eat is to eat low-fat, low-cholesterol foods.

9. FALSE. Studies show that even a little physical activity helps prevent high blood pressure and strengthens your heart. People who are overweight but active have lower blood pressure than those who aren't active. It's best to do some activity (e.g., walk, garden, bowl) for 30 minutes 4–5 times a week. If you don't have 30-minute blocks of time available, try doing something for 15 minutes twice a day. Every bit helps, so make activity part of your daily routine.

10. TRUE. Americans consume too much salt and sodium. African Americans, in particular, are sensitive to salt and sodium. Salt is made of sodium and chloride, and

continued

it's mostly the sodium that affects blood pressure. Salt is only one form of sodium, so you need to watch your use of salt and sodium, including what's added to foods at the table, in cooking, in processed foods, and snacks. Be especially careful of "TV dinners"—they're convenient, but one meal can contain much more sodium than you need daily. Americans, especially those with high blood pressure, should eat no more than approximately 6 grams of salt a day, which equals around 2,400 milligrams of sodium.

11. FALSE. Drinking too much alcohol can raise blood pressure. If you drink, have no more than two drinks a day. For overall health, women should limit their alcohol intake to no more than one drink a day. A drink would be 1 1/2 ounces of 80-proof whiskey, 5 ounces of wine, or 12 ounces of beer.

12. TRUE. High blood pressure *can* be treated and controlled. Usually, treatment includes making lifestyle changes—losing weight, becoming physically active, limiting salt and sodium, and avoiding drinking alcohol to excess—and, if needed, taking medication. The best way to avoid the dangers of high blood pressure is to prevent the condition.

For more information on high blood pressure, call 1 (800) 575-WELL (9355), or write to the National Heart, Lung, and Blood Institute Information Center, Post Office Box 30105, Bethesda, Maryland 20824-0105.

What Do I Know About Diabetes?

Circle "T" for true or "F" for false in response to the following statements:

1. You can have "just a touch of sugar" and not really have diabetes. T F
2. Diabetes always leads to other serious health problems such as blindness or kidney failure, no matter what you do. T F
3. Your blood sugar level is probably the most important factor in determining whether complications of diabetes will develop. T F
4. If your blood sugar is too low or too high, you will always have symptoms. T F
5. Eating a diabetic diet means that you can't eat the foods you like. T F
6. Nearly all people with diabetes should exercise regularly. T F
7. Everyone with diabetes must take insulin. T F
8. People with diabetes don't need to see a doctor unless they have a special problem because treatment is pretty much the same for everyone. T F
9. People who have had diabetes for a long time probably know all they need to know about managing it. T F
10. When someone has diabetes, friends and family are often affected. T F

Answers

1. FALSE. There is no such thing as "just a touch of sugar." Diabetes is a very serious disease, whether you take insulin or not. Without warning, diabetes can cause blindness, kidney failure, heart attack, or stroke.
2. FALSE. Research shows that the closer to normal that you maintain your blood sugar, the less likely you are to develop other serious health problems.
3. TRUE. Results from the Diabetes Control and Complications Trial (NIH, 1994) show that if you maintain your blood sugar at close to what is considered normal, you are likely to protect your future health. A good meal plan, exercise, blood sugar testing, and medications, if needed, work together to prevent your blood sugar from being too high or too low.
4. FALSE. There are always symptoms when your blood sugar is low. When your blood sugar is high, symptoms are barely noticeable or difficult to sense. Talk to your physician about how often you should check your blood sugar.
5. FALSE. A wide variety of foods, even some sweets, can be part of a healthful meal plan. A dietitian can help you plan your meals based on your likes, dislikes, and lifestyle.
6. TRUE. Regular exercise can help you control your blood sugar, reach or maintain your desired weight, and protect your heart. Check with your physician before starting any exercise program.
7. FALSE. Everyone with Type I diabetes needs insulin. Many people with Type II, the most common type of diabetes, control their disease through eating healthfully and exercising. Sometimes, pills, insulin shots, or both are needed to help them manage their disease. Check with your physician about the best treatment for you.
8. FALSE. People with diabetes require ongoing medical care. If you have diabetes, your health care team will work with you to develop a diabetes management plan that fits your lifestyle. The team needs to meet with you from time to time to monitor your progress and check for warning signs of complications.
9. FALSE. Scientists are learning more about diabetes every day, and research findings may affect how you care for your diabetes. Talk to your physician about current treatment options during your next visit.
10. TRUE. People who have diabetes need support from family and friends. The good news is that good meal and exercise plans for people with diabetes likely make friends and family feel better and healthier, too.

For more information on diabetes treatment and available diabetes programs and resources, contact your local American Diabetes Association office.

Source: National Institutes of Health. Publication No. 97-3874. September 1994.

Osteoporosis: The Silent Bone Thinner

What is osteoporosis?

Osteoporosis is a disease that thins and weakens bones to the point at which they break easily—especially bones in the hip, spine, and wrist. Osteoporosis is called "the silent disease" because a person may not notice any symptoms. People can lose bone mass over many years but not know that they have osteoporosis until a bone breaks. Approximately 25 million Americans have osteoporosis; 80% are women.

Experts don't fully understand all of the causes of osteoporosis. They do know that when women experience menopause, their estrogen levels drop. Lower hormone levels can lead to bone loss and osteoporosis. Other causes of bone loss and osteoporosis include a diet that is too low in calcium and a lack of exercise.

Who can get osteoporosis?

One in two women and one in eight men over age 50 will experience an osteoporosis-related fracture. Caucasian and Asian women are the most likely to develop osteoporosis. Women who have a family history of osteoporosis or early menopause or who have small body frames are at greatest risk. Men are at less risk because they do not experience the same types of hormone losses as do women. Osteoporosis can strike at any age, but the risk increases with age.

How is osteoporosis diagnosed?

Losing height or breaking a bone may be the first sign of osteoporosis. Your doctor may use one of several different tests to diagnose the disease: The dual energy X ray absorptiometry (DEXA) is the most exact way to measure bone density in the wrist, hip, and lower spine; single-photon absorptiometry, dual energy absorptiometry, and quantitative computed tomography are others. Ask your doctor about these tests if you think that you are at risk for osteoporosis.

Is osteoporosis preventable? How?

Osteoporosis is preventable. A diet that is rich in calcium and vitamin

continued

D and a lifestyle that includes regular weight-bearing exercise are the best ways to prevent osteoporosis. Getting enough calcium throughout life is important because it helps to build and maintain strong bones. Men and women ages 25–65 should have 1,000 milligrams of calcium every day. Women near or past menopause should have 1,500 milligrams of calcium daily.

Healthy foods that are rich in calcium are low-fat dairy products, such as cheese, yogurt, and milk; canned fish with bones you can eat, such as salmon and sardines; dark-green leafy vegetables, such as kale, collards, and broccoli; and breads made with calcium-fortified flour. If you don't always get enough calcium from your food, think about taking a calcium supplement, but check with your doctor first. Your body uses vitamin D to absorb calcium. Being out in the sun for even a short time every day gives most people enough vitamin D, and you can get it from supplements, cereal, and milk fortified with the vitamin. Exercise builds bone strength and helps prevent bone loss. It also helps older people remain active and mobile. Done on a regular basis, weight-bearing exercises—walking, jogging, playing tennis—prevent osteoporosis. Always check with your doctor before beginning any exercise program.

How is osteoporosis treated?

Treatment of osteoporosis aims to stop bone loss and prevent falls. Often, falls cause broken bones, which can mean a trip to the hospital or a long-term disabling condition. Osteoporosis is the cause of $1^1/_2$ million fractures a year, including more than 300,000 hip fractures. Doctors sometimes prescribe hormone-replacement therapy (HRT) with estrogen during menopause. HRT also protects against heart disease and stroke. Experts, however, do not know all of the risks of long-term use of HRT. Women should discuss the risks, benefits, and possible side effects of HRT with their doctors. Calcitonin is a naturally occurring hormone that increases bone density in the spine and can reduce the pain of fractures. This hormone can be administered as an injection or as a nasal spray. Alendronate also increases bone mass in women past menopause. The best way to prevent osteoporosis is to be aware of the disease and to maintain a healthful lifestyle. If you think that you might be at risk for osteoporosis, talk to your doctor. Ask about the bone density tests available in your area and your prevention and treatment choices.

Source: National Institute on Aging.

Taking Charge of My Pain

How would I describe my pain? ______________________

____

____

Where is my pain? ______________________

When does my pain occur? ______________________

____

What causes my pain (diagnoses)? ______________________

____

What makes my pain worse? ______________________

____

What makes my pain better? ______________________

____

I will develop a pain-control plan, which may include

- ❑ Visiting my doctor
- ❑ Physical therapy
- ❑ Exercise
- ❑ Recreation and leisure therapies
- ❑ Visiting a pain control clinic
- ❑ Occupational therapy
- ❑ Relaxation training
- ❑ Nonprescription drugs (if needed)
- ❑ Prescription drugs (if needed)

A Successful Doctor's Visit

DR. JONES: So, Mrs. Delaney, you say you've had this infection for about a week now? I'll give you something to take care of it. *[Begins writing]*

MRS. DELANEY: Thank you, doctor. What's the name of the medicine?

DR. JONES: Don't worry about it. I'll write it all down.

MRS. DELANEY: Well, no. I like to be aware of what's going into my body. I'd like to know the name, what it's supposed to do for me, and how it works.

DR. JONES: Oh, I see. Well, it's "betterthromycin." It's an antibiotic that gets into your bloodstream and kills the germs that are making you sick.

MRS. DELANEY: How and when should I take it?

DR. JONES: Take it with liquid twice a day after you eat.

MRS. DELANEY: Can I take it with my evening cocktail?

DR. JONES: No. Antibiotics and alcohol don't mix. Don't drink while you're on this medication.

MRS. DELANEY: I won't. Now, will I have any side effects or bad reactions? If I do, what should I do about them?

DR. JONES: You might get a little sleepy, so don't drive after you've taken a pill. Other than that, you shouldn't have any problem. But do call me if you develop a skin rash.

MRS. DELANEY: Does this medicine mix well with all my other medicines?

DR. JONES: *[Consults chart]* Shouldn't be a problem.

MRS. DELANEY: Should I stop taking it as soon as I feel better?

DR. JONES: No, I want you to continue taking the medicine until it's all gone, even if you feel better before you run out of it.

MRS. DELANEY: Is there a good generic substitute for it that costs less?

continued

DR. JONES: No, there's no generic.

MRS. DELANEY: When should I see you again?

DR. JONES: If the infection hasn't cleared up completely in two weeks, make an appointment to see me, but call me right away if it gets worse.

MRS. DELANEY: Thanks, Dr. Jones. I'll call you if I have any more questions. I really appreciate your time. You helped me understand my medicine. You know, I'm not as quick as I used to be.

[Mrs. Delaney walks across the street to the pharmacy]

MRS. DELANEY: I have a few questions for the pharmacist about this prescription.

CLERK: She's busy now. You'll have to wait.

MRS. DELANEY: Okay.

[A few minutes later, the pharmacist approaches Mrs. Delaney]

PHARMACIST: Yes, ma'am. You have some questions about your prescription?

MRS. DELANEY: Yes, I do. Are there any side effects to this medication, and how will it mix with the other medicines I'm taking?

PHARMACIST: Do we have your record on file here?

MRS. DELANEY: Yes, you do.

PHARMACIST: *[Checks record]* Mmmm. You shouldn't have any problems with this medication, except maybe some drowsiness, so you might want to stay home after you take it. If you get a rash, call your doctor right away. I'm going to give you some literature about the medicine that you can take home and read.

MRS. DELANEY: Okay, thank you. I forget things sometimes.

PHARMACIST: Did you want safety caps?

MRS. DELANEY: No. I want easy-open caps. I never can get the darn safety caps open. I have arthritis, you know.

PHARMACIST: Yes, that's on your record. I'll give you easy-open caps.

MRS. DELANEY: Thank you. I really appreciate your talking to me so I do the right thing.

Q: I started a new prescription yesterday, and today, I feel dizzy and confused. What should I do?

Q: My neighbor got the same bug I had last week and wants to use my medicine. Is that okay?

Q: I have the same bug this year that I had last year. Can I use the same bottle of medicine?

Q: I get my medicines from two different doctors, but neither of them knows what the other prescribes. Is that okay?

answers on back

A: No. Don't share medications with other people. They may not have the same "bug" after all, and they might be taking other drugs that wouldn't mix well with the one you gave them.

A: Always call your doctor immediately about side effects.

A: No. Make a list of all the medications you take to show to all of your doctors, or take them in a brown bag to the doctor.

A: See your doctor first, and take the medicine along. It may not be the same bug, your medicine may have expired, and now you might be taking another drug that wouldn't mix well with the old one.

Q: Sometimes I skip a pill or two because I'm tired of taking so much medicine. Is that okay?

Q: I take medicine for high blood pressure. Would a daily walk work just as well?

Q: Can I have a couple beers with my medicine?

Q: I'm really having trouble remembering to take all my medicines. What can I do?

answers on back

A: First, check with your doctor. Sometimes walking helps, but sometimes the medicines are necessary.

A: No. Talk this over with your doctor. He'll review your medications to see if you still need them all.

A: Ask a family member or trusted friend to help you. Tell your doctor you're forgetting. Maybe a container with compartments would help you.

A: Ask your doctor. A lot of medications don't mix with alcohol, but it might be okay with some.

Q: Is it okay to put my pills in a container with compartments to help me remember to take them?

Q: What if I can't afford to buy all the medicines I need?

Q: Do I need to tell my doctor about the over-the-counter drugs I take?

Q: My 50-year-old son takes the same medicine I do, but he takes twice as much. Should I be taking more?

answers on back

A: Talk to your doctor or social worker. You may be eligible for some assistance through programs like Medicaid.

A: Check with your doctor before you do that to see if any of your medications need to be kept in their original airtight container.

A: No. Older bodies absorb and process drugs differently from younger bodies. If you're not sure, ask your doctor.

A: Definitely. Even though they're not prescription drugs, you still need to be concerned about drug interactions.

Q: The pills the doctor gave me make me so sleepy, but I seem to take them all the time anyway. What should I do?

Q: Since my Ralph passed on, I've had trouble sleeping. I think it's because I miss him so much. I asked the doctor for some tranquilizers. Was that okay?

Q: I take 15 different medicines. I think that might be too many, but I don't think my doctor has ever given a thought to whether I still need them all. What should I do?

Q: My doctor is so busy that I'm afraid to bother him with all my questions about my pills. What should I do?

answers on back

A: Pills won't cure loneliness. You may want to think about trying some counseling.

A: Tell your doctor. Some drugs may cause dependency and you may need some help to stop taking them.

A: The doctor's job is to help you use your pills safely and effectively. Tell him you need more time and help to get all the information you need from him. If he won't take the time, look for a doctor who will.

A: Ask the doctor to review your drugs. If you don't feel your doctor pays enough attention to your problems, you may want to see another doctor.

Q: When I'm in the doctor's office, I get so nervous I forget to ask all the questions about my medicine that I could think of at home. What should I do?

Q: I can't see like I used to. It's gotten to where I can't read the labels on the medicine. What can I do?

Q: My neighbor has the same medical problem I do, but she takes only half the medicine I do. How come? Am I taking too much?

Q: My medicine expired last year. Can I still take it?

answers on back

A: Ask your pharmacist to use large-print labels.

A: You could write your questions down before you go to your appointment. You could try asking the pharmacist, or call the doctor's office to get the information you need. Ask the nurse to ask the doctor for you.

A: Probably not, but ask your pharmacist or doctor.

A: Talk it over with your doctor. Ask her if you are taking the lowest possible dose for your condition.

Q: I'd like to know why I have to take this medicine. Is that unreasonable?

Q: These childproof caps are a nuisance. Sometimes I just skip taking my medicine if I can't get the bottle open. Is that okay?

Q: The doctor didn't say *how* to take this pill. Can I take it with my dinner?

answers on back

A: If there are no small children living with you, ask your pharmacist to put your drugs in easy-open containers.

A: No, that's very reasonable. Ask your doctor and your pharmacist to put the purpose on the label.

A: Call your doctor to find out. It's very important to know how to take it and how long to take it.

Do I Have the Right Doctor?

Read the following statements and respond "agree" or "disagree" to each. For any statement to which you respond "disagree," you may want to find ways to improve interactions with your doctor. If that's not possible, you may want to find another doctor.

1. I feel comfortable with my doctor.
2. My doctor takes the time to answer all my questions.
3. My doctor listens and evaluates carefully each medical problem I report.
4. My doctor doesn't attribute my medical problems to "old age."
5. When my doctor prescribes a new medication, she explains what it is and how to use it.
6. My doctor reviews all my medications periodically.
7. I can call my doctor or the nurse with questions between office visits.
8. I can ask my doctor questions about personal concerns such as finances and family and emotional issues.
9. My doctor asks for my opinion about treatment options when possible.
10. My doctor encourages me to live a healthful lifestyle through regular exercise and proper nutrition.

Symptoms I Shouldn't Ignore

Stress Anxiety Insomnia Depression Paranoia
Alcohol abuse Medication problems
Financial abuse Abuse and neglect Addiction

1. After Mildred's friend has visited, she checks her jewelry box and wallet because she's afraid that he has taken her things. This may be a symptom of ____________.
2. Night after night Richard lies awake for hours and then is exhausted the following day. He is having trouble with ____________________.
3. The new medication Roy is taking makes him drowsy and gives him horrible nightmares. He's having _____________ __________________.
4. Marie seems to have lost interest in everything. She has no appetite and is losing weight. She may have__________ ____________________.
5. Ruth's daughter-in-law makes her sign over her Social Security and pension checks. Ruth gets none of the money. This could be _______________.
6. Hanako is taking more and more tranquilizers to calm her nerves. She could be having a problem with ______________________.
7. Often when Marion starts worrying about things, her heart pounds and she starts breathing hard and fast. This is _________________________.
8. Mateo needs to drink several beers to get to sleep each night. He may have a problem with ____________________.

continued

9. Julie lives with her children. They make her stay in her room all day and often yell at her. This is ______________________.

10. Joe is so worried about paying his bills that he gets headaches and stomachaches. These could be symptoms of illness caused by too much ______________________.

If you are experiencing any of these problems, please talk to your group facilitator or to a trusted friend or family member. The telephone number is ________________.

Answers

1. **Paranoia** is the false belief or suspicion that people are intentionally trying to bother you or harm you. These feelings may come from isolation, hearing loss, or other health problems that need medical attention. Talk to a trusted friend, a family member, or your group facilitator about your feelings.

2. **Insomnia** is the sleep disorder in which a person has problems getting to sleep, staying asleep, or both. If insomnia persists, you should try to find out why and develop a treatment program. Your doctor may be able to help.

3. **Medication problems** may be the result of side effects from a single medication, adverse reactions resulting from the interaction of several drugs, or developing a drug dependence. Talk to a trusted friend and your doctor.

4. **Depression**, often caused by stress or loss, is prolonged disturbance of mood. In older adults depression may be caused by a medical problem such as stroke or dementia. Talk to your group facilitator, who can refer you for help.

5. **Financial abuse** occurs when someone steals or mismanages your money, assets, or property. If you suspect financial abuse, ask your group facilitator for help.

6. **Addiction** is a dependence on something. It can result from taking certain drugs such as those for pain, depression, and

insomnia. If you suspect you are addicted or think that someone you love is addicted, consult your doctor.

7. **Anxiety** is fear without an obvious reason. It is a common experience in later life and can mean that you are having problems with coping or with psychological conflicts caused by loss or stress. Ask your group facilitator for help in seeking sources that can reduce your anxiety.

8. **Alcohol abuse** or dependence is a "secret disease" among more older adults than you might think. It can and should be treated. Ask your group facilitator or a trusted friend for help.

9. **Abuse and neglect** occurs when the family or caregiver of a dependent person does not meet his or her needs and/or causes physical pain and injury. It can result from a family or caregiver's feeling overwhelmed or exhausted, or there may be deeper psychological problems. Consult a trusted friend or your group facilitator if you feel you are being abused.

10. Illness related to **stress** results from a feeling of a lack of control over life or from an inability to cope with too many problems. Your group facilitator can help you to work through these feelings and/or refer you for help.

Symptoms of Depression

If you have several of the following symptoms and they last for more than 2 weeks, talk to your doctor or a family member about the possibility that you have depression. Remember that depression is a treatable physical illness.

- ❑ Sad or depressed mood
- ❑ Loss of interest or pleasure in usual activities
- ❑ Difficulty sleeping
- ❑ Severe restlessness or agitation or significant slowing of movement
- ❑ Decreased energy, easily fatigued
- ❑ Feelings of worthlessness or excessive guilt
- ❑ Decreased ability to think or concentrate
- ❑ Recurrent thoughts of death or suicide

A Safe Home Is No Accident

In Your Home

Yes	No	
		Do you have emergency phone numbers—police, fire, doctor, utilities—located next to the phone?
		Do you have smoke detectors in your home?
		Do you check the batteries every April and October (when you change the clocks for daylight saving and standard times)?
		Do you keep an approved fire extinguisher on each floor of the house?
		Do you check electrical outlets regularly for overloading?
		Do you know how to turn off gas and electricity?
		Do you use proper-size fuses for replacement?
		Do you have nonskid floors?
		Do you make sure that floor coverings are fastened down securely?
		Do you make sure that electrical extension cords are in good condition?
		Do you keep electrical extension cords from being stretched across heavily traveled areas of your home?
		Do you have a sturdy stepladder?

continued

Yes	No	*In Your Kitchen*
		Do you tie curtains away from the stove?
		Do you disconnect electrical appliances when they're not being used?
		Do you have a light over your stove and sink?
		Do gas appliances have flue ventilation?
		Do you keep drawers and cupboards closed?
		Do you keep knives in a rack or tray with compartments?
		Do you place pan handles away from the edge of the stove and other burners?
		Do you wipe up spilled liquids or foods immediately?
		Do you keep hot dish holders near the stove?
		In Your Bedroom
		Do you keep a lamp or a light by your bed that you can reach easily?
		Do you keep your room properly ventilated when you use a space heater, and do you turn it off at bedtime?
		Do all family members refrain from smoking in bed?
		In Your Hallways and Stairwells
		Do you keep stairway approaches uncluttered and free of throw rugs?
		Do stairways have strong banisters or railings?
		Do you keep steps and floors free of toys, tools, and other objects?

Yes	No	
		Do you keep stair treads or carpeting in good repair?
		Do you have stairways that are well lighted, with electrical switches located at the top and bottom?
		Do you provide night-lights in hallways and bed- and bathroom areas?
		In Your Bathroom(s)
		Do you use nonskid mats in bathtubs and showers?
		Do you make sure that medicines for "external use only" are labeled as such and kept separate from other medicines?
		Do you discard prescription drugs after their expiration date?
		Do you have hand grips mounted alongside the shower, tub, and toilet?
		Do you have a shower bench?
		Do you keep all electrical appliances away from water?
		Do you unplug them after each use?
		In Your Yard
		Do you keep steps and sidewalks free from toys, tools, and debris?
		Is your yard free of glass, nails, yard tools, and all items with jagged edges?
		Do you refrain from using poisonous garden sprays?
		Do you limit the amount of time that you work in the sun?

continued

Yes	*No*	
		Do you use sunscreen?

For every "no" answer, please correct the problem as soon as possible. You'll be making your home safe for yourself and the people you love.

This home safety checklist was adapted from materials provided by the Healthy Older Adult Program, National Health Information Center, Office of Disease Prevention and Health Promotion, Public Health Service, U.S. Department of Health and Human Services, Washington, DC.

All About Falls

Respond either "true" or "false" to each statement.

1. The age group that experiences the most falls is age 65 and older.
2. Falls are a normal part of the aging process.
3. About half of all falls are caused by environmental factors such as rugs that slip, objects left on the floor, and uneven sidewalks.
4. Nothing can be done about falls that are caused by muscular weakness.
5. Taking certain medications or too many medications may cause dizziness, which is a risk factor for falls.

Answers

1. FALSE. Children under 6 years old experience the most falls. Falls among people over age 65, however, result in nearly 250,000 hip fractures each year and are the sixth leading cause of death among older adults.
2. FALSE. Falls are not a normal part of aging. Often, they are due to things that can be changed, such as physical fitness, gait and balance disorders, environmental hazards, and misuse of medications and alcohol, often in interaction.
3. TRUE. Carefully checking your home and yard for safety hazards can greatly reduce your risk of falls.
4. FALSE. Exercises designed to improve muscular strength and balance can reduce an older person's chances of falling.
5. TRUE. People who suspect that their medications are causing dizziness or falls should ask their doctor what they can do about it.

Source: Jan Ferris Koltun, who developed the quiz during a student practicum with the Honolulu Gerontology Program.

Getting Help in an Emergency

The following are some suggestions for making sure that you can get emergency help when you need it.

1. ***Carrier alert***. Call your local post office and ask whether they have a carrier alert program. This program ensures that your letter carrier will check on you if you fail to remove your mail from the mailbox each day.

2. ***Buddy system***. Pair up with someone you know in your building or neighborhood and make a daily visit or telephone call to check on each other's welfare. Make arrangements ahead of time as to who should be called if the other person doesn't respond.

3. ***Telephone reassurance***. Ask a family member to call you at the same time each day to ensure that you're okay. If a family member isn't available, try an aging agency. Many of them offer daily telephone reassurance service.

4. ***Portable telephone***. Some people keep their portable telephone nearby in case there's an emergency. You can program in key telephone numbers to call in an emergency. Don't forget to program in 911.

5. ***Personal emergency response systems***. Personal emergency response systems provide you with a necklace or bracelet call button that you can press to summon help in an emergency. There are several variations. Some call a prearranged list of personal contacts; others call for ambulance or police assistance. Call your local Area Agency on Aging for a list of providers in your area.

Services for Older Adults

Place a check mark by the services you need.

At Home

- ❑ Personal care
- ❑ Home-delivered meals
- ❑ Emergency response system
- ❑ Chore services
- ❑ Friendly visitor program
- ❑ Telephone reassurance

In the Community

- ❑ Recreation program
- ❑ Seniors club
- ❑ Adult day services
- ❑ Board and care home
- ❑ Nursing facility
- ❑ Group dining program
- ❑ Restorative groups
- ❑ Affordable housing
- ❑ Assisted living facility

In the space below, list any service or assistance you need that is not listed above:

____

____

____

____

____

____

____

____

Name that Service!

Directions: Select a word from the list below to match the descriptions. Insert the appropriate phrase in the blank. Do the same thing on the second page.

Community Services

Restorative group for frail older adults *Adult day services*
Senior center *Group dining* *Board and care home*

1. Program for low-cost, nutritious group dining and socializing

   ____

2. Family home licensed to house several adults who need help in accomplishing activities of daily living ______________

   ____

3. Facility that offers recreational, financial, and counseling services ______________________________

4. Program of care offered during the day in a group setting

   ____

5. Program of exercise, education, and social support that's offered 2–3 times a week ______________________

continued

Home Services

Home-delivered meals *Chore service*
In-home respite *Telephone reassurance*
Home care *Friendly visitor program*

6. Program that delivers meals to a homebound person's residence ______________________
7. Program in which aides come to the home to relieve a weary or overburdened caregiver ______________________
8. Program of daily calls to ensure that client is okay ______________________
9. Regular visits by volunteer for in-home socializing ______________________
10. Help with cleaning and chores______________________
11. Physician-ordered home visits from nurses, social workers, and physical or occupational therapists ______________________

Answers

1. *Group dining*
2. *Board and care home*
3. *Senior center*
4. *Adult day services*
5. *Restorative group*
6. *In-home respite*
7. *Home-delivered meals*
8. *Telephone reassurance*
9. *Friendly visitor program*
10. *Chore service*
11. *Home care*

Tips for Independent Living

AARP makes the following suggestions for maintaining independence and avoiding the risk of abuse:

1. Remain sociable as you age. Maintain and increase your network of friends and acquaintances, especially if you move.
2. Develop a "buddy system" with a friend outside your residence. Plan for at least weekly contact, and share aspects of your life openly with your "buddy."
3. Make sure that you have your own telephone; post and open your own mail. If your mail is being intercepted, discuss the problem with postal authorities.
4. Take care of your personal needs. Keep regular medical, dental, barber, hairdresser, and other personal appointments.
5. Arrange to have your Social Security or pension check deposited directly to your bank account.
6. Get legal advice about arrangements you can make now for possible future disability, including powers of attorney, trusts, or joint ownership.
7. Keep records, accounts, and property available for examination by someone you trust, as well as by the person that you or the court has designated to manage your affairs in the event that you are disabled.
8. Give up control of your property or assets only when you decide that you cannot manage them.
9. Ask for help when you need it. Discuss your plans with your attorney, physician, or family.
10. Don't accept personal care in return for transfer or assignment of your property or assets unless a lawyer, advocate, or another trusted person who represents you acts as a witness to the transaction.
11. Don't sign a document unless someone you trust has reviewed it.
12. Don't allow anyone else to keep the details of your finances or property management from you.

Adapted from American Association of Retired Persons. (1992). *Tomorrow's choices: Preparing now for future legal, financial and health care decisions.* Brochure No. D13479. Washington, DC: Author.

Housing Options

The array of options for housing can be overwhelming. The following are some options, with a brief description of each.

YOUR OWN HOME. Your home can be adapted or renovated to make it safer and more comfortable in which to live. Adapting or renovating your living space allows you to remain in your old, familiar neighborhood. If you need help in the home, help can be arranged. A housemate or live-in companion may be possible, but sometimes these arrangements are hard to find, are costly, and/or don't work out.

A SMALLER, PERHAPS NEWER, HOME IN YOUR OWN NEIGHBORHOOD. Moving to a smaller and/or newer home that doesn't require the work and expense of a large yard and inside repairs may be the answer for some frail older adults.

AN APARTMENT OR CONDOMINIUM IN YOUR NEIGHBORHOOD. Moving to an apartment or a condo in your neighborhood would enable you to continue to see old friends.

A HOME OR APARTMENT IN ANOTHER COMMUNITY, NEARER TO YOUR CHILDREN. Adult children would be close by to socialize and to help you when you need it. Keep in mind that, sometimes, adult children are busy with their own lives, and that sometimes, you and your adult children don't get along.

RETIREMENT RESIDENCE WITH LIFE CARE SERVICES. Some retirement facilities provide a range of types of care, from independent apartment to full-time nursing care. Housekeeping and group dining may be available to independent older adults. This type of residence may be expensive.

continued

Privately or publicly (HUD) funded housing for low- to moderate-income older adults. Qualification for this type of housing is based on total income and thus is affordable for most older adults. Rent may be a proportion of income (e.g., one third of total income). Social activities and group dining may be available.

Assisted living facility. Assisted living facilities provide housekeeping, personal care assistance, and some medical procedures (e.g., insulin shots for diabetics) that allow very frail older people to maintain some level of independence.

Board and care home. In board and care homes, a number of older adults live together, sharing food and social activities. Life in a board and care home can be expensive, and it may require adjustment to people and foods of different cultures.

Intermediate care facility. Intermediate care facilities provide nursing care for people who need at least some nursing attention each day.

Skilled nursing facility. Skilled nursing facilities provide nursing care, with nurses and nursing assistants on duty 24 hours a day.

Learning About Life Care Planning

Fill in the blank for each statement using the list of terms below.

Nondurable power of attorney **Durable power of attorney**

Springing power of attorney **Will** **Living will**

1. A document that authorizes a certain individual to act on your behalf as long as you are competent ______________________

   ____

2. A document that authorizes a certain individual to act on your behalf even when you become incompetent ______________

   ____

3. A document that authorizes a certain individual to act on your behalf only if you become incompetent __________________

   ____

4. A document that provides advance instructions for your health care, which is followed only when you are no longer able to communicate or to make responsible decisions regarding medical care ______________________________________

5. A document that states your wishes for the distribution of your property after your death ______________________________

continued

Fill in the blank after each statement using the list of terms below.

Long-term care insurance   Supplemental Security Income

Medigap   Medicaid   Medicare

6. Private insurance that provides for in-home or institutional care of a dependent person ______________________
7. Federal health insurance for people age 65 and older and some people with disabilities ______________________
8. Federal/state program to help low-income individuals pay for certain health care services ______________________
9. Private health insurance designed to supplement Medicare ______________________
10. Federal program providing income for people who are old, blind, or disabled and are either not eligible for Social Security or not receiving adequate payment from Social Security ______________________

If you need help with any of these areas, talk to your attorney or to your group facilitator, who can refer you for help.

Answers

1. Nondurable power of attorney
2. Durable power of attorney
3. Springing power of attorney
4. Living will
5. Will
6. Long-term care insurance
7. Medicare
8. Medicaid
9. Medigap
10. Supplemental Security Income

Famous Couples

Ronald Reagan	Nancy Reagan
Hi	Lois
Richard Burton	Elizabeth Taylor
Dagwood	Blondie
Prince Philip	Queen Elizabeth
Roy Rogers	Dale Evans
FDR	Eleanor Roosevelt
Romeo	Juliet
Hansel	Gretel
Raggedy Ann	Raggedy Andy
Porgy	Bess
Adam	Eve
Harry Truman	Bess Truman
Bill Clinton	Hillary Rodham Clinton

Fun with Skits

I'm Not Forgetful

LUCY: My daughter thinks I'm forgetful.

ROSE: *[Sighs]* So does mine.

LUCY: Maybe I am, but so is she. Do you know what she forgot one day?

ROSE: No, what?

LUCY: She left the retainer for her teeth on her school lunch plate. She had to look in the garbage to find it.

ROSE: Did she ever find it?

LUCY: Yes. Guess what they had for lunch that day?

ROSE: What?

LUCY: Well, do you know what color a retainer is?

ROSE: I don't know. Red, I guess.

LUCY: Yep, and the dessert that day was strawberry Jell-O!

continued

I Can't See Anymore

JACK: I'm quitting golf. I can't see the ball anymore.

FRED: No! Don't quit! Take me with you. I can see good.

JACK: Hey, that's a good idea. Let's go!

[Jack and Fred walk to the golf course]

JACK: This is a great idea!

FRED: What's that?

JACK: To be my eyes.

FRED: Oh, yeah. Well, tee 'er up.

[Jack hits the ball]

FRED: That was a beautiful drive!

JACK: Thanks. Where'd it go?

FRED: I don't remember!

continued

Exercise

JOE: Cecile *[exercise leader]* says we need to exercise. I walk every morning. How about you, Tom?

TOM: Oh, sure, I work up a pretty good sweat watching football on TV.

JOE: That's not exercise! What about you, Molly?

MOLLY: You're darn right I exercise. My joints are so stiff that I have to exercise just to get out of bed in the morning!

TOM: Well, Joe, I guess you're the best of us. How many miles do you walk each day?

JOE: Miles? Who said anything about miles? I meant I walk from the bed to the sofa.

Sedentary Scavenger Hunt

Find or write the following items:

1. A bobby pin
2. "I love you" in three languages
3. A prescription for medicines or eyeglasses
4. A driver's license from another state
5. A picture of a member's spouse
6. A picture of a group member's grandchild
7. One verse of a nursery rhyme
8. A grocery store receipt
9. An all-white blouse or shirt (don't take it off, please)
10. A $2 bill or a silver dollar
11. Shoelaces
12. Eyeglasses cord
13. A gold chain
14. Earrings
15. Hearing aid (extra points for two)

Body Parts

List 10 body parts that are spelled with three letters.
No slang or abbreviations can be accepted.

1. ______________________
2. ______________________
3. ______________________
4. ______________________
5. ______________________
6. ______________________
7. ______________________
8. ______________________
9. ______________________
10. ______________________

Answers

1. Eye
2. Arm
3. Leg
4. Toe
5. Gum
6. Ear
7. Lip
8. Hip
9. Rib
10. Jaw

Name the States

Can you unscramble the names of these states?

1. DAAYLRNM
2. GOEONR
3. NSWIINOCS
4. IIISLOLN
5. AEOGGIR
6. ROTNHTKADOA
7. ESENSETNE
8. MHOAKOAL
9. HDIOA
10. DEAVAN
11. AWIO
12. MNYGOWI
13. NAALNSEVPIYN

Answers

1. Maryland
2. Oregon
3. Wisconsin
4. Illinois
5. Georgia
6. North Dakota
7. Tennessee
8. Oklahoma
9. Idaho
10. Nevada
11. Iowa
12. Wyoming
13. Pennsylvania

References

Preface

Institute for Health and Aging, University of California–San Francisco. (1996, August). *Chronic care in America: A 21st century challenge*. Princeton, NJ: The Robert Wood Johnson Foundation.

Chapter 1

American Association of Retired Persons. (1995). *The power of memories: Creative use of reminiscence*. [Brochure No. D14930]. Washington, DC: Author.

Berdit, M. (1995, December). Muscles: Use them or lose them. *Aging Network News*, pp. 15–18.

Berkman, L.F., Leo-Summers, L., & Horwitz, R.I. (1992). Emotional support and survival after myocardial infarction. A prospective population study on the elderly. *Annals of Internal Medicine*.

Bonder, B.R., & Wagner, M.B. (1994). *Functional performance in older adults*. Philadelphia: F.A. Davis.

Burnette, J.D., & Mui, A.C. (1994). Determinants of self-reported depressive symptoms by frail elderly persons living alone. *Journal of Gerontological Social Work, 22*(1–2), 3–19.

Burnside, I., & Schmidt, M.G. (1994). *Working with older adults: Group process and techniques* (3rd ed.). Boston: Jones & Bartlett.

Butler, R.N. (1963). The life review: An interpretation of reminiscence in the aged. *Psychiatry, 26*, 65–76.

Butler, R.N. (1975). *Why survive? Being old in America*. New York: Harper & Row.

Butler, R.N. (1981). The life review: An unrecognized bonanza. *International Journal of Aging and Human Development, 12*(1), 35–58.

Butler, R.N., & Lewis, M.I. (1982). *Aging and mental health*. St. Louis: C.V. Mosby.

de St. Aubin, E., & McAdams, D.P. (1995). The relations of generative concern and generative action to personality traits, satisfaction/happiness with life, and ego development. *Journal of Adult Development, 8*, 115–118.

Dungan, J.M., Brown, A.V., & Ramsey, M.A. (1996). Health maintenance for the independent frail older adult: Can it improve physical and mental well-being? *Journal of Advanced Nursing, 23*, 1185–1193.

Dychtwald, K. (1986). *Wellness and health promotion for the elderly*. Rockville, MD: Aspen Publications.

Erikson, E.H. (1963). *Childhood and society* (2nd ed.). New York: Norton.

Erikson, E.H., Erikson, J.M., & Kivnick, H.Q. (1986). *Vital involvement in old age: The experience of old age in our time*. New York: Norton.

Femia, E., Zarit, S.H., & Johansson, B. (1997). Predicting change in activities of daily living: A longitudinal study of the oldest old in Sweden. *Journal of Gerontology, 52B*(6), 294–302.

Fiatarone, M.A., Marks, E.C., Ryan, N.D., Meredith, C.N., Lipsitz, L.A., & Evans, W.J. (1990). High intensity strength training in nonagenarians: Effects on skeletal muscle. *Journal of the American Medical Association. 263*, 3029–3034.

Fiatarone, M.A., O'Neill, E.F., Ryan, N.D., Clements, K.M., Solares, G.R., Nelson, M.E., Roberts, S.B., Kehayias, J.J., Lipsitz, L.A., & Evans, W.J. (1994). Exercise training and nutritional supplementation for physical frailty in very elderly people. *New England Journal of Medicine, 330*, 1769–1775.

Guralnik, J.M., Ferrucci, L., Simonsick, E.M., Salive, M.E., & Wallace, R.B. (1995). Lower extremity function in persons over the age of 70 years as a predictor of subsequent disability. *New England Journal of Medicine, 332*(9), 556–561.

Haber, D. (1994). *Health promotion and aging*. New York: Springer.

Kaplan, B.H., Cassel, J.C., & Gore, S. (1977). Social support and health. *Medical Care, 15*(Suppl. 5), 47–58.

Lewis, H. (1984). Self-determination: The aged client's autonomy in service encounters. *Journal of Gerontological Social Work, 7*, 51–63.

Lorig, K. (1993, Fall). Self-management of chronic illness: A model for the future. *Generations*, 11–14.

Mack, R., Salmoni, A., Viveras-Dressler, G., Porter, E., & Rashmi, G. (1997). Perceived risks to independent living: The views of older community-dwelling adults. *Gerontologist, 37*, 6.

Mazzuca, S.A. (1982). Does patient education in chronic disease have therapeutic value? *Journal of Chronic Diseases, 35*(7), 521–529.

McAdams, D.P., de St. Aubin, E., & Logan, R.L. (1993). Generativity among young, midlife and older adults. *Psychology and Aging, 8/2*, 221–230.

McAuley, E. (1993). Self-efficacy, physical activity and aging. In J.R. Kelly (Ed.), *Activity and Aging: Staying involved in later life* (Sage Focus Editions, Vol. 161, pp. 187–205). Thousand Oaks, CA: Sage Publications.

Mor-Barak, M.E., & Miller, L.S. (1991). *Social networks and health of the frail elderly*. New York: Garland.

Mosher-Ashley, P.M., & Barrett, P.W. (1997). *A life worth living: Practical strategies for reducing depression in older adults*. Baltimore: Health Professions Press.

Munnings, F. (1993, April). Strength training: Not only for the young. *Physician and Sports Medicine, 21*(4), 133–140.

Oxman, T.E., & Hull, J.G. (1997). Social support, depression and activities of daily living in older heart surgery patients. *Journal of Gerontology, 52B*(1), 1–14.

Roberts, R.E., Kaplan, G.A., Shema, S.J., & Strawbridge, W.J. (1997). Prevalence and correlates of depression in an aging cohort: The Alameda County Study. *Journal of Gerontology, 52B*(5), S252–S258.

Robinson, R.G., Lipsey, J.R., & Price, T.R. (1984). Depression: An often overlooked sequela of stroke. *Geriatric Medicine Today, 3*, 71.

Sharpe, P.A., Jackson, K.L., White, C., Vaca, V., Hickey, T., Jakook, G., & Herness, C.O. (1997). Effects of a one-year physical activity intervention for older adults at congregate nutrition sites. *Gerontologist, 37*, 2.

Shephard, R.J. (1993). Exercise and aging: Extending independence in older adults. *Geriatrics, 48*(5), 61–64.

Stevenson, J.S., & Topp, R. (1990). Effects of moderate and low intensity long-term exercise by older adults. *Research in Nursing and Health, 13*, 209–218.

Strawbridge, W., Shema, S.J., Balfour, J., Higby, H.R., & Kaplan, G.A. (1997). Antecedents of frailty over three decades in an older cohort. *Journal of Gerontology, 53B*(1), S9–S16.

Thompson, M.G., & Heller, K. (1990). Facets of support related to well-being: Quantitative social isolation and perceived family support in a sample of elderly women. *Psychology and Aging, 5*(4), 535–544.

Tobin, G. (1988, April). Workshop presentation at the Hawaii Pacific Gerontological Society. Honolulu, HI.

Toseland, R.W. (1995). *Group work with the elderly and their family caregivers*. New York: Springer.

Verbrugge, L.M. (1997). Windows to their world: The effect of sensory impairments on social engagement and activity time in nursing home residents. *Journal of Gerontology, 52B*(3), S135–S144.

Yalom, I.D. (1985). *The theory and practice of group psychotherapy*. New York: Basic Books.

Zimmer, Z., Hickey, T., & Searle, M.S. (1997). The pattern of change in leisure activity behavior among older adults with arthritis. *Gerontologist, 37*, 3.

Chapter 2

American Association of Retired Persons. (published annually). *A profile of older Americans*. Washington, DC: Author.

Freiberg, P. (1995, December). A calculated gamble: The benefits of bingo. *American Psychological Association Monitor,* 33.

Reminisce: The magazine that brings back the good old times. Subscription fulfillment center, P.O. Box 5282, Harlan, IA 51593-2782.

Stock, G. (1987). *The book of questions*. New York: Workman Publishing.

Stock, G. (1989). *The book of questions: Love and sex*. New York: Workman Publishing.

Stock, G. (1991). *The book of questions: Business, politics and ethics*. New York: Workman Publishing.

Chapter 3

Fillenbaum, G.G. (1988). *Multidimensional functional assessment of older adults: The Duke Older Americans Resources and Services procedures*. Hillsdale, NJ: Lawrence Erlbaum Associates.

Mosher-Ashley, P.M., & Barrett, P.W. (1997). *A life worth living: Practical strategies for reducing depression in older adults*. Baltimore: Health Professions Press.

Tideiksaar, R. (1998). *Falls in older persons: Prevention & management* (2nd ed.). Baltimore: Health Professions Press.

Chapter 4

Middleman, R. (1987). Workshop presentation at the annual meeting of the Association for the Advancement of Social Work Groups, Boston.

Shulman, L. (1984). *The skills of helping individuals and groups* (2nd ed., pp. 85–87). Itasca, IL: F.E. Peacock Publishers.

Weisman, C.B., & Schwartz, P. (1989). Worker expectations in group work with the frail elderly: Modifying the models for a better fit. *Social Work with Groups, 12*(3), 47–55.

Chapter 5

Bass, D.S. (1990). *Caring families: Supports and interventions*. Silver Spring, MD: NASW Press.

Older Americans Act of 1965, Pub. L. No. 89-73, 42 U.S.C. § 3001 *et seq.*

Part 3

National Institute on Aging. (1991). *What's your aging IQ?* [Brochure No. 281-837/40019]. Gaithersburg, MD: Author.

Appendix A

Resources for Handouts & Games

- **Alzheimer's Association**
  919 North Michigan Avenue, Suite 1000
  Chicago, Illinois 60611-1676
  Telephone: (800) 272-3900, (312) 335-8700, and (312) 335-8882 (TTY)
  FAX: (312) 335-1110
  World Wide Web site: http://www.alz.org

  The Alzheimer's Association aims to optimize the quality of life for individuals with Alzheimer's disease and their families while working toward a cure for the disease. They do so by promoting, developing, and disseminating educational programs and training guidelines for health and social services professionals; increasing the public's awareness and concern for people with Alzheimer's disease; and expanding access to services, information, and best practices for caring for people with Alzheimer's disease.

- **Alzheimer's Disease Education and Referral Center (ADEAR)**
  Post Office Box 8250
  Silver Spring, Maryland 20907-8250
  Telephone (800) 438-4380
  World Wide Web site: http://www.alzheimers.org
  email: adear@alzheimers.org

  Materials available: Information about Alzheimer's disease and related dementias

- **American Association of Retired Persons (AARP)**
  c/o AARP Fulfillment
  601 E Street, NW
  Washington, DC 20049
  Telephone: (800) 424-3410
  World Wide Web site: http://www.aarp.org
  email: member@aarp.org

  AARP is the leading advocacy group for people age 50 and older. The organization provides information, education, and community services, which are provided by a network of local chapters and experienced volunteers throughout the United States. The organization also offers members a wide range of special benefits and services, including *Modern Maturity* magazine and the monthly *AARP Bulletin*.

- **American Cancer Society (ACS)**
  Telephone: (800) 227-2345
  World Wide Web site: http://www.cancer.org
  Materials available: Numerous free brochures, information on services, the ACS breast cancer network, alternative therapies, detection and prevention guidelines, and patient and family information

- **American Council of the Blind (ACB)**
  1155 15th Street, NW, Suite 720
  Washington, DC 20005
  Telephone: (800) 424-8666 and (202) 467-5081
  FAX: (202) 467-5085
  World Wide Web site: http://acb.org (email can be sent from the home page)
  ACB's mission is to improve the quality of life of all blind and visually impaired people by elevating their social, economic, and cultural levels; improving educational and rehabilitation facilities and opportunities; and cooperating with institutions and organizations that are concerned with blind services. Services available: *The Braille Forum* (a free monthly national magazine that contains articles on employment, legislation, sports and leisure activities, new products and services, human interest, and other information), "ACB Reports" (a monthly radio reading-information service), toll-free information and referral on all aspects of blindness, scholarships for blind/visually impaired postsecondary students, public education and awareness training, support to consumer advocates and legal assistance on blindness-related matters, leadership and legislative training, and employment consultation.

- **American Diabetes Association**
  1660 Duke Street
  Alexandria, Virginia 22314
  Telephone: (800) DIABETES (342-2383) and (703) 549-1500
  World Wide Web site: http://www.diabetes.org
  The American Diabetes Association is dedicated to preventing and curing diabetes and to improving the lives of people affected by diabetes. The Association funds research, publishes scientific findings, and provides information and other services such as the Diabetes Information and Action Line (800-DIABETES), which provides information on all aspects of diabetes management and refers callers to local diabetes programs and services; *Diabetes Forecast*; *Diabetes Advisor*; and a vast library of cookbooks, meal-planning guides, and food-exchange lists.

- **American Dietetic Association**
  216 West Jackson Boulevard
  Chicago, Illinois 60606-6995

Telephone: (800) 366-1655 and (312) 899-0040
FAX: (312) 899-4845
World Wide Web site: http://www.eatright.org

The American Dietetic Association disseminates sound nutrition information to the public through publications, national events, and marketing (its national media program is represented by 26 registered dietitian spokespersons). The Association establishes and enforces quality standards for training and practice in medical nutrition therapy, foodservice systems management, and community dietetics. The National Center for Nutrition and Dietetics (NCND) is the Association's public education center. It maintains a toll-free consumer nutrition hotline, which includes a referral service for registered dietitians and a resource library that provides access to numerous databases. NCND sponsors National Nutrition Month®, celebrated each March under the theme "Eat Right America®," and promotes Project LEAN (Low-Fat Eating for America Now), which encourages low-fat eating and the increased availability of low-fat, flavorful foods.

- **American Heart Association**
  7272 Greenville Avenue
  Dallas, Texas 75231
  Telephone: (800) 242-1793 and (214) 373-6300
  World Wide Web site: http://www.amhrt.org
  email: email addresses are specific to the type of information sought and are contained within the AHA web site.

  Materials available: Educational brochures

- **American Institute for Preventive Medicine (AIPM)**
  30445 Northwestern Highway, Suite 350
  Farmington Hills, Michigan 48334
  Telephone: (800) 345-2476 and (810) 539-1800
  FAX: (810) 539-1808
  World Wide Web site: http://www.aipm.healthy.net
  email: aipm@healthy.net

  AIPM promotes wellness programs and produces self-care publications. The Institute works with more than 5,000 hospitals, HMOs, corporations, and government agencies throughout North America, and is an invited member of the Healthy People 2000 project, which has set the U.S. health goals for the 21st century.

- **American Lung Association**
  1740 Broadway
  New York, New York 10019-4374
  Telephone: (800) LUNG-USA (586-4872) and (212) 315-8700
  FAX: (212) 265-5642
  World Wide Web site: http://www.lungusa.org

- **American Optometric Association (AOA)**
243 North Lindbergh Boulevard
St. Louis, Missouri 63141
Telephone: (314) 991-4100
FAX: (314) 991-4101
World Wide Web site: http://www.aoanet.org
email: mamoptnews@aol.com

  AOA represents more than 32,000 doctors of optometry, students of optometry, and paraoptometric assistants and technicians in more than 6,600 communities around the world. AOA helps its members to conduct their practices in accordance with the highest standards of patient care and efficiency and represents the optometric profession to government and other organizations related to health care.

- **American Society on Aging (ASA)**
833 Market Street, Suite 511
San Francisco, California 94103
Telephone: (415) 974-9600
FAX: (415) 974-0300
World Wide Web site: http://www.asaging.org
email: info@asa.asaging.org

  ASA makes available numerous informational services, including its publication *Aging Today* and its newly established Multicultural Aging Network, open to anyone in the field of aging seeking to expand his or her organization's diversity efforts. The network offers training, technical assistance, information sharing, and networking. *Diversity Currents*, the network's quarterly newsletter, contains information about resources, activities, and issues related to multicultural aging.

- **Arthritis Foundation**
1330 West Peachtree Street
Atlanta, Georgia 30309
Telephone: (800) 283-7800 and (404) 872-7100
World Wide Web site: http://www.arthritis.org

  The Arthritis Foundation supports research toward the prevention of and a cure for arthritis and the improvement of the quality of life of people with arthritis and their families. The Foundation provides fact sheets; public information memoranda; news releases; and brochures in English and Spanish on self-management, daily living, family life, charitable estate planning, advocacy, treatments and medications, and types of arthritis. "Quick Answers" can be accessed through the web site or requested by calling the toll-free number.

- **Bi-Folkal Productions, Inc.**
809 Williamson
Madison, Wisconsin 53703

Telephone: (800) 568-5357
FAX: (608) 251-2874
email: bifolks@globaldialog.com

Materials available: Visual and programming aids for reminiscence activities

- **Catholic Charities**
  Answers for the Aging
  Telephone: (888) 50-ASKUS (501-7587)

  Information and referral service for older adults; addresses retirement communities, nursing facilities, adult day services, and housing and community services

- **Center for Science in the Public Interest (CSPI)**
  1875 Connecticut Avenue, NW, Suite 300
  Washington, DC 20009-5728
  Telephone: (202) 332-9110
  FAX: (202) 265-4954
  World Wide Web site: http://www.cspinet.org
  email: circ@cspinet.org

  CSPI is a nonprofit education and advocacy organization that attempts to improve the safety and nutritional quality of the food supply and to reduce the adverse effects of drinking alcoholic beverages. CSPI is supported by more than 1 million member-subscribers to its *Nutrition Action Healthletter* and through grants and sales of educational materials.

- **Center for the Study of Aging**
  706 Madison Avenue
  Albany, New York 12208
  Telephone: (518) 465-6927
  FAX: (518) 462-1339

  Materials available: Exercise materials

- **Channing L. Bete Co.**
  200 State Road
  South Deerfield, Massachusetts 01373
  Telephone: (800) 628-7733
  FAX: (800) 499-6464
  World Wide Web site: www.channing-bete.com
  email: custsvcs@channing-bete.com

  Materials available: Scriptographic booklets

- ***Consumer Information Catalog***
  Pueblo, Colorado 81009
  email: cic.info@pueblo.gas.gov

  Write "send info" in your email message for a catalog of free and low-cost government publications on numerous subjects.

- **Gerontological Society of America (GSA)**
  1030 15th Street, NW, Suite 250

Washington, DC 20005-1503
Telephone: (202) 842-1275
FAX: (202) 842-1150
World Wide Web site: http://www.geron.org
email: geron@geron.org

GSA's Information Service comprises an expert referral program through which experts in almost any area in the field of aging can be identified. In addition, GSA can do bibliographic searches for articles published since 1990 in GSA's journals (e.g., *The Gerontologist*). Information on experts and searches can be requested by email.

- **Interactive Aging Network (IANet)**
  World Wide Web site: http://www.ianet.org

  IANet is a nonprofit corporation that helps aging-related organizations enhance their productivity through the use of technology, especially the Internet. This easy-to-use site organizes many practical, helpful resources. It maintains a link called "Fundraising Resources," which lists numerous organizations that fund aging projects.

- **Journeyworks Publishing**
  Post Office Box 8466
  Santa Cruz, California 95061-8466
  Telephone: (800) 775-1998
  FAX: (408) 423-8102

  Materials available: Educational pamphlets

- **Krames Communications**
  1100 Grundy Lane
  San Bruno, California 94066-3030
  Telephone: (800) 333-3032
  World Wide Web site: http://www.Krames.com

  Krames publishes easy-to-read, inexpensive, consumer-oriented health education information. More than 850 booklets, brochures, instruction sheets, videos, CD-ROMs, and posters are available.

- **National Aging Information Center/Administration on Aging**
  330 Independence Avenue, SW
  Room 4656
  Washington, DC 20201
  Telephone: (202) 619-7501 and (202) 401-7575 (TTY)
  FAX: (202) 401-7620
  World Wide Web site: http://www.ageinfo.org
  email: naic@ageinfo.org

  Materials available: Information and publications on aging issues; a valuable resource is AoA's "Elderpage," the web address for which is http://www.aoa.dhhs.gov/elderpage.html. *(See also NIA.)*

- **National Association for Continence *(formerly Help for Incontinent People)***
  Post Office Box 8310

Spartanburg, South Carolina 29305-8310
Telephone: (800) BLADDER (800-252-3337) and (864) 579-7900
FAX: (864) 579-7902
World Wide Web site: http://www.nafc.ioffice.com

A leading source of education, advocacy, and support to the public and health care professionals about the causes, prevention, diagnosis, treatments, and management alternatives for incontinence, NAFC's primary goal is to destigmatize incontinence. Publications and services include *Quality Care; The Resource Guide—Products and Services for Incontinence* (a directory of products and manufacturers that assists people in finding the most helpful product[s] for their type of incontinence); and pamphlets, audiovisuals, and books. Online information on incontinence can be accessed from http://www.incontinent.com.

- **National Council on the Aging (NCOA)**
Department 5087
Washington, DC 20061-5087
Telephone: (800) 867-2755 and (202) 479-1200
FAX: (202) 479-6959
World Wide Web site: http://www.ncoa.org
email: info@ncoa.org

NCOA promotes the dignity, self-determination, well-being, and contributions of older adults through leadership, education and training, community services, employment programs, coalition building, public policy, and advocacy. Among the programs offered are Family Friends, an intergenerational volunteer program; Discovery Through the Humanities; and The National Clergy Leadership Project.

Materials available: Educational materials, including *NCOA Publications*, a catalog of books and reports, brochures, program resources and kits, and videos, which is free upon request.

- **National Information Center on Deafness**
Gallaudet University
800 Florida Avenue, NE
Washington, DC 20002-3695
Telephone: (202) 651-5051 and (202) 651-5052 (TTY)
FAX: (202) 651-5054
email: nicd@gallaudet.edu

NICD is a central source of accurate, up-to-date information on deafness and hearing loss.

Materials available: NICD's catalog lists publications that are available for free or a small charge.

- **National Institute on Aging (NIA)**
Information Center

Post Office Box 8057
Gaithersburg, Maryland 20898-8057
Telephone: (800) 222-2225 and (800) 222-4225 (TTY) between 8:30 A.M. and 5:00 P.M., EST
FAX: (301) 589-3014
World Wide Web site: http://www.nih.gov/nia/health/health.htm
email: niainfo@access.digex.net

Materials available: Age Pages and other relevant material such as the *Resource Directory for Older People*. The directory contains names, addresses, telephone numbers, and fax numbers of organizations that provide information and other resources on matters that are relevant to the needs of older people. Inclusion in the directory does not imply endorsement or a recommendation by NIA or AoA. You can access the directory on the Internet at www.aoa.dhhs.gov/aoa/resource.html, where you will find the online version of the hard-copy publication. The printed version can be purchased from the U.S. Government Printing Office for $11.00 (prepaid). The publication number is 0106200145-6. Credit card orders (VISA or MasterCard) may be placed by calling (202) 512-1800. Written order accompanied by check or money order (payable to the Superintendent of Documents) may be mailed to Superintendent of Documents, Post Office Box 371954, Pittsburgh, PA 15250-7954. Bulk orders are accepted. *(See also NAIC/AoA.)*

- **National Osteoporosis Foundation (NOF)**
  1150 17th Street, NW, Suite 500
  Washington, DC 20036-4603
  Telephone: (800) 223-9994 and (202) 223-2226
  FAX: (202) 223-2237
  World Wide Web site: http://www.nof.org

  NOF makes available numerous booklets and brochures (in English and Spanish, and in large-print format; priced low in bulk; single copies of patient/public education publications are free); questionnaire cards (pack of 50 cards); a patient education sample pack (contains 10 brochures); the "Osteoporosis Education Kit" (updated annually; includes age-targeted materials, nutrition information, and osteoporosis fact sheets that are easily duplicated, as well as samples of NOF brochures); a fully scripted 42-slide presentation for training/education; posters; graphs; and *Osteoporosis Report* (newsletter). NOF members receive a discount on their orders.

- **National Parkinson Foundation, Inc. (NPF)**
  1501 Northwest 9th Avenue/Bob Hope Road
  Miami, Florida 33136
  Telephone: (800) 327-4545 and (305) 547-6666
  FAX: (305) 243-4403
  World Wide Web site: http://www.parkinson.org
  email: mailbox@npf.med.miami.edu

NPF is dedicated to finding the cause of and cure for Parkinson's disease and related neurodegenerative disorders through research; to educating medical practitioners about early detection; to educating patients, their caregivers, and the public about Parkinson's disease; to providing diagnostic and therapeutic services; and to improving the quality of life of patients and their caregivers. A variety of free publications, in both English and Spanish, are available, and numerous articles, books, and videos are offered at low cost or via a small donation to NPF.

- **National Sleep Foundation (NSF)**
  1367 Connecticut Avenue, NW, Suite 200
  Washington, DC 20036
  Telephone: (202) 785-2300
  World Wide Web site: http://www.sleepfoundation.org
  email: natsleep@erols.com

  The National Sleep Foundation seeks to increase the public's understanding of the importance of sleep to good health and productivity; to prevent/cure health and safety problems that are related to insufficient sleep and untreated sleep disorders; to expand scientific research; and to implement public policy that promotes sleep education, research, and treatment. NSF programs include Drive Alert . . . Arrive Alive (warning about the dangers of drowsy driving); Towards the Cause of Narcolepsy Program (includes the National Narcolepsy Registry, research grants, and public education); *Sleep and Aging* (explains common sleep problems, including insomnia, and the impact of menopause, drugs, nicotine, and travel on sleep); the *Doctor, I Can't Sleep Training Manual* (a comprehensive course manual for primary care physicians and the public; outlines basic facts about epidemiology, sleep hygiene, relaxation techniques, diagnosis, and treatment; $25.00); press releases and brochures on melatonin (a hormone that, when taken internally, induces drowsiness), narcolepsy, pain and sleep, sleep apnea, and drowsy driving; and *The NSF Connection*.

- **National Stroke Association (NSA)**
  96 Inverness Drive East, Suite I
  Englewood, Colorado 80112-5112
  Telephone: (303) 649-9299 (Stroke Information and Resource Center: [800] STROKES [787-6537])
  FAX: (303) 649-1328
  World Wide Web site: http://www.stroke.org (email link is contained within the site)

  NSA offers many services, including the Stroke Information and Resource Center (national clearinghouse of information on stroke statistics, medical referral sources, support groups for survivors and caregivers, as well as rehabilitation facility listings), the Stroke Center Network, the Stroke Prevention Screening Program (provides hospitals and other organizations with information and tools to conduct public screenings to identify and counsel stroke-at-risk individuals), STROKE PREVENT[SM] (personalized stroke risk assessment), and *Be Stroke Smart*, NSA's monthly newsletter. NSA also makes available books, brochures, videotapes, posters, slides, T-shirts, and pins on stroke public awareness, professional education, and survivor/caregiver resources for older Native Americans.

- **Native Elder Health Care Resource Center (NEHCRC)**
  University of Colorado Health Sciences Center
  4455 East 12th Avenue, Room 329
  Denver, Colorado 80220
  Telephone: (303) 372-3250
  FAX: (303) 372-3579
  World Wide Web site: http://www.uchsc.edu/sm/nehcrc
  email: jeanene.diana@uchsc.edu

  The NEHCRC applies research, disseminates information through a computerized telecommunications system, provides training/technical assistance, and enhances professional education. NEHCRC focuses on ascertaining health status and conditions, improving practice standards, increasing access to care, and mobilizing community resources for older Native Americans.

- **Parlay International**
  Post Office Box 8817
  Emeryville, California 94662-0817
  Telephone: (800) 457-2752 and (510) 601-1000
  FAX: (510) 601-1008
  World Wide Web site: http://www.parlay.com

  Parlay International markets KOPY KIT® Reproducible Resources, a collection of one-page handouts on a variety of topics related to a theme. The materials can be customized to fit individual needs.

- **Restless Legs Syndrome Foundation, Inc.**
  4410 19th Street, NW, Suite 201
  Rochester, Minnesota 55901-6624
  World Wide Web site: http://www.rls.org
  email: rlsf@millcomm.com

  The Restless Legs Syndrome Foundation publishes a quarterly newsletter, *NightWalkers*, and has placed Patient Information and Bibliography (geared to health care professionals) links on its web site.

- **Signal Hill Publications**
  Department FB4, Box 888
  Syracuse, New York 13210
  Telephone: (800) 506-READ
  Materials available: *Aging with Confidence*

- **Talicor, Inc.**
  8845 Steven Chase Court
  Las Vegas, Nevada 89129
  Telephone: (800) 433-4263
  FAX: (909) 596-6586
  Materials available: Icebreaker and reminiscing games, including the Ungame

- **United Seniors Health Cooperative**
  1331 H Street, NW, Suite 500
  Washington, DC 20005-4706
  Telephone: (800) 637-2604
  FAX: (202) 783-0588
  Materials available: Eldergames and other materials such as information on legal and financial issues associated with aging

- **U.S. Consumer Product Safety Commission**
  Washington, DC 20207
  Telephone: (800) 638-2772
  Materials available: Brochures on home safety

- **U.S. Department of Health and Human Services, Office of Disease Prevention and Health Promotion (ODPHP)**
  Humphrey Building, Room 738G
  200 Independence Avenue, SW
  Washington, DC 20201
  Telephone: (800) 336-4797 and (202) 205-8611
  FAX: (301) 984-4256
  World Wide Web site: http://nhic-nt.health.org
  email: nhicinfo@health.org
  ODPHP is part of the U.S. Public Health Service. The ODPHP National Health Information Center is an information and referral service that offers free publications on national health observances (a calendar), federal health information centers and clearinghouses, and toll-free numbers for health information. A list of materials is available on request.

- **Wellness Reproductions and Publishing, Inc.**
  23945 Mercantile Road, Suite W5
  Beachwood, Ohio 44122-5924
  Telephone: (800) 669-9208
  FAX: (800) 501-8120
  World Wide Web site: http://www.wellness-resources.com
  email: wri@wellness.resources.com
  Wellness Reproductions and Publishing, Inc., is a hands-on resource center offering creative, ready-to-use therapeutic and educational products (including reproducible handouts) focusing on mental health.

Appendix B

State Units on Aging

- **Alabama (Region IV)**
  Martha Murphy Beck, Executive Director
  Alabama Commission on Aging
  RSA Plaza, Suite 470
  770 Washington Avenue
  Montgomery 36130
  Telephone: (334) 242-5743
  FAX: (334) 242-5594
- **Alaska (Region X)**
  Jane Demmert, Director
  Alaska Commission on Aging
  Division of Senior Services
  Department of Administration
  Juneau 99811-0209
  Telephone: (907) 465-3250
  FAX: (907) 465-4716
- **American Samoa (Region IX)**
  Lualemaga E. Faoa, Acting Director
  Territorial Administration on Aging
  Government of American Samoa
  Pago Pago 96799
  Telephone: (684) 633-2207
  FAX: (684) 633-2533
- **Arizona (Region IX)**
  Henry Blanco, Program Director
  Aging and Adult Administration
  Department of Economic Security
  1789 West Jefferson Street, #950A
  Phoenix 85007
  Telephone: (602) 542-4446
  FAX: (602) 542-6575
- **Arkansas (Region VI)**
  Herb Sanderson, Director
  Division of Aging and Adult Services
  Arkansas Department of Human Services
  Post Office Box 1437, Slot 1412
  7th and Main Streets
  Little Rock 72201
  Telephone: (501) 682-2441
  FAX: (501) 682-8155
- **California (Region IX)**
  Dixon Arnette, Director
  California Department of Aging
  1600 K Street
  Sacramento 95814
  Telephone: (916) 322-5290
  FAX: (916) 324-1903
- **Colorado (Region VIII)**
  Rita Barreras, Director
  Aging and Adult Services
  Department of Social Services
  110 16th Street, Suite 200
  Denver 80202-5202
  Telephone: (303) 620-4147
  FAX: (303) 620-4189
- **Connecticut (Region I)**
  Christine M. Lewis, Director of Community Services
  Division of Elderly Services
  25 Sigourney Street, 10th Floor
  Hartford 06106-5033
  Telephone: (860) 424-5277
  FAX: (860) 424-4966

- **Delaware (Region III)**
  Eleanor Cain, Director
  Delaware Division of Services for Aging and Adults with Physical Disabilities
  Department of Health and Social Services
  1901 North DuPont Highway
  New Castle 19720
  Telephone: (302) 577-4791
  FAX: (302) 577-4793

- **District of Columbia (Region III)**
  E. Veronica Pace, Director
  District of Columbia Office on Aging
  One Judiciary Square, 9th Floor
  441 Fourth Street, NW
  Washington, DC 20001
  Telephone: (202) 724-5622
  FAX: (202) 724-4979

- **Florida (Region IV)**
  Bentley Lipscomb, Secretary
  Department of Elder Affairs
  Building B, Suite 152
  4040 Esplanade Way
  Tallahassee 32399-7000
  Telephone: (904) 414-2000
  FAX: (904) 414-2002

- **Georgia (Region IV)**
  Judy Hagebak, Director
  Division of Aging Services
  Department of Human Resources
  2 Peachtree Street, NE, 18th Floor
  Atlanta 30303
  Telephone: (404) 657-5258
  FAX: (404) 657-5285

- **Guam (Region IX)**
  Arthur San Augstin, Administrator
  Division of Senior Citizens
  Department of Public Health & Social Services
  Post Office Box 2816
  Agana 96932
  Telephone: (671) 475-0263
  FAX: (671) 477-2930

- **Hawaii (Region IX)**
  Marilyn Seely, Director
  Hawaii Executive Office on Aging
  250 South Hotel Street, Suite 107
  Honolulu 96813
  Telephone: (808) 586-0100
  FAX (808) 586-0185

- **Idaho (Region X)**
  Arlene Davidson, Director
  Idaho Commission on Aging
  Room 108–Statehouse
  700 West Jefferson—Post Office Box 83720-0007
  Boise 83720-0007
  Telephone: (208) 334-3833
  FAX: (208) 334-3033

- **Illinois (Region V)**
  Maralee Lindley, Director
  Illinois Department on Aging
  421 East Capitol Avenue, Suite 100
  Springfield 62701-1789
  Telephone: (217) 785-2870
  FAX: (217) 785-4477
  Chicago Office: (312) 814-2630

- **Indiana (Region V)**
  Geneva Shedd, Director
  Bureau of Aging and In-Home Services
  Division of Disability, Aging and Rehabilitative Services
  Family and Social Services Administration
  402 West Washington Street, #W454
  Post Office Box 7083
  Indianapolis 46207-7083
  Telephone: (317) 232-7020
  FAX: (317) 232-7867

- **Iowa (Region VII)**
  Betty Grandquist, Executive Director
  Department of Elder Affairs
  Celemens Building, 3rd Floor
  200 Tenth Street
  Des Moines 50309-3609
  Telephone: (515) 281-5187
  FAX: (515) 281-4036
- **Kansas (Region VII)**
  Thelma Hunter Gordon, Secretary
  Department on Aging
  New England Building
  503 South Kansas Avenue
  Topeka 66603-3404
  Telephone: (785) 296-4986
  FAX: (785) 296-0256
- **Kentucky (Region IV)**
  Jerry Whitley, Director
  Kentucky Division of Aging Services
  Cabinet for Human Resources
  275 East Main Street, 6 West
  Frankfort 40621
  Telephone: (502) 564-6930
  FAX: (502) 564-4595
- **Louisiana (Region VI)**
  Paul "Pete" F. Arcineaux, Jr., Director
  Governor's Office of Elderly Affairs
  Post Office Box 80374
  412 North 4th Street, 3rd Floor
  Baton Rouge 70802
  Telephone: (504) 342-7100
  FAX: (504) 342-7133
- **Maine (Region I)**
  Christine Gianopoulos, Director
  Bureau of Elder and Adult Services
  Department of Human Services
  35 Anthony Avenue
  State House–Station #11
  Augusta 04333
  Telephone: (207) 626-5335
  FAX: (207) 624-5361
- **Maryland (Region III)**
  Sue Fryer Ward, Director
  Maryland Office on Aging
  State Office Building, Room 1007
  301 West Preston Street
  Baltimore 21201-2374
  Telephone: (410) 767-1100
  FAX: (410) 333-7943
  email: sfw@mail.ooa.state.md.us
- **Massachusetts (Region I)**
  Lillian Glickman, Acting Secretary
  Massachusetts Executive Office of Elder Affairs
  One Ashburton Place, 5th Floor
  Boston 02108
  Telephone: (617) 727-7750
  FAX: (617) 727-9368
- **Michigan (Region V)**
  Lynn Alexander, Director
  Office of Services to the Aging
  Post Office Box 30026
  Lansing 48909-8176
  Telephone: (517) 373-8230
  FAX: (517) 373-4092
- **Minnesota (Region V)**
  James G. Varpness, Executive Secretary
  Minnesota Board on Aging
  444 Lafayette Road
  St. Paul 55155-3843
  Telephone: (612) 296-2770
  FAX: (612) 297-7855
- **Mississippi (Region IV)**
  Eddie Anderson, Director
  Division of Aging and Adult Services
  750 State Street
  Jackson 39202
  Telephone: (601) 359-4925
  FAX: (601) 359-4370
  email: ELANDERSON@msdh.state.ms.us

- **Missouri (Region VII)**
  Andrea Routh, Director
  Division on Aging
  Department of Social Services
  Post Office Box 1337
  615 Howerton Court
  Jefferson City 65102-1337
  Telephone: (573) 751-3082
  FAX: (573) 751-8493

- **Montana (Region VIII)**
  Charles Rehbein, State Aging Coordinator
  Senior and Long-Term Care Division
  Department of Public Health & Human Services
  Post Office Box 8005
  48 North Last Chance Gulch
  Helena 59604
  Telephone: (406) 444-7788
  FAX: (406) 444-7743

- **Nebraska (Region VII)**
  Mark Intermill, Administrator
  Department of Health and Human Services
  Division on Aging
  Post Office Box 95044
  301 Centennial Mall South
  Lincoln 68509-5044
  Telephone: (402) 471-2307
  FAX: (402) 471-4619

- **Nevada (Region IX)**
  Carla Sloane, Administrator
  Nevada Division for Aging Services
  Department of Human Resources
  State Mail Room Complex
  340 North 11th Street, Suite 203
  Las Vegas 89101
  Telephone: (702) 486-3545
  FAX: (702) 486-3572

- **New Hampshire (Region I)**
  Catherine A. Keane, Director
  Division of Elderly and Adult Services
  State Office Park South
  115 Pleasant Street, Annex Building #1
  Concord 03301-3843
  Telephone: (603) 271-4680
  FAX: (603) 271-4643

- **New Jersey (Region II)**
  Ruth Reader, Assistant Commissioner
  Department of Health and Senior Services
  Division of Senior Affairs
  Post Office Box 807
  Trenton 08625-0807
  Telephone: (609) 588-3141
  Telephone: (800) 792-8820
  FAX: (609) 588-3601

- **New Mexico (Region VI)**
  Michelle Lujan Grisham, Director
  State Agency on Aging
  La Villa Rivera Building, 4th Floor
  224 East Palace Avenue
  Santa Fe 87501
  Telephone: (505) 827-7640
  FAX: (505) 827-7649

- **New York (Region II)**
  Walter G. Hoefer, Executive Director
  New York State Office for the Aging
  2 Empire State Plaza
  Albany 12223-1251
  Telephone: (518) 474-5731
  Telephone: (800) 342-9871
  FAX: (518) 474-0608

- **North Carolina (Region IV)**
  Karen E. Gottovi, Director
  Division of Aging
  693 Palmer Drive, CB 29531
  Raleigh 27626-0531
  Telephone: (919) 733-3983
  FAX: (919) 733-0443

- **North Dakota (Region VIII)**
  Linda Wright, Director
  Department of Human Services
  Aging Services Division
  600 South 2nd Street, Suite 1C
  Bismarck 58504
  Telephone: (701) 328-8910
  FAX: (701) 328-8989
- **Northern Mariana Islands (Region IX)**
  Ana D.L.G. Flores, Administrator/Director
  CNMI Office on Aging
  Post Office Box 2178
  Commonwealth of the Northern Mariana Islands
  Saipan 96950
  Telephone: (670) 233-1320/1321
  FAX: (670) 233-1327/0369
- **Ohio (Region V)**
  Judith V. Brachman, Director
  Ohio Department of Aging
  50 West Broad Street, 9th Floor
  Columbus 43215-5928
  Telephone: (614) 466-5500
  FAX: (614) 466-5741
- **Oklahoma (Region VI)**
  Roy R. Keen, Division Administrator
  Services for the Aging
  Department of Human Services
  Post Office Box 25352
  312 NE 28th Street
  Oklahoma City 73125
  Telephone: (405) 521-2281/2327
  FAX: (405) 521-2086
- **Oregon (Region X)**
  Roger Auerbach, Administrator
  Senior and Disabled Services Division
  500 Summer Street, NE, 2nd Floor
  Salem 97310-1015
  Telephone: (503) 945-5811
  FAX: (503) 373-7823
- **Palau (Region X)**
  Lillian Nakamura, Director
  State Agency on Aging
  Republic of Palau
  Koror 96940
  Telephone: (680) 488-2736
  FAX: (680) 488-1662/1597
- **Pennsylvania (Region III)**
  Richard Browdie, Secretary
  Pennsylvania Department of Aging
  Commonwealth of Pennsylvania
  555 Walnut Street, 5th Floor
  Harrisburg 17101-1919
  Telephone: (717) 783-1550
  FAX: (717) 772-3382
- **Puerto Rico (Region II)**
  Ruby Rodriguez Ramirez, M.H.S.A., Executive Director
  Commonwealth of Puerto Rico
  Governor's Office of Elderly Affairs
  Call Box 50063
  Old San Juan Station 00902
  Telephone: (787) 721-5710/4560/6121
  FAX: (787) 721-6510
- **Rhode Island (Region I)**
  Barbara Raynor, Acting Director
  Department of Elderly Affairs
  160 Pine Street
  Providence 02903-3708
  Telephone: (401) 277-2858
  FAX: (401) 277-2130
- **South Carolina (Region IV)**
  Constance C. Rinehart, Deputy Director
  Office on Aging
  South Carolina Department of Health and Human Services
  Post Office Box 8206
  Columbia 29201-8206
  Telephone: (803) 253-6177
  FAX: (803) 253-4173
  email: Rinehart@dhhs.state.sc.us

- **South Dakota (Region VIII)**
  Gail Ferris, Administrator
  Office of Adult Services and Aging
  Richard F. Kneip Building
  700 Governor's Drive
  Pierre 57501-2291
  Telephone: (605) 773-3656
  FAX: (605) 773-6834

- **Tennessee (Region IV)**
  James S. Whaley, Executive Director
  Commission on Aging
  Andrew Jackson Building, 9th Floor
  500 Deaderick Street
  Nashville 37243-0860
  Telephone: (615) 741-2056
  FAX: (615) 741-3309

- **Texas (Region VI)**
  Mary Sapp, Executive Director
  Texas Department on Aging
  4900 North Lamar, 4th Floor
  Austin 78751
  Telephone: (512) 424-6840
  FAX: (512) 424-6890

- **Utah (Region VIII)**
  Helen Goddard
  Division of Aging & Adult Services
  120 North 200 West, Box 45500
  Salt Lake City 84145-0500
  Telephone: (801) 538-3910
  FAX: (801) 538-4395

- **Vermont (Region I)**
  David Yavocone, Commissioner
  Vermont Department of Aging and Disabilities
  Waterbury Complex
  103 South Main Street
  Waterbury 05676
  Telephone: (802) 241-2400
  FAX: (802) 241-2325
  email: dyaco@dad.state.vt.us

- **Virginia (Region III)**
  Ann Magee, Commissioner
  Virginia Department for the Aging
  1600 Forest Avenue, Suite 102
  Richmond 23219-2327
  Telephone: (804) 662-9333
  FAX: (804) 662-9354

- **Virgin Islands (Region II)**
  Ms. Sedonie Halbert, Acting Commissioner
  Senior Citizen Affairs
  Virgin Islands Department of Human Services
  Knud Hansen Complex, Building A
  1303 Hospital Ground
  Charlotte Amalie 00802
  Telephone: (809) 774-0930
  FAX: (809) 774-3466

- **Washington State (Region X)**
  Ralph Smith, Assistant Secretary
  Aging and Adult Services Administration
  Department of Social & Health Services
  Post Office Box 45050
  Olympia 98504-5050
  Telephone: (360) 586-8753
  FAX: (360) 902-7848

- **West Virginia (Region III)**
  Patricia F. Bradford, Commissioner
  West Virginia Bureau of Senior Services
  Holly Grove–Building 10
  1900 Kanawha Boulevard East
  Charleston 25305-0160
  Telephone: (304) 558-3317
  FAX: (304) 558-0004

- **Wisconsin (Region V)**
  Donna McDowell, Director
  Bureau of Aging and Long-Term Care Resources
  Department of Health and Family Services
  Post Office Box 7851
  Madison 53707
  Telephone: (608) 266-2536
  FAX: (608) 267-3203

- **Wyoming (Region VIII)**
  Wayne Milton, Program Coordinator
  Office on Aging, Department of Health
  117 Hathaway Building, Room 139
  Cheyenne 82002-0480
  Telephone: (307) 777-7986
  FAX: (307) 777-5340

Index

Additional Titles from Health Professions Press on Activities for Older Adults

The Arts/Fitness Quality of Life Activities Program: Creative Ideas for Working with Older Adults in Group Settings, by Claire B. Clements, Ed.D. / Stk. No. 2459 / *$44.95*

I Can't Draw A Straight Line: Bringing Art into the Lives of Older Adults, by Shirley Hubalek, B.F.A. / Stk. No. 0343 / *$30.95*

More Than Movement for Fit to Frail Older Adults: Creative Activities for the Body, Mind and Spirit, by Pauline Postiloff Fisher, M.A. / Stk. No. 0211 / *$24.00*

The Power of Music: A Complete Music Activities Program for Older Adults, by Bill Messenger, M.L.A. / Stk. No. 0270 / *$24.95*

A Life Worth Living: Practical Strategies for Reducing Depression in Older Adults, by Pearl M. Mosher-Ashley, Ph.D., & Phyllis W. Barrett, Ph.D. / Stk. No. 2033/ *$31.95*

Prices are subject to change

Ordering Information

Please send me the following book(s):

Stk. No.	Author	Title	Qty.	Price

❏ Check or money order enclosed *(payable to Health Professions Press)*
❏ Bill my institution *(attach purchase order)*
❏ MasterCard ❏ VISA ❏ American Express

Card No.________________________________ Exp. Date___/___

Signature________________________________

Name *(please print)* ________________________________

Address________________________________

City/State/ZIP____________________ Day Phone (   )__________

❏ *Please send me a copy of your current catalog.*

Health Professions Press P.O. Box 10624 Baltimore, MD 21285-0624
Toll-Free (888) 337-8808 Fax (410) 337-8539
E-mail hpp@pbrookes.com